Moral Maturity

Measuring the Development of Sociomoral Reflection

Moral Maturity

Measuring the Development of Sociomoral Reflection

John C. Gibbs
The Ohio State University

Karen S. Basinger
Marshall University

Dick Fuller
The Columbus College of Art and Design

LAWRENCE ERLBAUM ASSOCIATES, PUBLISHERS
1992   Hillsdale, New Jersey   Hove and London

Lawrence Erlbaum Associates, Inc., Publishers
365 Broadway
Hillsdale, New Jersey 07642

Library of Congress Cataloging-in-Publication Data

Gibbs, John C.

   Moral maturity : measuring the development of sociomoral
reflection / John C. Gibbs, Karen S. Basinger, Dick Fuller
     p.   cm.

Includes bibliographical references and indexes.
ISBN 0-8058-0425-0
1. Social ethics. 2. Judgment (Ethics). 3. Moral development.-
-Testing 4. I. Basinger, Karen S. II. Fuller, Dick. III. Title.
IV. Title: Sociomoral reflection.
HM216.G452   1991
303.3'72--dc20   91-6552
                                                     CIP

Printed in the United States of America
10 9 8 7 6 5 4 3 2 1

Dedicated to the
Memory of
Larry Kohlberg

Contents

Preface

This book is dedicated to the memory of Larry Kohlberg (1927–1987), a caring and brilliant person. In his last years, Kohlberg witnessed the empirical and theoretical establishment of his cognitive-developmental approach to morality. Kohlberg's 20-year longitudinal study culminated in support for his cognitive-developmental theory of morality, in which moral judgment is viewed as a progression through standard, sequential stages (Colby, Kohlberg, Gibbs, & Lieberman, 1983). He also published his assessment instrument (Colby & Kohlberg, 1987; Colby, Kohlberg, Speicher, Hewer, Candee, Gibbs, & Power, 1987); his overall psychology (Kohlberg, 1984); and his philosophy of moral development (Kohlberg, 1981). Kohlberg is one of the most frequently cited psychologists in the contemporary social and behavioral science literature (Endler, Rushton, & Roediger, 1978). His theory and research have been given space in every major developmental psychology textbook and in virtually every introductory psychology textbook.

This book is the culmination of John Gibbs' work on moral judgment assessment since his participation in Kohlberg's longitudinal research team at the Harvard University Center for Studies in Moral Development (from 1975 to 1979). During these years, the Center developed the current Standard Issue method for scoring Kohlberg's Moral Judgment Interview (MJI) data.

Use of the MJI is demanding. The instrument requires laborious individual interviewing, using moral dilemmas to elicit reasoning that must then be inferentially scored. Standard Issue scoring is intricate. Indeed, the scoring system taxed the patience and ability of Gibbs, who, as one of the co-authors, was intimately familiar with the system. How easily, then, could a novice learn the assessment method? Each summer, researchers traveled (many from considerable distances) to a workshop at the Harvard Center to become expert in moral judgment assessment. As one of the workshop leaders, Gibbs spent many hours training others to score the MJI, but was concerned that many more hours of post-workshop practice would be necessary for the participants to achieve reliable and valid scoring. Did moral judgment data collection and scoring really have to be so difficult? Could a less cumbersome measure be developed -- one that could be group-administered and efficiently scored without workshop training.

Jim Rest, one of Gibbs' predecessors at the Harvard Center, harbored the same questions. As a result, Rest developed the Defining Issues Test (DIT; Rest, 1979), which uses moral dilemmas but eliminates the need for inferential moral judgment assessment. The DIT requires subjects to *evaluate* moral considerations or reasoning. However, this procedure sacrifices an essential feature of moral judgment assessment: It eliminates the opportunity

ix

for subjects to produce spontaneously their own moral justifications. Gibbs wondered whether a measure could be developed that would both elicit a subject's spontaneous reasoning and save time and labor for the researcher. Gibbs consulted Larry Kohlberg, who agreed that such a version of the MJI, if it could be created, would be a worthy contribution.

Heartened, Gibbs began to develop a less daunting questionnaire. The DIT and the MJI ask subjects to evaluate the importance of moral considerations or values on some dilemma-based questions. On the MJI, this procedure clearly facilitates the scorability of subjects' responses. If this evaluation procedure is so useful, why not ask subjects to evaluate all of the questions? In his new questionnaire, Gibbs began to elicit evaluations as part of *every* question—resulting in a breakthrough.

The work on the new questionnaire continued when Gibbs joined the faculty of The Ohio State University in 1979. Gibbs, along with Keith Widaman (now a Psychology Department faculty member at the University of California at Riverside), received a National Institute of Mental Health (NIMH) Small Grant to fund the instrument development. Valuable advice on scoring criteria was contributed by Gibbs' Harvard Center colleague Anne Colby, who is now director of Radcliffe College's Henry A. Murray Center for the Study of Lives. These efforts resulted in the Sociomoral Reflection Measure (SRM; Gibbs & Widaman, 1982).

By and large, the SRM was a success. Reliability (internal consistency, test–retest, and interrater) and validity (concurrent and construct) were good (see Gibbs, Widaman, & Colby, 1982). Especially important was its concurrent validity with the MJI, even though the SRM defined moral judgment maturity somewhat differently (see Gibbs, 1977, 1979; and chapter 1 of this volume).

Supported in 1982 by another NIMH Small Grant, we developed a recognition or objective measure based on the SRM, the Sociomoral Reflection Objective Measure (SROM; Gibbs, Arnold, Morgan, et al., 1984). The SROM asks subjects to select stage-significant reasons that are "close" and "closest" to the ones they would give to justify the importance of moral values, and thereby provides an indirect index of sociomoral reflection or justification. This measure differs from the DIT. Whereas the DIT asks respondents what they "appreciate" (Rest, 1975) or rate as important among moral considerations or values, our test asks respondents what reasoning they would use to justify that which they evaluate as important. Like the SRM, the SROM turned out to have generally good reliability and validity.

In one respect, however, the SROM failed where the SRM had succeeded. In fully controlled comparisons, the SROM did not confirm the construct validity hypothesis that juvenile offenders would score lower in moral judgment than non-delinquents (Gavaghan, Arnold, & Gibbs, 1983). We suspected that this failure might be partly attributable to the greater reading and attention-span demands of the objective measure. Accordingly, Gibbs and Karen Basinger designed a streamlined, simplified version of the objective measure. In most respects, the Sociomoral Reflection Objective Measure–Short Form (SROM-SF) performed as well as its long-form counterpart. However, like the SROM, it failed to discriminate delinquents from non-delinquents in fully controlled comparisons (Basinger & Gibbs, 1987). Hence, the attempt to accomplish satisfactory measurement of sociomoral reflection through objective measures proved limited.

The SRM distinguished delinquents from non-delinquents. However, many subjects from the delinquent sample and the non-delinquent sample, as well as elementary school subjects, were confused by some of the dilemma-based questions. Although the SRM is slightly less taxing than the SROM (its long-form recognition counterpart), the SRM still requires that subjects have a considerable attention span. The thought occurred to us: Were *dilemmas* really necessary? This thought was the stimulus for our most recent endeavor. A new measure—which came to be called the Sociomoral Reflection Measure–Short Form (SRM-SF) was designed, eliminating the use of dilemmas and introducing certain other efficiencies. This measure is a straightforward four-page form, rather than a sometimes confusing eight-page SRM. The SRM-SF is less daunting for subjects and saves the researcher administration and scoring time.

In sum, the SRM-SF and this book is the culmination of 12 years of work on the measurement of moral judgment maturity by Gibbs and his colleagues. Chapter 1 provides an overview of the cognitive-developmental approach to morality, including our view of the stages and their relationship to other areas of cognitive development. The implicit theme of chapter 1—that maturity in moral-cognitive development is no less valid a construct than in other areas of cognitive development—underlies the title of this book. Chapter 2 discusses the background and rationale for the SRM-SF, and presents the results of recent psychometric evaluations of the measure. Chapter 3 provides guidance for self-training and test administration, and rules for protocol scoring. Chapters 4 through 8 comprise the scoring manual. These chapters provide the criteria to which the scorer refers when rating a subject's responses on the SRM-SF questionnaire. Appendix A provides the SRM-SF questionnaire and scoring form. Appendices B and C contain the materials for the self-training program presented in chapter 3.

Many persons and institutions made major contributions to the success of this project. Personnel of The Ohio State University, the Reynoldsburg Public Schools, the Galion Middle School, the Plain City Elementary School, and the Ohio Department of Youth Services provided crucial assistance in our data collection. We especially thank Kevin Arnold, Bob Casey, Vicki Kilberry, Bruce Layne, Leonard Leeman, Bud Potter, and Paul Steinman. Nancy Eisenberg of Arizona State University provided very helpful and insightful comments on a preliminary version of the scoring manual chapters. Keith Widaman provided valuable advice concerning the statistical analysis of our data. Brenda Brown, Ginny Jelinek, Tiffany Malcolm, and Maureen Lach did diligent, conscientious, and thoughtful work as self-training trainees. The notes in Appendices B and C owe much to their suggestions. Similarly, Ginny and Tiffany deserve special thanks for their high quality editorial work on the reference chapters. Jane Fuller made inportant contributions to the design of the manuscript. Lawrence Erlbaum Associates Editor Judi Amsel provided consistent encouragement and support throughout the preparation of the book's manuscript. Assistant Editor Chava Casper scrutinized the format and consistency of our manuscript with tireless zeal. Finally, we thank our families for their patience, especially during the final phases of manuscript preparation.

John C. Gibbs
Karen S. Basinger
Dick Fuller

Background

Chapter 1

Moral-Cognitive Development and Maturity

This chapter relates moral development to general processes of cognitive development, and within that framework provides an introductory description of moral judgment stages. The young child's moral judgment is superficial. The growing child's expanding working memory, as well as increasing social role-taking opportunities, enable him or her to attend simultaneously to multiple features of the environment. These processes eventuate in the achievement of a mature understanding of the intrinsic or underlying meaning of moral values. The child whose moral development has reached a relatively mature level might suggest, for example, that one should keep a promise to a friend to preserve the trust on which the friendship is based, or because mutual respect is the basis for any relationship. Mature or profound moral understanding pertains not only to keeping a promise, but also to a broad spectrum of cross-culturally pervasive moral norms and values such as telling the truth, refraining from stealing, helping others, and saving a life.

MORAL-COGNITIVE DEVELOPMENT

It is evident that natural moral development is grossly defined by a trend toward an increasingly internal orientation to norms. Our moral stages . . . clearly represent increasingly interiorized orientations. . . . but this development cannot be defined as a direct internalization of external cultural norms. If students of socialization ignore [the] maturity components of social development in favor of simpler conformity or internalization concepts, they will . . . fail to describe "natural development" correctly. (Kohlberg, 1984, pp. 90–93)

According to Kohlberg, then, it is a mistake to interpret the "increasingly internal orientation" in moral development simply as the outcome of a direct internalization of prevailing cultural norms. Rather, the internal moral orientation represents a mature product of natural development. "Natural"

3

moral development entails movement toward "moral adequacy" (Kohlberg, 1971, p. 213), which we characterize as a progression from superficial to profound moral judgment.

This superficial-to-profound movement or progression entails four stages of moral judgment similar in many respects to those originally described by Kohlberg. The superficiality of immature moral judgment is most readily illustrated by Stage 1, which reflects "the natural tendency of young children to embody . . . moral notions in concrete places or events" (Damon, 1988, p. 15). Stage 1 morality entails a physicalistic understanding of moral authority (e.g., "The father is the boss because he's bigger"; Kohlberg, 1984, p. 624), or a physicalistic understanding of the moral worth of a human life (one of the subjects in Kohlberg's longitudinal study suggested that saving the life of more than one person is especially important because "one man has just one house, maybe a lot a furniture, but a whole bunch of people have an awful lot of furniture"; p. 192). Similarly, keeping a promise might be justified by appeal to physical consequences (otherwise the person "will beat you up"). Perceptually impressive features of a situation (e.g., size, objects, or actions), then, tend to capture the young child's attention or imagination; it is these features that dominate the child's reasons for obeying authority, saving a life, keeping a promise, or adhering to other moral prescriptions.

Stage 2 reasoning goes beyond physical appearances to interrelate psychological perspectives, but this stage, as well, can be characterized as superficial. Kohlberg described the perspective at Stage 2 as:

> . . . pragmatic—to maximize satisfaction of one's needs and desires while minimizing negative consequences to the self. The assumption that the other is also operating from this premise leads to an emphasis on instrumental exchange. . . . For example, it is seen as important to keep promises to in- sure that others will keep their promises to you and do nice things for you, or . . . in order to keep them from getting mad at you. (Kohlberg, 1984, pp. 626–628)

Snarey (1985) provided illustrations of Stage 2 pragmatic or egoistic- instrumental thinking in five different cultures (pp. 221-222; but see also Keller, Eckensberger, & Von Rosen, 1989). Insofar as empathic concern for another is expressed in Stage 2 moral judgment, the concern is in terms of the other person's practical needs or desires (Eisenberg, Boehnke, Schuler, & Silbereisen, 1985).

With the advent of Stage 3, moral judgment advances beyond superficiality to a mature understanding of moral norms and values. Stage 3 refers to an interrelating of egoistic-instrumental perspectives sufficient to bring about an understanding of the mutuality or trust that underlies mature interpersonal relationships. Kohlberg suggested that:

> . . . at Stage 3 the separate perspectives of individuals are coordinated into a third-person perspective, that of mutually trusting relationships. . . . Stage 3 reciprocity . . . [allows] one to understand reciprocity as going beyond concrete notions of equal exchange to maintaining relationships, mutuality of expectations, and sentiments of gratitude and obligation. (Kohlberg, 1984, pp. 628–629)

Piaget, whose (1932/1965) study of moral judgment was seminal for Kohlberg's work, characterized this progression from instrumental exchange to a "mutuality of expectations" as a transition from "reciprocity as a fact" to "reciprocity as an ideal," or the prescription of:

> . . . behavior that admits of indefinitely sustained reciprocity. The motto "Do as you would be done by," thus comes to replace the conception of crude equality. The child sets forgiveness above revenge, not out of weakness, but because "there is no end" to revenge (a boy of 10). (pp. 323–324)

"Do as you would be done by" represents a transformation in the nature of reciprocity reasoning. In "reciprocity as a fact" (Stage 2), one evaluates whether one's prospective action has been or will be matched by a reciprocal action; that is, one's action and its effect on another person are considered in the context of an exchange of rewards or punishments ("You scratch my back, I'll scratch yours"). In "reciprocity as an ideal" (Stage 3), one reflectively evaluates one's prospective action as if it *were* the reciprocal action; that is, one's action and its effects on another person are hypothetically inverted and used as a guide for how one person should treat another in a relationship ("If you were to treat me that way, how would I feel?; if I were to treat you that way, how would you feel?"). Mature moral reciprocity is neglected in reductionistic sociobiological (Alexander, 1987) and exchange-theory (Burgess & Huston, 1979) accounts, which generally depict moral reciprocity in Stage 2 terms (cf. Losco, 1986).

Stage 3 moral judgment does not fully represent moral-cognitive adequacy or maturity for individuals living in a society more complex than a small community. As adolescents or adults move beyond local communities to universities or complex work settings, they increasingly deal with anonymous individuals and relate to individuals with diverse or heterogeneous values. As a result of this experience and the reflection it stimulates, their appreciation of the need for mutual trust (Stage 3) expands into an appreciation of the need for commonly accepted, consistent standards and requirements (Stage 4; cf. Edwards, 1975, 1982; Whiteford & Gibbs, 1991). In the words of one 18-

year-old, the purpose of laws is "to set up a standard of behavior for people, for society living together so that they can live peacefully and in harmony with each other" (Adelson, B. Green, & O'Neil, 1969, p. 328). Commonly accepted standards and requirements, then, "promote cooperation or social contribution and act as regulations designed to avoid disagreement and disorder" (Kohlberg, 1984, p. 632). As one of the subjects in Kohlberg's longitudinal study said, "You've got to have certain understandings in things that everyone is going to abide by or else you could never get anywhere in society, never do anything" (Colby et al., 1987, p. 375). In other words, individuals in a complex society must generally understand their interdependence with others. They must accept a balance between their rights or freedoms and their responsibility to respect others' rights as well as to contribute to society. In the absence of such commonly accepted "understandings," not only will society "never get anywhere," but (in the words of another subject) "chaos will ensue, since each person will be following his or her own set of laws" (p. 375).

The general age-related progression from a superficial (physicalistic, egoistic-instrumental) orientation to a profound orientation (mutual trust or caring underlying relationships, commonly accepted standards or interdependencies underlying society) in moral judgment has been found in longitudinal studies (Colby et al., 1983; Page, 1981; Walker, 1989) and in cross-cultural research. In a review of Kohlbergian moral judgment studies in 27 countries, Snarey (1985) concluded that Kohlberg's Stages 1 through 4 are "represented in a wide range of cultural groups" (p. 218). At least Stages 1 through 3 are discernible in Damon's (1977; cf. Leahy, 1983) study of children's reasoning concerning fair distribution and legitimate authority, Youniss's (1980) study of friendship conceptions, Selman's (1980; Selman & Shultz, 1990; cf. Bigelow, 1977) broader investigation of interpersonal thought and action; and Eisenberg's (1982) study of prosocial reasoning.

C. C. Peterson, J. L. Peterson, and Seeto (1983) described superficial-to-profound transitions in children's developing conceptions of lying. In response to the question, "What happens when lies are told?," 92% of 5-year-olds referred to punishment by an authority or agency (e.g., "You get sick/belted/into trouble," p. 1533), whereas only 28% of 11-year-olds did so. Underlying intangible effects of lying, such as a guilty conscience and the loss of trust, were mentioned, respectively, by 0% and 10% of the 5-year-olds, in contrast to 28% and 48% of the 11-year-olds. The older children were more likely to take underlying intentions and situational circumstances into account, as indirectly suggested by their general unwillingness to state that lying is "always wrong" (28% versus 92% of the 5-year-olds), or to define inaccurate guesses as lies (8% versus 55% of the 5-year-olds).

The superficial-to-profound progression in morality is strikingly similar to age trends in other areas of social cognitive development. A transition from physicalistic or egoistic responses to mutualistic or system-level responses is evident in studies of ego development (Loevinger & Wessler, 1970) and development of the self-concept (Harter, 1983; Montemayor & Eisen, 1977). Similarly, a progression from judgment based on superficial, immediate appearances or actions to judgment based on underlying, inferred meaning is evident in children's developing social explanations (J. G. Miller, 1986), person descriptions (Livesley & Bromley, 1973), narrative comprehension (Paris & Upton, 1976), and understanding of gender constancy (Kohlberg, 1966; Maccoby, 1990; Marcus & Overton, 1978; Smetana & LeTourneau, 1984; but cf. Bem, 1989).

Finally, the superficial-to-profound progression is discernible in the development of reasoning concerning physical objects. Flavell (1985) has described the child's development from judgment based on "perceived appearances" to judgment based on "inferred reality" with reference to the widely studied conservation phenomenon:

Piaget's test for conservation of liquid quantity illustrates the meaning of this and other [progressions]: (1) the child first agrees that two identical glasses contain identical amounts of water; (2) the water from one glass is poured into a third, taller and thinner glass, while the child is watching; (3) the child is then asked if the two amounts of water are still identical, or whether one glass now contains more water than the other. The typical preschool nonconserver is apt to conclude, after the liquid has been poured, that the taller and thinner glass now has more water . . . [the preschooler] is more given than the older child to make judgments on the basis of the immediate, perceived *appearances* of things. . . . The conserver . . . may also think that the tall glass *looks* like it contains more water because the liquid column is higher, but goes beyond mere appearances to *infer* from the available evidence that the two quantities *are really* still the same. That is, the child makes an *inference* about *underlying* reality [last two italics added]. (pp. 93–94)

The Role of Decentration

The development of mature moral judgment (especially, the transition from instrumental to ideal reciprocity) reflects a constructive process of decentration, that is, attending to and interrelating multiple features of situations (cf. Grueneich, 1982; Kaplan, 1989; Leahy, 1983). In the conservation example,

. . . the preschooler is more prone to concentrate or *center* (hence *centration*) his attention exclusively on some single feature or limited portion of the stimulus array that is particularly salient and interesting to him, thereby neglecting other task-relevant features. In the present [conservation] example, the difference in the heights of the two liquid columns is what captures most of his attention. . . . In contrast, the older child is likelier to achieve a more balanced, "decentered" (hence, *decentration*) perceptual analysis of the entire display. While, of course, attending to the conspicuous height differences, just as the younger child does, he also carefully notes the correlative differences in container width. (Flavell, 1985, p. 94)

Flavell (following Piaget), then, accounted for the progression from superficial appearances to inferred underlying meanings—in social as well as non-social development—by reference to decentration. Accounts similar to Flavell's can be found elsewhere in the cognitive developmental literature. Case (1985) discerned in both the child's non-social (problem-solving, exploration) and social (imitation, social conflict, social cooperation) activities a "common set" of decentration-like processes (cf. Damon, 1977). Going beyond the idea that decentration can be social as well as non-social is Doise and Mugny's (1984) claim that decentration as facilitated by *social* conflict is of pre-eminent importance in *physical* cognitive development. In any event, the interrelating of situational features or perspectives may bring about inferential or intrinsic understanding, whether the interrelating and resulting understanding take place in the physical realm or the social. As Feffer (1970) put it: "A stable *construction* [italics added] of the interpersonal event depends, as in the impersonal realm, on a reconciliation of . . . complementary dimensions" (p. 206). The cognitive emergents attributable to decentration become more impressive as the child's working memory expands (Chapman & Lindenberger, 1989; Pascual-Leone, 1970, 1987).

In a 1989 review of research on social causal reasoning, P. H. Miller and Aloise noted that young children "tend not to consider" information concerning psychological states or motives unless it "is explicit and salient" (p. 268; cf. Nunner-Winkler & Sodian, 1988), that is, clearly manifested in behavior. They furthermore found that older children tend to "more effectively integrate multiple information about causes, . . . integrate information over time, and consider conflicting emotions" (p. 278). In other words, older children in sociomoral problem-solving tend to consider and interrelate motives or psychological states, even when explicit or salient *physical* determinants or consequences are present. In short, older children decenter.

Miller and Aloise also noted young children's tendency to evidence superficial, object- and action-oriented, reasoning. However, they emphasize that even very young children are able to go beyond a superficial (at least a physicalistic) understanding of interpersonal events, in that young children attribute much behavior to psychological causes. Hence, Miller and Aloise rejected simplistic characterizations of young children's social causal reasoning as "external." Construed as an increasing cognitive *tendency*, however, the age trend from external to internal (or from superficial to profound) social judgment is clear.

Decentration and Its Outcomes

As already noted, Flavell (1985) characterized *decentration* as a shift from judgment captured by attention to the most salient or interesting aspects of a situation, to judgment based on a more extensive, equally distributed, and "balanced" attention to a real or imagined situation. Extending from Flavell's analysis, we suggest that decentration processes naturally lead to certain outcomes: the reduction of self-centered judgment or egocentrism and the emergence of equality and reciprocity prescriptions in the physical and social realms. In the social realm, equality and reciprocity constitute elements of justice.

Decentration in the social realm is functionally linked to the decline of "egocentric bias" (Flavell, 1985, p. 124), or what Piaget (1932/1965) referred to as egocentrism. The child's own claims, needs, or desires (or those of someone similar and familiar to the child) are the features of a social situation that are often most salient and interesting to the child. Hence, the child's own viewpoint is likely to capture most of his or her attention (at least in the absence of an adult authority figure). This egocentric bias accounts, at least in part, for the young child's unfair, yet unabashed, self-serving allocations in distributive justice tasks (Damon, 1977).

Although egocentric bias may decline with decentration, it probably is never eliminated entirely (Gibbs, in press-a). Even with cognitive maturity, it remains true that "we experience our own points of view more or less directly, whereas we must always attain the other person's in more indirect manners. . . . Furthermore, we are usually unable to turn our own viewpoints off completely, when trying to infer another's" (Flavell, 1985, p. 125).

As the child's social attention becomes less self-centered and more extensively and equally distributed, an ideal of social equality or impartiality tends to emerge, including, for example, prescriptions that rewards be shared equally in a distributive justice task (Damon, 1977). Such an ideal is central to moral development. As Maccoby (1980) suggested, "The essence of moral maturity is giving [initially] equal weight to all moral claims" (p. 349).

The balanced aspect of the child's decentered attention gives rise to prescriptions of *reciprocity*. Damon (1977) characterized reciprocity as the correction of an "imbalance" closely related to equality, that is, as a "compensatory act . . . which consists of an *equal* [italics added] reaction to an initial action" (p. 284). Feffer (1970) virtually equated reciprocity with decentration by defining decentration as a "coordination and *reciprocal* [italics added] correction between complementary physical [or social] dimensions" (p. 204).

Reciprocity is discernible in the development of the child's judgments with respect to physical objects. In the conservation example, one type of reciprocity refers to the child's consideration of the "correlative" (Flavell, 1985) or reciprocally compensating changes in height and width dimensions of the liquid quantity. Reciprocal compensation or counter-balancing of possible acts would also seem to be implied in conservers' suggestions "that the experimenter . . . merely poured the water from one container to the other . . . without *spilling* or *adding* [italics added] any" (Flavell, 1985, p. 95). "Temporal" decentration (i.e., compensatory acts across past, present, and future states) relates to "inversion" reciprocity, as when the child suggests "that the continuing equality of amounts could be proved by pouring the liquid back into its original container" (p. 95). Temporal decentration may account for the older child's expanded temporal perspective not only in physical but also in social cognition.

Piaget (1932/1965) argued that equality and reciprocity prescriptions naturally emerge as peers facilitate social decentration by confronting and reacting to one another's viewpoints (Doise & Mugny, 1984; Youniss, 1980). As described earlier, reciprocity undergoes transformation as the child develops from Stage 2 (pragmatic exchange or reciprocity as a fact) to Stage 3 (hypothetical reversal or reciprocity as an ideal, expanded to encompass society at Stage 4). Indeed, Kohlberg (1984) suggested that "moral stages represent successive forms of reciprocity" (p. 73).

According to Kohlberg (1984), "conceptions of equality and reciprocity" constitute the structure for "sentiments of justice" (p. 41). Kohlberg chose to study "justice reasoning," in fact, because it was "the cognitive factor most . . . [likely to] provide reasoning material where structuring and equilibratory operations (e.g., reversibility) could be seen" (pp. 304–305). Although Kohlberg did not specifically utilize the concept of decentration (let alone relate decentration to equality and reciprocity), it would appear that decentration provides a plausible articulation of the cognitive "structuring" and equilibration processes to which Kohlberg referred.

Decentration and Moral Motivation

Studies of decentration in cognitive development imply that equality and reciprocity prescriptions generated through decentration can play an important motivational role. Conservation, transitivity, and other decentration-based constructions are experienced "as necessary, as something that *must* be true," rather than "as merely one of many facts that happen to be true about the world" (S. A. Miller, 1986, p. 3; cf. Nicholls & Thornkildsen, 1988; Piaget,

1971a, 1971b). The characterization of the decentration-based prescriptions in terms of "necessity" connotes their compelling or obligatory—that is, motivating—quality.

In non-social cognitive development, the motivational implications of decentration can be discerned in the responses of children in "counter-suggestion" research. In these studies, children who make conservational or other largely logic-based judgments are confronted with (false) evidence of non-conservation (e.g., the experimenter may surreptitiously add or remove material). Although interpretations of the counter-suggestion research are controversial (S. A. Miller, 1976), the general finding is that children who make logic-based judgments are surprised and upset when the experimenter confronts them with an apparent violation of "necessary" reality as they have inferred it (S. A. Miller, 1986, p. 17). They seek, for example, some explanation, some logical means of accounting for or correcting, an apparent non-conservation (Robert & Charbonneau, 1978; Smedslund, 1961; but cf. Winer, Hemphill, & Craig, 1988). In general, they act as if illogical imbalances or violations of reciprocity and equality "shouldn't be." The pertinent cognitive structuring of the situation as wrong generates a motivation to restore the "necessary" reciprocity or equality.

The parallel with the compelling or obligatory quality of prescriptive *moral* feelings is straightforward. Injustices, like violations of logic, shouldn't be. The cognitive structuring of a situation as unfair generates a motivation to restore the "necessary" reciprocity or equality (cf. Hammond, Rosen, Richardson, & Bernstein, 1989). As Kohlberg (1984) put it, "Violation of logic and violation of justice . . . arouse . . . affects" (p. 63). The motivation to correct a "reciprocity imbalance" (Gouldner, 1961, p. 167) in the social context may be no less cognitively based than is the corresponding motivation in the physical-cognitive context. This intimate relationship of morality and logic is captured in Piaget's (1932/1965) intriguing assertion that "logic is the morality of thought just as morality is the logic of action" (p. 398). Similarly, Rest (1983) suggested that the sentiment of justice may have "a counterpart in people's sense of logical necessity derived from the application of basic logical schemas to phenomena" (p. 616).

Although logic and morality may be intimately related, Kohlberg (1984) argued that the experiential requisites for moral-cognitive development are more complex than are those for physical-cognitive development. He further posited that physical-cognitive development is necessary, but not sufficient, for sociomoral-cognitive development. Kohlberg emphasized the particular role of social interaction in making possible the attainment, in the sociomoral domain, of the developmental "ceiling" set by the physical cognitive domain (see Walker, 1988, pp. 48–53; but cf. Damon, 1975; Helkama, 1988; Leahy, 1983, pp. 318–322).

Kohlberg grouped diverse social interaction experiences in the environment under the rubric of "role-taking opportunities":

> If moral development is fundamentally a process of the restructuring of modes of role-taking, then the fundamental social inputs stimulating moral development may be termed "role-taking opportunities." . . . Participation in various groups . . . [stimulates] development. . . . The child lives in a total social world in which perceptions of the law, of the peer group, and of parental teaching all influence one another. . . . Various people and groups . . . [stimulate] *general moral development.* . . . The more the social stimulation, the faster the rate of moral development. (pp. 74–78)

Particularly noteworthy is Kohlberg's analysis of the child's socialization experiences in the home. He argued that "parental socialization is not unique or critically necessary for moral development," because the role-taking opportunities it provides can alternatively be provided by "other primary groups" (p. 75). Hence, parents who, as part of discipline, induce a child to consider how he has hurt another (what Hoffman, 1983, termed *inductive discipline*), are viewed by Kohlberg as providing but one of many possible types of social role-taking opportunities for the child to attend to and consider another's perspective (cf. Keasey, 1971; Sedikides, 1989; Whiteford & Gibbs, 1991).

In summary, then, the child progresses in moral judgment from a relatively superficial (physicalistic, egoistic-instrumental) level to a more profound and mature level in which he or she gains insight into the psychological meaning and functional basis of human interpersonal relationships (mutuality of expectations) and society (commonly accepted standards and interdependencies). The progressive construction of moral judgment stages results from a decentering process that operates upon environmental "input," such as social role-taking opportunities, and establishes a cognitive basis (equality and reciprocity, i.e., justice) for moral motivation.

A REVISIONIST VIEW OF KOHLBERG'S THEORY

In general, as we have seen, Kohlberg contended that moral development represents at least in part a "natural" constructive process distinguishable from internalization processes. Furthermore, Kohlberg contended that as a result of this constructive process, a cross-culturally standard sequence of stages of moral judgment development and maturity could be identified (see Kohlberg, 1971, 1984; for a review of pertinent research, see Walker, 1988). Our view is consistent with—indeed, is based on—both of these general contentions concerning moral development and maturity. Nonetheless, our view entails certain revisions pertaining to problems in Kohlberg's specific formulation of these contentions, namely: (a) his confusion of construction with internalization in "natural" moral developmental processes, and (b) his misrepresentation of moral judgment maturity.

Discussion of both of these points requires familiarity with Kohlberg's developmental typology. Kohlberg classified six stages of moral judgment development in terms of three developmental levels: preconventional, conventional, and postconventional. Drawing upon certain early 20th-century writings (Dewey & Tufts, 1908; McDougall, 1908), Kohlberg (1984) characterized his first two stages as preconventional (preceding the understanding and acceptance of social conventions); Stages 3 and 4 as conventional, "conforming to and upholding the rules and expectations of conventions of society or authority just because they are society's rules, expectations, or conventions" (p. 172); and Stages 5 and 6 as postconventional, "based on formulating and accepting the general moral principles that underlie these rules" (p. 173). The postconventional level is considered mature not only because of the discernment of underlying moral principles, but also because the moral principles are "self-chosen" and independent of social approval or disapproval:

> One way of understanding the three levels is to think of them as three different types of relationships between the *self* and *society's rules and expectations*. From this point of view, Level I is a preconventional person, for whom rules and social expectations are something *external* [italics added] to the self; Level II is a conventional person, in whom the self is identified with or *has internalized* [italics added] the rules and expectations of others, especially those of authorities; and Level III is a postconventional person, who has differentiated his or her self from the rules and expectations of others and defines his or her values in terms of *self-chosen* [italics added] principles. (p. 173)

Developmental Processes in Kohlberg's Theory

Kohlberg is, in some respects, self-contradictory in his discussions of the processes accounting for moral judgment development. Internalization of the initially external rules and expectations of others is explicitly referred to by Kohlberg in accounting for the preconventional-to-conventional transition. On the other hand, as quoted earlier, Kohlberg suggested that "natural" moral development (presumably even at the lower levels) "cannot be defined as a direct internalization of external cultural norms" (p. 93).

The apparent contradiction could be resolved if Kohlberg did not intend to discard models of *indirect* internalization in moral development. To account for specific transitions from stage to stage, Kohlberg suggested that role-taking opportunities would only be developmentally stimulating if they provided an optimal (i.e., moderately more advanced) moral judgment "match" relative to the individual's developmental level. Hoffman (1988) correctly pointed out, however, that the optimal-match process still entails "an implicit moral internalization concept" (p. 523), because a match still requires an external referent. Hence, internalization figures into Kohlberg's depiction of development, at least from the preconventional to the conventional level, even if the child is actively constructing (or re-constructing) the initially external morality.

Construction can be distinguished from internalization (Gibbs & Schnell, 1985). This point is perhaps best illustrated in the non-social cognitive realm. Ames and Murray (1982) found that the acquisition of conservation could result from the confrontation of one preconservational child by another, for example, the confrontation of a child who believes a taller, narrower glass holds more liquid by a peer who (centering instead on the narrowness) argues it holds less. In these studies, cognitive development results from reciprocally stimulating social interaction between children with opposing types of centration (Doise & Mugny, 1984). The conflict brings home to each child the alternative feature (narrower or taller) and the need to resolve the contradiction (the glass cannot hold both more water and less water; Feffer, 1970). The acquisition of conservation cannot be attributed to internalization in the sense that the child copies the concept from an external model. There is no model in this situation, because both children are preconservational! Hence, this achievement of a deeper understanding cannot be construed as an internalization, but must instead be interpreted as a "pure" de novo construction (Murray, 1983). Analogous constructions take place in moral-cognitive development as well (Walker, 1988, p. 61).

We hasten to acknowledge that cognitive development is not exclusively constructive in this "pure" sense; it almost certainly includes at least modified internalization processes. It is probably important that the environmental role-taking opportunities in natural moral-cognitive development typically include exposure to higher stage reasoning:

> The constructive process, whatever its precise nature, does not take place in a vacuum. In the course of their everyday experience, children encounter all sorts of implicit or explicit examples of the higher level concepts which they themselves will acquire. That does not imply that they internalize the examples to which they are exposed in any direct or automatic way. But it is equally unlikely that they systematically ignore them. . . . The objective . . . must be to understand the specific ways in which the individual's constructive activity utilizes these external data. (Kuhn, 1988, p. 229)

Maturity in Kohlberg's Theory

Kohlberg strongly implied that moral judgment maturity is most properly defined by the postconventional level (his Stages 5 and 6). In contrast, we argue that the postconventional or so-called "principled" level should not be regarded as the exclusive repository of moral judgment maturity or even as a part of a standard stage sequence. Indeed, it is time, finally, to discard the very terms *preconventional, conventional,* and *postconventional* so that a more valid understanding of moral judgment maturity can emerge. We regard Stages 3 and 4 as already representing mature moral reasoning. We defend this view on the basis of a critique of Kohlberg's Stages 5 and 6.

Kohlberg's changing criteria for defining postconventional moral judgment are noteworthy. During his longitudinal work in the 1960s, Kohlberg discovered that some students who were scored at Stage 5 or 6 during high school (Kohlberg, 1963) were scored at Stage 2 when retested later as college students. This discovery presented a theoretical problem: If the high school scores were correct—if these students' reasoning in high school really had been postconventional—then approximately 20% of the sample's moral judgment stage development would have evidenced stage regression (Kohlberg & Kramer, 1969). Such a regression would fly in the face of one of the basic contentions of Kohlberg's theory, namely, the notion of invariant stage sequence: that stages progress in a regular, consecutive order. This invariance would be invalidated by such longitudinal results. To solve this problem, Kohlberg (1973, 1984; Colby et al., 1987) innovated two reclassifications: (a) ostensible Stage 2 judgments in college protocols were reconstrued as in fact postconventional (albeit not yet principled, i.e., a relativistic moral-philosophical level labelled "4 1/2"—Kohlberg, 1973); and (b) ostensible principled-sounding moral judgments in high school were reconstrued as actually indicative of Stages 3 and 4. For example, certain judgments by high school students that "the moral value of life [takes] precedence over obedience to laws or authority" (Kohlberg, 1984, p. 447) were re-interpreted as at the conventional rather than postconventional level.

Kohlberg thereby restored the invariant, non-regressive stage sequence. However, in the process of solving this problem he created a new one: a contradiction between the principled-sounding moral ideality now included in Stages 3 and 4 and the traditional designation of those stages as "conventional." In particular, how could a subject whose moral judgment represents an internalization of and conformity to "the rules and expectations of others, especially those of authorities" (Kohlberg, 1984, p. 173) produce moral judgment conceptualizing "the moral value of life as taking precedence over obedience to laws or authority" (Kohlberg, 1984, p. 447)?

We do not believe that Kohlberg fully solved, or even fully recognized, this contradiction. We do believe, however, that two of his theoretical innovations during the last years of his life represented, in effect, efforts (although not altogether successful ones) to cope with this contradiction. First, consider Kohlberg's (1984) claim that even the newer Stage 3 and 4 moral judgment is still conventional because it still embodies a "member-of-society perspective" rather than a "prior-to-society perspective" (as at the postconventional level; p. 177). In practice, establishing this distinction in perspective proves quite elusive. Even Kohlberg's prime illustration of the distinction seems problematic. Joe, one of his longitudinal subjects, answered the question, "Why should a promise be kept?," at age 17, and again at 24. Joe's justification at 17 was that "friendship is based on trust. If you can't trust a person, there's little grounds to deal with him." At 24, Joe's justification was that "human relationships in general are based on trust, on believing in other individuals. If you have no way of believing in someone else, you can't deal with anyone else and it becomes every man for himself." Kohlberg suggested that in the first answer, Joe "expects trust of others in general . . . as a member of society" (ostensibly rendering the moral judgment scorable at the conventional level), whereas in the second answer, he considers "why any society or social relationship presupposes trust, and why the individual, if he or she is to contract into society, must be trustworthy" (ostensibly rendering the moral judgment scorable at the postconventional level; pp. 179–180).

Is there really such a difference in perspective in these examples? Granted, the second justification is broader in scope ("human relationships" rather than "friendship") and mentions the chaotic consequences if social dealings are not based on trust ("it becomes every man for himself"). But both responses essentially state that trust is a necessary basis for relationships. Why should the first moral judgment not also be considered "mature"? In our scoring system (as presented initially in Gibbs & Widaman, 1982, and refined further in this book), the developmental difference between the justifications is more modest (Transition 3/4 vs. Stage 4). We believe that moral judgment at the so-called conventional level can already be hypothetical or prior-to-society, in light of adolescents' hypothetically reflective responses to the "desert island" problem and questions concerning law and community (Adelson, B. Green, & O'Neil, 1969; Adelson & O'Neil, 1966).

In addition to innovating the member-of-society/prior-to-society distinction, Kohlberg (1984) also innovated the construct of *moral sub-stage* or *moral type* in an effort to resolve the contradiction. Roughly speaking, in Kohlberg's 1960s revision, traditional Stage 3 (conventionally expressed interpersonal ideals) and Stage 4 (conventionally expressed societal ideals) moral judgment became designated as Stage 3 Type A and Stage 4 Type A, whereas the principled-sounding moral judgment imported from the postconventional level became designated as Stage 3 Type B (basic and universalized interpersonal ideals) and Stage 4 Type B (basic and universalized societal ideals). Although 3B and 4B embody moral ideality, Kohlberg argued that they are still at the "conventional" level because they only implicitly or "intuitively [give] priority to moral values over legal and customary ones" (p. 451). As with the member-of-society/prior-to-society distinction, however, the implicit-explicit distinction seems rather difficult to establish in practice. An example of a 3B moral justification is that "life is more important than anything else, it's more important than money or anything in this world" (Colby & Kohlberg, 1987, p. 355). A corresponding Stage 5 justification is that "it's all well and good to talk about property rights, but I don't think they mean much in a society that doesn't value human life higher" (Colby et al., 1987, p. 55). Granted, the second justification explicitly refers to property rights and society, but couldn't this justification represent a 4B societal version of the 3B fundamental valuing of life? After all, 4B moral judgment recognizes human life as a fundamental value or right in any society's balance between human rights and responsibilities. Although the Moral Type distinction is an interesting and useful one (indeed, it is incorporated into our own work), the "intuitive" or implicit quality of Moral Type B reasoning does not constitute valid grounds for classifying such reasoning as merely conventional or immature.

The intuitive/explicit distinction is not only difficult to establish in practice; it is also poor developmental theory. Granted, some respondents enhance the explicitness of their sociomoral justifications by references to explicitly formulated ethical theory or philosophical reflection. Kohlberg (1973; cf. 1984) described such discourse as "defining a moral theory and justifying basic moral terms or principles" (p. 192); Brandt (1959) described it as "the explicit formulation of principles about obligations" (p. 14). In our view, however, such reasoning does not entail any additional stages beyond Stage 4. We do not see that it makes any theoretical sense to characterize the explicit use of ethical philosophy as a higher natural developmental stage, any more than it would make sense to characterize the use of a systematic philosophy of language or mathematics as a higher natural stage in language or logical development. This approach would misrepresent moral judgment maturity as the exclusive province of the philosophically articulate.

Nonetheless, we recognize that such discourse can be functionally helpful for enhancing the clarity or ideality of one's normative ethics; the systematic study of ethics, for example, may augment the likelihood of a Type B orientation in one's moral reflection. Consistent with our view is Brandt's reference to the:

. . . enrichment of personal insight to be gained from the study of [philosophies of] ethics. . . . Merely the explicit formulation of principles about obligations should make us more sensitive to those obligations. It should make us less liable to be deceived by selfish ethical reasoning in ourselves or others. It should make us more perceptive in our moral assessment of ourselves and our motivation. (Brandt, 1959, p. 14)

It is in this sense of development in terms of greater clarity or veridicality—but not stage advance—that the value of advancing from intuitive to explicit moral judgment should be understood.

Again, our view is that Stages 3 and 4—especially 3B and 4B—evidence moral-cognitive maturity. We believe that the only valid solution to the problem with which Kohlberg struggled is to jettison the preconventional –conventional–postconventional trichotomy; once this is done the mature character of Stages 3 and 4 can finally be recognized. Even 3A and 4A judgments represent a profound moral understanding of the bases for viable interpersonal relationships and social systems. However, 3A and 4A thinking is more embedded in existing social arrangements—and hence is less clearly ideal—than is that of 3B and 4B reasoning. Because field dependence/field independence correlates with Type A/Type B (Gibbs et al., 1986), we suspect that the greater differentiation from social conventions or conformity of Type B reflects a more field-independent cognitive style expressed in the context of moral judgment. Indeed, Gibbs et al. (1986) found that Stage 3B/4B high school students were more likely than their Type A counterparts to be rated high in "moral courage" (a kind of social-behavioral field independence) by their teachers. In contrast, the social conformist tendencies of Stage 3A high school students provide some basis for Lickona's (1983) concern that Stage 3 (at least Type A) relationship-oriented thinkers sometimes "care so much about what others think of them that they can turn into moral marshmallows, willing to do something because 'everybody's doing it'" (p. 161).

On the basis of our revisionist view, we can critique alternative revisionist suggestions, most notably those of Snarey (1985) and Turiel (1989). Snarey's suggestion, based on a cross-cultural review, stems from the problem that Kohlberg's postconventional level is cross-culturally rare. Such rarity is inconsistent with Piagetian expectations that mature stages should be "commonly in evidence throughout humanity" (Gibbs, 1977, p. 50), and relatively spontaneous or unconfounded with cultural ideology (Gibbs, 1979). It is important to note that this problem led Kohlberg himself to announce a startling theoretical retreat. Because *none* of Kohlberg's longitudinal subjects reached Stage 6 (as defined in terms of the late 1960s stage revisions), Kohlberg (1984) suspended his empirical claims for Stage 6, acknowledging that his contemporary definition "came from the writings of a small elite sample, elite in the sense of its *formal philosophical training* [italics added] and in the sense of its ability for and commitment to moral leadership" (p. 270). As for Stage 5, Snarey found that the frequency of Stage 5s within any sample is rarely high, and that it was not found at all in "tribal or village folk societies" (p. 218). Furthermore, Snarey noted that Stage 5 is based on the individualistic philosophies of "Kant, Rawls, and other Western philosophers [and hence is] incomplete" (p. 228). In this connection, it should be noted that it is now rare for a subject to be scored at Stage 5 in production measures. For example, Kohlberg (1984; cf. Colby, Kohlberg, Gibbs, & Lieberman, 1983) found that only 13% of his longitudinal subjects reached Stage 5 (even counting stage mixtures including Stage 5 as a major or minor stage), and all of these subjects had some graduate education.

Snarey suggested that Kohlberg's characterization of Stage 5 be supplemented with more "collective" postconventional principles from non-Western societies (cf. Vasudev & Hummel, 1985), and that, through such supplementations, Stage 5 would become a valid stage construct. In our view, however, even a Snarey-revised Stage 5 would be an inappropriate definer of moral judgment maturity because it would still confuse maturity with philosophical articulateness or verbal sophistication.

Our dissatisfaction with Kohlberg's reserving mature or intrinsic morality for the postconventional level is shared by Turiel (1983, 1989), although our interpretation differs from Turiel's. He presented evidence that even young children can distinguish moral right and wrong from social conventions, and can appreciate morality's intrinsic character: for example, that hitting someone is always wrong, whereas addressing a teacher by a first name may or may not be wrong, depending on the particular social convention. Turiel's distinction between morality and social convention may still be problematic, however, because "violation of a social convention that has no intrinsic harmful effect can, nevertheless, cause human suffering by hurting another's feelings or showing contempt for the other's dignity" (Rest, 1983, pp. 609–610; cf. Kagan, 1987, p. xviii). Furthermore, Turiel did not present evidence that young children's moral judgment is intrinsic in the sense of inferring an underlying meaning, for example, that breaking a promise is wrong because it destroys trust. Indeed, an unqualified rejection of hitting that fails to consider situational circumstances (prior provocation, self-defense, absence of hostile intent, etc.), suggests possibly superficial judgment concerning the immorality of aggression. Understood as the progression from superficial appearances to inferred underlying meanings, the extrinsic-intrinsic trend is clear in cognitive development generally and moral judgment in particular.

THE STAGES

In the remainder of this chapter, moral-cognitive development and maturity are discussed in greater detail. We discuss the developmental stages of moral judgment—or more precisely, sociomoral reflection—as the stages have been articulated in our research. Although interesting in their own right, the descriptions will also be valuable for the stage assessment work in the succeeding chapters.

Our concern is with sociomoral justification. Sociomoral justifications are the reasons one gives for decisions or values (keeping a promise, telling the truth, helping a friend, saving a life, not stealing, etc.) pertaining to benevolent and fair behavior. We prefer "sociomoral" to "moral" because the unadorned "moral" is for many people rife with misleading solipsistic or privatistic connotations. In the Piagetian/Kohlbergian approach, "morality" is understood as deeply and inextricably rooted in social interaction (see Gibbs, in press-b). One's sociomoral justification is structured by one's understanding of "the nature of the *relations* between persons (or between persons and their institutions) and the *transactions* that serve to regulate, maintain, and transform these relations" (Damon, 1977, p. 2).

A given sociomoral stage, then, refers primarily to the character or "structure" of one's justifications pertaining to prescriptive relations and transactions between people. Consider the following four paragraphs, each of which provides a "structure" for justifying the value or importance of keeping promises or telling the truth in human relations:

"You should always keep your promise, and never be a tattletale. If you made a promise to a friend, it wouldn't be nice to break your promise because then he wouldn't play with you and wouldn't be your friend any more. Or he'd cry or beat you up. Not only that, but your parents will punish you if you lie or break a promise."

"Your friend has probably done things for you and may return the favor if you help him by keeping your promise. Besides, you may like your friend, and this could be your only friend. Lies catch up with you sooner or later, and once they do you'll be in worse trouble because the other person may get even. If it's parents and children, then parents should keep their promises to the children if the children have kept their promises to their parents. But if the promise is to someone you hardly know, then why bother? They'll probably never know whether you kept it or not."

"Your friend has faith in you, and you shouldn't betray that trust or hurt their feelings. After all, you'd expect them to keep their promises to you, and having a friend to share feelings with means a lot. Even if it's not a friend, honesty is still the best policy and it's just common courtesy. It's selfish to break promises, and once you make a bad impression people won't think much of you. If it's a child and the parents don't keep promises, the children will stop believing in their parents and will start thinking that lying is all right. Even if it's someone you hardly know, you may start a good relationship by showing that you care and can be trusted."

"Society is based on trust, and keeping promises is necessary for the sake of the social order. Honesty is a standard everyone can accept, and you wouldn't want to live in a society where you couldn't trust anyone. After all, promises have intrinsic value, and a relationship is meaningless if there is no trust. In the case of a child, parents have an obligation to keep their word and to provide an example of character so that the child develops a sense of responsibility. Keeping a promise is a commitment and a matter of honor—failing to keep it, even if it's to someone you hardly know, reflects on your integrity. People must be consistent and not break promises whenever they feel like it, so that they earn others' respect to say nothing of their own."

As cognitive developmentalists, we claim that these four paragraphs justifying the importance of keeping promises or telling the truth are: (a) qualitatively different, and (b) progressively more adequate or mature. In fact, in light of the preceding discussion, one should recognize that these paragraphs exemplify moral judgment at Stages 1 through 4, respectively. Such paragraphs summarizing the reasoning stages are called "montages" and are utilized in moral judgment scoring (see chapters 4 through 8).

The Immature Level

As described earlier, Stages 1 and 2 constitute the immature level of sociomoral reflection. Both are relatively concrete or superficial, confusing morality with physical power (Stage 1) or pragmatic deals (Stage 2).

Stage 1: Unilateral and Physicalistic

Sociomoral justification at Stage 1 represents a morality of unilateral authority, especially the authority of physically powerful persons. Piaget's (1932/1965) description of this morality as "heteronomous" (literally, "rules from others") aptly captures its extrinsic and authority-oriented character. Although the Stage 1 thinker can recognize different perspectives over time, there is little discernible coordination of these perspectives; hence, the perspective-taking is "unilateral" (Selman, 1980) and is often expressed in absolute terms ("always" or "never"). The facets or "aspects" that define Stage 1 thinking are as follows.

Aspect 1: Edicts of Unilateral Authority (Unilateral Authority)

This aspect consists of a simple appeal to an authority figure (parent, spouse, God) or other embodiment of authority (the law, the Bible). There is no differentiation of the position of authority from the person of authority. The appeal to authority is usually not elaborated, as if the very invocation of the authority's name were a sufficient justification in itself. The authority seems to be taken as a given prior presence (e.g., "The law is there for you to follow"). Anything an authority—especially a physically powerful authority—declares is, ipso facto, morally right.

Aspect 2: Immediate or Physical Status (Status)

Evaluations at Stage 1 may also be justified by an appeal to the most salient role or status of the person or persons involved. For example, helping one's parents might be important because they're "big," "older," or "grown up." Saving a life might be justified because the person saved might "own a lot of furniture." Occasionally the "status" may refer to an object: Not stealing might be justified by the consideration that the object stolen "might cost a lot of money." The appealed-to status is "immediate" in that it is conceptualized without an appreciation of underlying psychological mediators.

Aspect 3: Coercive Rules, Maxim-Like Prescriptions, or Absolute Proscriptions (Rules)

This aspect of Stage 1 justification consists of flat assertions that have a maxim-like ring and that are often couched in absolute terms. For example, saving a stranger's life may be seen as *not* important because "you should never go near strangers." The assertions are usually proscriptive, but may sometimes be prescriptive ("you should always keep your promises"). The adverbs *always* and *never*, especially as in "you should always/never . . .," are strongly suggestive of Stage 1 reasoning. The Rules aspect entails a quite rigid, constraint-oriented, or coercive view of roles. For example, the importance of sending lawbreakers to jail may be supported with the suggestion that "a judge has to send people to jail."

Aspect 4: Unqualified Positive or Negative Labels (Labels)

This facet of Stage 1 thinking consists of the superficial application of gross or undifferentiated labels (e.g., good/bad, nice/mean, right/wrong) in moral justification. (The use of even simple psychological labels, e.g., happy/sad, can be more advanced and is designated as Transition 1/2.) Thus one should keep a promise "to be nice" or because otherwise "you'd be a tattletale" or the other person "won't be your friend." Note that certain assertions, such as "You should never tattletale," would be classified under Rules, not Labels.

Aspect 5: Physical or Punitive Consequences (Physical Consequences)

This aspect consists of the justification of moral values in terms of physicalistic—usually punitive—consequences for violating the normative value, for example, one will be punished for disobeying laws. The anticipation of punitive consequences is expressed in the simple future tense, suggesting that the punishment is felt to be inevitable or unavoidable. The punitive event is represented in physical or action terms (being spanked, beaten up, killed, found out, punished, put in jail). Although the physical consequences are usually punitive, they may also be positive, for example, keeping a promise to get a treat.

Stage 2: Exchanging and Instrumental

The unilateral heteronomy of Stage 1 is succeeded at Stage 2 by an "autonomous" (Piaget, 1932/1965) morality of social interaction. In other words, sociomoral justifications now reflect a moral understanding that derive not from salient appearances such as physical power, but instead from the perspectives that arise through one's interaction with others. Accordingly, Stage 2 represents a more "rational" morality than does Stage 1. On the other hand, the "rationality" of Stage 2 thinking is peculiarly narrow in that social ethics are treated as a matter of pragmatic deals or exchanges (cf. Piaget's "reciprocity as a fact"). One helps a friend who has done you favors because he or she may return the favor. In its own way, then, Stage 2 morality is still extrinsic and superficial. There are six aspects of Stage 2.

Aspect 1: Quid Pro Quo Deals or Exchanges (Exchanges)

This aspect of Stage 2 reflection is comprised of justification by appeal to "tit-for-tat" exchanges or deals with others. For example, helping one's parents is important because "they've done things for you" or, by the same token, helping a friend is not important if the friend "hasn't done anything for you lately." Also included under Exchanges are anticipations of reciprocation, either positive (the friend "might return the favor") or negative (otherwise the friend "might get even"). Legal justice is justified as a negative reciprocation that the lawbreaker should be able to accept as a fair deal if he is caught ("If you can't do the time, don't do the crime"). Anticipations of benefits not explicitly reciprocative are classified under Advantages.

Aspect 2: Strict Equalities or Inequalities (Equalities)

In contrast to the authoritarian relations so congenial to Stage 1 thinking, Stage 2 moral cognition is emphatically egalitarian, a quality described by Piaget (1932/1965) as "crude equality" (p. 323). For example, helping one's parents may not be important because "the children are equal, so parents shouldn't boss them around." People shouldn't take things that belong to others because "I don't steal so they shouldn't either." Judges should sometimes be lenient because "the judge might have stolen something, too."

Aspect 3: Concrete Rights or Unfettered Freedoms (Freedoms)

This aspect generally covers appeals to unfettered or unconstrained freedoms as concrete rights. For example, saving a stranger's life may be evaluated as unimportant because "you shouldn't stick your nose in someone else's business." "Living even when you don't want to" may be evaluated as unimportant because "if you don't want to live you don't have to." Judges should sometimes be lenient to lawbreakers if free choice was restricted ("maybe he was forced into stealing").

Aspect 4: Contingent Preferences or Dispositions (Preferences)

This aspect generally covers justifications where the favorable evaluation is made contingent on the actor's wishes, desires, or inclinations. For example, helping a friend is important "if you want to" or "if you like your friend." Occasionally, the appeal to preferences is generalized ("no one wants to go to jail"), explicitly prescriptive ("you should want to live"), or referring to others (not stealing is important because other people "like their things").

Aspect 5: Pragmatic Needs (Needs)

This aspect consists of appeals to assumed or probable pragmatic needs. For example, not stealing is important because "you may not need to steal" or other people "need their things." Helping others is important "if they need you" to help them or because "this might be your only friend."

Aspect 6: Calculated Advantages or Disadvantages (Advantages)

This aspect of Stage 2 thinking bases moral values on the calculation of anticipated practical benefits or liabilities. Living even when you don't want to is important because "you could still have fun." Helping a friend is important if they "might do you a favor some day" (note that reference to a reciprocation in kind, e.g., "might return the favor," is classified under Exchanges). Obeying the law may be evaluated as important because "you shouldn't take the risk" involved in breaking a law, because "you don't know what you're getting into," or because "stealing gets you nowhere." Sending lawbreakers to jail is important so that they "don't go out and steal again." On the other hand, keeping a promise to someone you hardly know is "stupid because that person will never know" that you didn't keep your promise.

The Mature Level

As described earlier in this chapter, continued cognitive decentration through social role-taking opportunities brings about a more mature level of sociomoral reflection. The mature moral reasoner "penetrates" through superficial or extrinsic considerations to infer the bases of interpersonal relationships (Stage 3) or society (Stage 4). The mature level of sociomoral reflection is described in terms of both moral type and stage.

Moral Type

As noted earlier, the Type A/Type B distinction pertains to the extent to which the prescriptive ideals of the mature stages are evidenced. Ethical ideals are expressed in Type B thinking, whereas Type A indicates an "embedding" of the stages' ethical ideality in social conventions, or an assimilation of basic, universalizable interpersonal and societal ideals to existing social arrangements. Moral Type B is:

> . . . more balanced in perspective. A 3A decides in terms of What does of good husband do? What does a wife expect? A 3B decides in terms of What does a good husband who is a partner in a good mutual relationship do? What does each spouse expect of the other? Both sides of the equation are balanced; this is fairness. At 4A, the subject decides in terms of the question, What does the system demand? At 4B the subject asks, What does the individual in the system demand as well as the system, and what is a solution that strikes a balance? . . .
>
> Because of this balance, B's are more prescriptive or internal, centering more on their judgments of what ought to be. They are also more universalistic, that is, more willing to carry the boundary of value categories, like the value of life, to their logical conclusion. (Kohlberg, 1984, p. 185)

Accordingly, our articulation of the ethical ideality of Moral Type B features three components: balancing, fundamental valuing, and conscience.

Balancing

According to Kohlberg Moral Type B is more balanced in perspective. Whereas Moral Type A emphasizes given expectations in an interpersonal relationship (Stage 3) or society (Stage 4), Moral Type B designates an orientation to the ideal *mutuality* of interpersonal or societal expectations. For example, a father should not expect to be respected if he has not tried to treat his child fairly, that is, if he has not earned his child's respect. In a broader realm, although society legitimately expects a judge to apply legal sanctions consistently, the judge should apply the law flexibly or equitably when there are extenuating circumstances in particular cases.

Fundamental Valuing

Moral Type B thinking is also universalistic, that is, it extends or generalizes values such as life to all humanity, and not just to those in particular given relationships or societies, as Moral Type A would. For example, a stranger's life should be valued because all life is "precious" or "sacred," or people shouldn't just care about those in given relationships but about "all humanity." The possible basis of Fundamental Valuing in Balancing is suggested by the reasoning often associated with appeals to intrinsic values such as life: "How would you feel, if you were the stranger and no one cared enough to save your life?"

Conscience

Finally, Kohlberg describes Moral Type B as more prescriptive and internal than Type A. In other words, the ideals of mature morality are felt "from within" (Piaget, 1932/1965), or are integral to the self-definition of Type B individuals (cf. Blasi, 1984). Hence, a failure to live up to the ethics of Balancing and Fundamental Valuing results in an adverse self-judgment or "pangs of conscience." One experiences either a global self-disapproval (Stage 3) or a loss of self-respect for having violated one's standards of integrity (Stage 4).

Stage 3 and 4 aspects entailing a Moral Type B component are so indicated in the following sections.

Stage 3: Mutual and Prosocial

Stage 3 thinking transcends the pragmatics of instrumental preferences and exchanges to construct the intrinsic mutualities or interpersonal expectations of prosocial feeling, caring, and conduct. Stage 3 is represented in terms of six aspects.

Aspect 1: Relationships or Mutualities (Relationships)

This aspect consists of appeals to the mutual sentiments that emerge once the individual has attained an understanding of the psychological meaning of interpersonal relationships. Keeping promises is important for the sake of "a good relationship," because a friend "becomes a part of you," or so that the other person won't "lose faith in you." In contrast to the Stage 2 concern with the consequences for oneself of benefit or harm to another person, Stage 3 takes into account consequences to another person (especially, another person's feelings) as a consideration in its own right for determining how one should act toward others. An ideal form of reciprocity is effected by determining the moral status of an act by the criterion of how one would feel if one were the recipient of that act. For example, not stealing is important because "how would you feel if someone stole something of yours?" Helping a friend is important because "you would expect your friend to help you." Responses appealing to ideal reciprocity represent one manifestation of the Balancing component of Moral Type B reasoning.

Aspect 2: Empathic Role-Taking or Intrinsic Concern (Empathic Role-Taking)

This aspect is comprised of explicitly or strongly empathic references to another's psychological or emotional welfare. Not stealing is important because "people work so hard for their things and become very attached to them." There may be a concern for compassion, expressed in role-taking appeals to be "forgiving" or "understanding" of others. Although there is some empathic appreciation that another person will "cry" at Stage 1, or that another person may "need" or "want" something at Stage 2, empathy at Stage 3 involves a clear and direct imagining of oneself in another's place on a socioemotional level. For example, one should keep promises to avoid "hurting the other person's feelings," or should save a life because "you wouldn't want to watch someone die."

Aspect 3: Normative Expectations

This aspect consists of appeals to normally expected role conduct or to the consequences if normative expectations are violated. Illustrative responses are: "that's what friends are for," "that's what's expected of judges," and "children are supposed to honor their parents." Normative expectations are also evident in appeals to "common decency" or to the legitimacy of the expectations of hard-working people who "don't deserve to be stolen from." There is also a concern that if laws are broken or are not enforced normative expectations will break down, resulting in "chaos," "confusion," or "havoc."

Aspect 4: Underlying Prosocial or Antisocial Intentions or Personality (Prosocial Intentions)

This aspect generally covers appeals to the prosocial intentions or features of the normal social personality. Prosocial prescriptions of sympathy or sacrifice or judgments of antisocial intentions ("inhuman," "selfish," "greedy") are used not as unqualified labels (Stage 1), but rather as characterizations reflecting underlying motivational features of personality. For example, helping a friend is important not in order "to be good" or because "that's nice" (Stage 1, Labels aspect), but rather in order "to show his love" or to act "out of love" (Stage 3). The latter phrasing indicates an understanding of love as an underlying sentiment that needs to be expressed in, or is a wellspring for, prosocial conduct. Justifying appeals to "making a good impression" or not giving the wrong impression are also scored under Prosocial Intentions.

Aspect 5: Generalized Caring or Valuing (Generalized Caring)

This aspect covers appeals that generalize normative prosocial prescriptions or values beyond the context of particular relationships or roles. For example, saving a life is important because "you shouldn't just care about your friends," "even a stranger is a human life," or "life is precious." Parents should keep their promises to children because "children are people, too." Instances of Generalized Caring represent one manifestation of the Fundamental Valuing component of Moral Type B.

Aspect 6: Intrapersonal Approval or Disapproval (Intrapersonal Approval)

This aspect supports the importance of moral values by references to feelings of a clean conscience or pride, or to self-disapproval for misconduct. Keeping a promise, for example, may be justified on the grounds that it "makes you feel good inside." Not stealing is important for the sake of "peace of mind" or because otherwise "how could you live with yourself?" Sending a lawbreaker to jail may not be so important if the lawbreaker "has punished himself enough already." Instances of Intrapersonal Approval represent one manifestation of the Conscience component of Moral Type B.

Transition 3/4: Relativism of Personal Values

The transitional phases generally do not lend themselves to distinct discussion because their content categories are blends of aspects of the adjacent stage levels. For example, during the transition from Stage 3 to Stage 4, adolescents or adults normally manifest in their moral reasoning concerns that extend beyond particular interpersonal relationships, but that do not yet clearly address the functional requirements of social systems. Illustrative of such reasoning is the suggestion that keeping promises is important because "relationships are based on trust": Such a suggestion generalizes "a friendship" (Stage 3) to relationships in general, and discerns trust as an underlying requirement, but does not explicitly apply this requirement to *society* at large (as in "society is based on trust," Stage 4). Some individuals in their movement from Stage 3 to Stage 4, however, do evidence a distinct type of intermediate reasoning—*Relativism of Personal Values (RPV)*—as in the suggestion that whether keeping promises is important "depends on one's morals." Transition 3/4 RPV starts with Stage 3; its justifications refer to intentions or feelings. The RPV orientation extends beyond Stage 3, however, by relativizing those intentions or feelings as subjectively defensible values, that is, values which, if sincerely held by a person, cannot be questioned or invalidated by others (the prescriptive internality of RPV means that RPV is an indicator of the Conscience component of Moral Type B). There is generally a strong emphasis on "adhering to your own values" or "following your own judgment." Individuals who carry this emphasis to an extreme may eventually come to realize its anarchistic implications and reflect upon the need to establish commonly accepted standards if society is to survive and function smoothly (i.e., to construct Stage 4). Although transitional phases are almost by definition unstable, we suspect that Transition 3/4 RPV can remain functionally stable in a person's sociomoral reflection for an indefinite period of time, especially because of the cultural support it receives from popular ideological themes of Western societies.

Stage 4: Systemic and Standard

As described earlier in this chapter, Stage 4 extends to a complex social system the maturity accomplished at Stage 3 in the interpersonal sphere. There are seven aspects of Stage 4.

Aspect 1: Societal Requirements

This aspect covers those justifications where a moral value is supported as a requirement for society or one of its institutions. For example, obeying the law is important to "keep society in order" or because otherwise "the system would break down." Lawbreakers must be sent to jail because "the law is the backbone of our society." Keeping promises is important because "friendships require truth" or "society is based on trust." Helping one's parents is important because "the family must come before individual desires." Saving a life is important because "the world won't survive if no one cares for anyone else."

Aspect 2: Basic Rights or Values

This aspect generally relates to justifications of the importance of moral norms by appeals to basic rights or values applicable to any viable society. For example, keeping promises may be justified by the suggestion that "honesty is a standard everyone can accept." Not stealing is important because one "should respect the rights of others," and stealing is "against the morality which society has set up for itself." Helping one's parents is important because one thereby "contributes to the family unit." Life is important because "everyone has something to offer society." Where the right or value is explicitly characterized as a functional *necessity* for society, it is scored under Societal Requirements. Certain generalized assertions of basic value, for instance, "Life is sacred," illustrate the Fundamental Valuing component of Moral Type B.

Aspect 3: Societal Responsibilities or Contractual Obligations (Responsibility)

In terms of this aspect, adherence to moral norms is supported as a responsibility, obligation, or commitment that the actor has incurred or should accept. For example, keeping a promise is important because a promise is a "pact" or a "matter of honor." Sending lawbreakers to jail may be evaluated as important because "the judge has sworn to uphold the law." On the other hand, exceptions to obeying the law may be justified "if one is prepared to accept the consequences." Included here is the suggestion that with entitlement or privilege comes responsibility. For example, obeying the law may be justified on the grounds that one cannot expect to enjoy the benefits of living in society if one does not also accept the responsibilities that must go along with those benefits (this contractual version of Societal Responsibilities is one manifestation of the Balancing component of Moral Type B).

Aspect 4: Responsible Character or Integrity (Character)

This aspect of Stage 4 reflection refers to justifications that appeal to considerations of responsible character or integrity. For example, keeping promises may be justified as "a sign of character," "a reflection of one's integrity," or "showing self-respect." This concern with character may also be expressed in terms of its development: Keeping promises to one's children may be evaluated as important because parents should "provide a model of integrity, honor, or character."

Aspect 5: Procedural Precedents or Consistent and Standard Practices (Consistent Practices)

This aspect refers to justifications of the consistent or standard practice of normative moral values on the grounds that the alternative—subjective actions or decisions—is arbitrary and can be disastrous for society. For example, sending lawbreakers to jail is important "to avoid setting a dangerous precedent," or because "inconsistencies will lead to anarchy." Not stealing is important because otherwise "theft can be rationalized by anyone who steals." Similarly, saving even a stranger's life is important because "who is to say that one life is 'worth less' than another?"

Aspect 6: Procedural Equity or Social Justice (Procedural Equity)

This aspect complements the Responsibility and Consistent Practices aspects discussed above. Whereas Responsibility stresses what the individual owes the society or social institutions, Procedural Equity emphasizes what society or authority owes the individual, that is, social justice. For example, keeping promises to one's children is important because parents "should not abuse their authority" or "must earn or deserve their children's respect." (A concern with not *losing* respect is coded under Character.) Whereas the emphasis in Consistent Practices is on the need for standard procedures in order to avoid unfairness in the sense of arbitrariness, the emphasis in Procedural Equity is on the adjusted, case-by-case application of those standards for the sake of fairness in the sense of equity. The consideration may be raised that laws cannot take into account every particular case or circumstance, or the respondent may point out the judge should "interpret the law" or "realize that each case is different." Procedural Equity illustrates the Balancing component of Moral Type B.

Aspect 7: Standards of Conscience

This aspect justifies moral values by appeal to standards of individual or personal conscience: to one's "self-respect," "sense of self-worth," "personal satisfaction," "dignity," "honor," "consistency," or "integrity." (An appeal specifically against "compromising one's integrity" is scored under Character.) Use of the Standards of Conscience aspect is one manifestation of the Conscience component of Moral Type B.

Chapter 2

The Sociomoral Reflection Measure–Short Form

The main aim of this book is to provide researchers with a valid and practical instrument for assessing the maturity of moral judgment: the Sociomoral Reflection Measure–Short Form (SRM-SF). In this chapter, we describe the background and rationale for the SRM-SF, and summarize recent results concerning the reliability, validity, and practical advantages of the SRM-SF.

BACKGROUND: PRODUCTION AND RECOGNITION MEASURES

Instruments for assessing Kohlbergian stages of moral judgment fall into two categories: production and recognition. The most prominent production measure of moral judgment has been the Moral Judgment Interview (Colby & Kohlberg, 1987). The MJI uses moral dilemmas to elicit moral judgment (both reasoning and decision-making). One dilemma, for example, concerns whether a man should break the law by stealing an otherwise unobtainable drug in order to save his wife's life—Kohlberg's famous Heinz dilemma. Subjects are asked to make moral decisions (initially, whether Heinz should or should not steal the drug). They are also asked to evaluate certain moral values, for example, life (whether it is "important for people to do everything they can to save another's life") and law (whether people should "try to do everything they can to obey the law").

Subjects' moral decisions and evaluations are of secondary importance for moral judgment assessment on the MJI, however. Questions requiring moral decisions or evaluations are used to elicit moral reasoning or justification. Once they make a decision or evaluate a value, subjects are asked to explain or justify their choice or evaluation. It is subjects' sociomoral justifications that constitute the aspect of moral judgment used to assess Kohlbergian stages on the MJI. Scoring requires inferential assessment, that is, a content (or, more properly, "structural") analysis of subjects' moral justifications by the criteria provided in a scoring manual (Colby et al., 1987).

33

Most recognition measures of moral judgment have been derived from production measures, and they contain some interesting similarities and differences. Recognition measures are, in effect, multiple-choice tests, requiring subjects to evaluate or rank-order—but not to produce—statements of moral reasoning. The most prominent recognition measure derived from the MJI is the Defining Issues Test (Rest, 1979). Like the MJI, the DIT uses moral dilemmas to elicit moral evaluations. The DIT requires subjects to evaluate (rate and rank) the importance of Kohlbergian stage-significant statements of moral reasoning (derived from an early MJI scoring manual) concerning six moral dilemmas. In connection with the Heinz dilemma, for example, subjects evaluate the importance of moral reasoning appeals, such as "Isn't it only natural for a loving husband to care so much for his wife that he'd steal?" (indicative of Stage 3 moral reasoning). Such evaluations identify the reasoning justifications or issues that the subject sees as most relevant to or definitive of the moral dilemma (hence the name "Defining" Issues Test). Differential patterns of evaluation permit developmentally relevant distinctions among subjects' performances. A subject who consistently rates and ranks higher-stage reasoning as "most important" evidences a higher level of moral judgment than a subject whose highest evaluations go to lower-level considerations.

Rest (1975) argued that the evaluation of moral reasoning constitutes a sense of "moral judgment" worth assessing in its own right:

> In a great many cases in life, it is important what people recognize and appreciate in moral arguments rather than what moral arguments they spontaneously produce. For instance, a politician who only gives back to his constituency the kind of statements that he hears from them may be underestimating what his constituents can appreciate. (p. 748)

Nonetheless, it is clear that the developmental level of the moral arguments one most appreciates (or of the moral reasoning justifications one evaluates as most important) is not necessarily identical to the developmental level of the moral arguments one spontaneously produces. Hence, it is perhaps not surprising that correlations between the DIT and the MJI tend to be modest (Davison & Robbins, 1978; Froming & McColgan, 1979). On both conceptual and empirical grounds, then, it is inappropriate to use the DIT as a substitute for the MJI to assess the reasoning or justification aspect of moral judgment.

Some recognition measures ask the subject to identify from an array of reasoning justifications which one best approximates his or her own reasoning (Basinger & Gibbs, 1987; Gibbs, Arnold, Morgan, et al., 1984; Maitland & Goldman, 1974; Page & Bode, 1980). Some of these measures report good concurrent validity with production measures, as well as minimal vulnerability to self-presentational bias. Like the DIT, such measures offer certain practical advantages: They can be group-administered and quickly scored (because the scorer need merely code, rather than inferentially assess, the responses).

On the other hand, the chief disadvantage of recognition measures of moral judgment is that they are lengthy and, in places, difficult for children to read. Even the shortest and least demanding of these measures, the Sociomoral Reflection Objective Measure–Short Form (Basinger & Gibbs, 1987), includes two moral dilemmas and 48 moral reasoning justifications—including fairly sophisticated ones, such as "parents who abuse their authority are not worthy of their children's respect"—for subjects to evaluate in terms of closeness to "the reason that you would give." For similar reasons, Rest (1979) acknowledged that the DIT "cannot be used with subjects who have lower than 12-year-old reading level" (p. 256). Perhaps because of their formidable reading and attention-span requirements, the DIT and other recognition measures have generally proven to be of limited use—relative to the MJI and other production measures (Gibbs & Widaman, 1982)—with younger subjects and others with limited attentional and reading capacities, such as juvenile delinquents (Basinger & Gibbs, 1987; Blasi, 1980; Gavaghan et al., 1983; but cf. McColgan et al., 1983; Rest, 1986).

RATIONALE FOR THE SRM-SF

Based on our experience, we have concluded that recognition measures have limited value for assessing moral judgment in children and other subjects with limited reading skills. Might production measures have greater potential in this regard? The chief advantage of production measures is that, although subjects must produce statements of reasoning, at least they need not read and evaluate them. This advantage may account, in part, for the greater applicability of production measures to children, as well as for the generally greater discriminant validity of production measures in distinguishing the moral judgment of delinquents from that of nondelinquents.

Production measures are not without their own practical disadvantages, however. Inferential assessment is difficult to learn and time-consuming to accomplish. For example, MJI protocol scoring is conducted according to an intricate procedure entailing use of a several-hundred page manual (Colby et al., 1987). For many years, the only way to learn to do MJI scoring was to attend an intensive 1–2-week workshop taught by Lawrence Kohlberg and his associates at Harvard. Workshop attendance is no longer necessary because self-training materials are now available (Colby & Kohlberg, 1987), but the materials only make possible "progress *toward* [italics added] reliable scoring" (p. 241). Prospective raters presumably must continue to learn as best they can on their own with their own collected protocols. Administrators of the MJI must study and practice interview techniques modeled after Piaget's *method clinique* (described in Colby & Kohlberg, 1987, pp. 153-158), and then conduct individual oral interviews. Although the respondents' reasoning can be written down verbatim by the interviewer, the preferred procedure is to tape record the interview and then transcribe it. Written, group-administered interviews are considered marginally acceptable (with certain precautions) for college-age and older subjects (Colby & Kohlberg, 1987). Although deservedly prominent for the quality of the moral judgment assessment it makes possible, the MJI is not exemplary in practical terms.

Because of the practical difficulties of the MJI, we have for many years been working to develop simpler measures. Even before our work on new recognition measures (Basinger & Gibbs, 1987; Gibbs, Arnold, Morgan, et al., 1984), we initiated the development of new production measures of moral judgment. Our first product was the Sociomoral Reflection Measure (SRM; Gibbs & Widaman, 1982; Gibbs et al., 1982). The SRM can be group-administered, because the questionnaire format elicits a high percentage of scorable responses even without individual probing. It also allows a more straightforward assessment procedure because the questionnaire format obviates certain preliminary work necessary in MJI scoring, and because the SRM scoring system is less complex. Finally, the SRM self-training materials are sufficiently extensive to make possible the attainment of reliable scoring competence.

The SRM was a success, evidencing good reliability (internal consistency, test–retest, and interrater) and validity (concurrent and construct; see Gibbs et al., 1982). The SRM detected gender-related differences in the expression of moral judgment, while replicating findings of no gender-related stage-level differences (Gibbs, Arnold, & Burkhart, 1984). Mature moral judgment stages and "ideal" (Moral Type B) aspects, as measured by the SRM, are related to adolescents' morally courageous actions (Gibbs et al., 1986). Delinquents were found to be developmentally delayed relative to non-delinquents even in fully controlled comparisons (Gavaghan et al., 1983). Also, delinquents participating in a moral judgment group treatment evidenced significant gains (relative to control subjects) on the SRM (Gibbs, Arnold, Ahlborn, & Cheesman, 1984). Overall, S. A. Miller (1987) evaluated the SRM as one of two main alternatives to the MJI in the field of moral judgment assessment (the other alternative being the DIT).

Nonetheless, we began to suspect that an even more practical and efficient, but still valid and reliable, production measure might be feasible. Although the SRM is not as lengthy or as complex as most recognition measures, it still cannot be characterized as brief or simple. The SRM entails two moral dilemmas and 15 questions, spanning eight pages. Subjects require approximately 35–45 minutes to complete the SRM (comparable to the administration time for the DIT and the individual interview time for the

MJI); in secondary schools, administration of a measure that lengthy effectively precludes the administration of virtually any other major research measure during a single class period. Furthermore, some younger subjects and delinquents found the SRM format to be confusing at certain points.

It occurred to us that a moral judgment assessment measure could be briefer and more straightforward if it did not contain moral dilemmas. Such a direction seemed unrealistic, however. We believed that moral dilemmas play an essential role in the collection of valid moral judgment data. The moral dilemma, after all, makes at least two contributions to moral judgment assessment. First, it provides concrete situational details—a dying wife, a concerned husband, a life-saving drug, a greedy druggist—that can lead into and facilitate the process of abstract sociomoral reflection. Subjects seem to "warm up" to reasoning about moral values such as human life, affiliation, property, and the laws of society as they attend to the relevant details of the dilemma. Second, the moral dilemma promotes the likelihood that one can elicit from subjects moral "reflection without interference from preconceptions" (Walker, 1990, p. 2). In other words, moral dilemmas "set the mind working" (Brown & Herrnstein, 1975, p. 310) in fresh and spontaneous ways, rendering more likely the production of scorable reasoning, that is, patterns of thinking that are generic rather than idiosyncratic.

On the other hand, the moral dilemma—especially the hypothetical dilemmas used on the MJI—has not been without its critics. Such dilemmas have been criticized as artificial, inappropriate, or irrelevant for children (Damon, 1977; Stein, Trabasso, & Garfin, 1979), females (Gilligan, 1982), individuals in certain cultures (Boyes & Walker, 1988), and practical moral situations (Haan, Aerts, & Cooper, 1985). Some critics (e.g., Walker, 1990) have advocated the innovation and use of ecologically more valid moral dilemmas as a means to accomplish more appropriate moral judgment stages and assessment.

Again, however, we raise the question: What if moral dilemmas are not necessary at all in moral judgment assessment? To the best of our knowledge, most researchers in moral judgment methodology assume that a moral dilemma (or at least conflicting moral stories; cf. Piaget, 1932/1965) is essential to accomplish a valid, standard moral judgment measure, but no one has investigated that assumption in empirical research. If moral judgment assessment could be accomplished without moral dilemmas, and if the moral reasoning thereby elicited were found to be structurally indistinguishable from the reasoning elicited via the dilemma instruments, then dilemma-based attacks on Kohlbergian moral judgment stages would be seriously undercut. More pertinent to the present concern, however, is that a more practical (quicker to administer, easier to score) measure of moral reasoning would result. Such a product would represent an important methodological contribution to the field.

Is there any alternative to the moral dilemma in moral judgment assessment? Our aim was to explore such an alternative in developing the Sociomoral Reflection Measure–Short Form (SRM-SF). First, we suspected that brief stimulus materials could be substituted successfully for the concrete specifics of the moral dilemma. We discovered that as lead-in's for sociomoral reflection, simple statements such as "Think about when you've made a promise to a friend of yours," "Think about when you've helped your mother or father," or "Let's say a friend of yours needs help and may even die, and you're the only person who can save him or her," seem to provide sufficient contextual support for reflection even with children and delinquents. Indeed, such stripped-down contextual statements seem to preclude or reduce the extraneous details through which one must otherwise labor when scoring responses elicited by dilemma-based instruments.

Second, we suspected that the process of moral evaluation, used intermittently on the MJI and systematically on the SRM and DIT, was itself a stimulus for moral reflection. On the SRM-SF, following concrete lead-ins such as "Think about when you've made a promise to a friend of yours," subjects are asked evaluation questions such as "How important is it for people to keep promises, if they can, to friends?" Subjects are then asked to consider whether such a value is "very important," "important," or "not important." (Most respondents evaluate the values as "very important" or at least "important," implying that the moral contexts for SRM-SF moral judgment are widely accepted.) Finally, subjects are asked to explain *why* the value is important. Again, we suspect that the process of moral justification is facilitated by the prior process of moral evaluation.

Both devices (brief contextual statements and moral evaluation questions) are utilized in the SRM-SF (see Appendix A). The SRM-SF is roughly half the length of the SRM (11 items with no moral dilemmas versus 15 items and two moral dilemmas, respectively), and entails a simpler question format. Furthermore, SRM-SF scoring requires reference to only five chapters, streamlined from the eight chapters required for SRM assessment. Based on our study of the SRM-SF (described in the remainder of this chapter), we believe it is a highly successful and practical production measure of moral reasoning.

PSYCHOMETRIC AND PRACTICAL PROPERTIES
OF THE SRM-SF

We designed the SRM-SF, then, to be a production measure of moral judgment that would combine reliability and validity with a maximum degree of practical efficiency for research use. Our psychometric investigation explored five considerations pertaining to the SRM-SF: (a) It should be comparable to the MJI and SRM, in reliability (test-retest and internal consistency) and validity (concurrent, convergent, and discriminant); (b) it should be reliably scorable on the basis of relatively easy self-training exercises, rather than workshop training, as was traditionally required for scoring the MJI, or the extensive self-training now needed to score the MJI; (c) it should be less time-consuming to administer than the MJI and SRM; (d) it should be group administrable; and (e) it should be less time-consuming to score than the MJI and SRM. We now summarize the results of our investigation (Basinger, 1990; Basinger, Gibbs, & Fuller, 1991).

SRM-SF data were collected from a sample of 509 subjects representing a wide range of ages. Subjects included public school students from 4th grade, 6th grade, 8th grade, and high school (9th to 12th grade); delinquent youths; university students; and adults. The instrument was group-administered to all subjects except adults (who individually self-administered the questionnaire). Of 509 participants, 473 provided usable SRM-SF data.

Reliability and Validity

The SRM-SF evidences acceptable levels of reliability. For all subject populations sampled, test-retest correlations were highly significant. The test-retest correlation for the entire sample was $r(234) = .88, p < .0001$. Mean test-retest discrepancies (both signed and absolute) were comparable in magnitude with those obtained for the SRM (Gibbs et al., 1982). SRM-SF item responses proved to be homogeneous on the basis of the results of a Cronbach's alpha computation ($.92, N = 374$), a split-half reliability computation, and an exploratory factor analysis. Interrater reliability is summarized in a later section.

The measure also achieves acceptable validity. Acceptable concurrent validity was shown between the SRM-SF and the MJI: The correlation was highly significant, $r(43) = .69, p < .0001$. The SRM-SF demonstrates good convergent validity through positive correlations (significant at the .0001 level) with the theoretically relevant variables of age, $r(372) = .66$; verbal intelligence, $r(319) = .49$ (with age partialled out); and socioeconomic status (SES), $r(349) = .20$. Also, the SRM-SF evidenced discriminant validity by showing no correlation with a measure of social desirability. In additional investigations of the instrument's construct validity, analyses of variance showed that the SRM-SF successfully discriminated among diverse age samples (fourth graders through adults; $F(5, 368) = 199.4, p < .0001$, with each group differing from all other age groups at the .05 level of significance), indicating that the instrument is sufficiently sensitive for investigating developmental age trends (see Table 1). Further, SRM-SF scores of delinquent adolescent males differed significantly from those of nondelinquent adolescent males in an analysis of covariance controlled for age, SES, and verbal intelligence, $F(1, 154) = 8.2$, $p < .005$.

Table 1

N, MEAN SRM-SF, MEAN GLOBAL STAGE, AGE, AND SES BY SAMPLE

Sample	N	SRM-SF Score Mean	Adjusted[a]	Global Stage	Age[b]	SES
Fourth Grade	48	215.17	227.21	2	10.05	46.15 (47)[c]
Sixth Grade	43	236.83	237.70	2(3)[d]	12.06 (42)[c]	49.83
Eighth Grade	74	259.96	260.80	3(2)	14.11	47.04 (72)
High School	89	296.27	293.28	3	17.30	53.87 (87)
University	72	312.00	304.98	3	19.18	54.32 (69)
Adult	58	350.28	—	4(3)	50.66	53.99 (41)
Total	384	283.59	—	3	20.61 (383)	51.11 (359)

[a]Mean score adjusted for SES and verbal IQ.
[b]Age is represented in years and months.
[c]Numbers within parentheses indicate, in case of discrepancy, the number of subjects providing scorable data for the variable.
[d]Numbers within parentheses for the Global Stage rating represent minor-stage usage.

Finally, gender differences in moral judgment level were examined. In a comparison matched for chronological age and controlled for Verbal IQ and SES, females evidenced more mature moral judgment than males, $M = 277.1$ versus $M = 266.8$, $F(300) = 10.0$, $p < .005$. The Gender × Grade Level interaction term was also significant, $F(300) = 3.14$, $p < .05$, and permits an interpretation of the main effect. Inspection at each age level revealed that the gender difference was significant for the 6th and 8th graders but not for the 4th and 10th graders or for the college students. Hence, the moral judgment difference favoring females was evident exclusively during the pubescent years, when females are known to be maturing more rapidly than males in a number of respects. The sensitivity of the SRM-SF in this regard can be interpreted as further evidence of its construct validity.

Interrater Reliability After Self-Training

The SRM-SF shows high interrater reliability even when scored by relatively inexperienced raters. One first-year graduate student in developmental psychology and two undergraduate students studied the SRM-SF reference manual and completed the self-training exercises in Appendices B and C. They then volunteered to score, independently, 25 SRM-SF protocols each to determine whether the self-training exercises are sufficient practice to make possible acceptable interrater reliability with expert raters. Interrater reliability between two expert raters (the first two authors, John Gibbs and Karen Basinger) was also assessed. Interrater reliability was high, as measured by interrater correlations and global stage agreements (see Table 2). Hence, the SRM-SF shows higher interrater reliability than the SRM. Not only were extremely high agreements found between expert raters, but high interrater correlations, low mean maturity score discrepancies, and good global stage index agreements were found between expert and novice raters. Indeed, a high level of interrater agreement within one level was found even among the novice raters.

Table 2

CORRELATIONS, MEAN SRM-SF DISCREPANCIES, AND GLOBAL STAGE AGREEMENTS AMONG EXPERT RATERS AND TRAINEES

Raters	N	Interrater Correlation[a]	Mean SRM-SF Discrepancy		Percent Global Stage Agreement	
			Signed[b]	Absolute	Exact	Within 1 level
Experts:						
1 and 2	23	.99	0.1	7.9	73.9%	100.0%
Experts and Trainees:						
1 and 3	23	.97	3.6	12.1	65.2%	100.0%
1 and 4	22	.96	8.6	15.7	54.5%	95.4%
1 and 5	22	.97	10.1	13.7	77.2%	100.0%
2 and 3	24	.96	3.2	13.0	54.1%	95.8%
2 and 4	22	.96	8.8	15.7	59.1%	90.9%
2 and 5	23	.96	8.9	14.1	69.6%	95.6%
Trainees:						
3 and 4	22	.95	4.6	15.5	36.3%	95.4%
3 and 5	24	.94	4.8	16.7	54.1%	95.8%
4 and 5	22	.94	1.5	18.3	59.1%	95.4%

[a]All correlations are significant (p < .0001).
[b]All signed discrepancies indicate a higher mean SRM-SF rating by the former rater.

Administration

The SRM-SF is less time-consuming to complete than the SRM. Generally, the SRM-SF requires approximately 15 to 20 minutes of administration time. This is less than half the time needed for the SRM (35–45 minutes) and the MJI (at least half an hour, and sometimes longer than an hour for individual interviewing).

The SRM-SF can be group-administered successfully, as indicated by the high percentage of subjects who produced scorable protocols under group-testing conditions: Of 509 subjects who participated, only 36 subjects were dropped; 473 subjects remained in the usable samples. Thus, the attrition rate, due to failure to meet the criterion of at least seven scorable items for protocol scorability, was only 7.1%. This rate is lower than the 10% generally obtained in the use of moral judgment production measures. It is noteworthy that the attrition rate for the fourth-grade sample is actually lower than that for the high school sample (4% versus 8%, respectively), which would suggest that the SRM-SF may be used with subjects even younger than those we tested. Preferably, however, moral judgment assessment methods with preschool children should utilize concrete task materials (e.g., Damon, 1977).

The SRM-SF is less time–consuming to score than the SRM. Estimates indicate that it takes a trained rater about 20 to 25 minutes to score an SRM-SF protocol as compared with 25 to 30 minutes for an SRM protocol. Even inexperienced raters can score the SRM-SF reasonably quickly. One of the trainees noted an average time of 25 minutes per protocol to score the interrater sample of 25 SRM-SF protocols, although more time was sometimes needed for rating marginally scorable protocols. An experienced MJI scorer takes 30 minutes to an hour to score a single MJI protocol, even when the protocol has been transcribed, as recommended.

CONCLUSION

Overall, then, the SRM-SF evidences impressive reliability (test-retest, interrater, and internal consistency) and validity (concurrent, convergent, and discriminant). The SRM-SF is an efficient and practical measure: It can be group-administered in a short time (with low attrition rates even among young children), and can be scored reasonably quickly and reliably even by self-trained undergraduate scorers. The SRM-SF is a psychometrically sound and useful contribution to assessment and methodology in the study of moral development.

Chapter 3

Using the Sociomoral Reflection Measure–Short Form

The SRM-SF questionnaire (see Appendix A) is comprised of 11 short-answer items that address sociomoral values, such as saving a life, not stealing, and keeping a promise. (For example, item 1 asks: "Think about when you've made a promise to a friend of yours. How important is it for people to keep promises to friends? Very important/important/not important [circle one]. Why is that very important/important/not important [whichever one you circled]?") Subjects respond, in writing, to the 11 items. The responses elicited by each "why" question are scored for moral judgment level using chapters 4 through 8, which constitute the "reference manual." After all responses have been scored, a summary score representing the subject's overall level of moral judgment is calculated.

This chapter discusses administering the questionnaire, instructions for self-training in moral stage assessment, and procedures for calculating questionnaire ratings.

SRM-SF ADMINISTRATION

General Guidelines

Administration of the SRM-SF to most subject populations is an easy and relatively quick task. Because the SRM-SF instructions and format are self-explanatory for most subjects, it readily can be administered to groups of subjects as a pencil-and-paper test. Indeed, with some populations (such as adults), it can even be administered by mail. Most subjects can complete the questionnaire within 25 minutes.

For group-administration to subjects younger than 12 (i.e., elementary-school classes below sixth grade) it is advisable to read the instructions and the first item aloud. When all the children have completed the first item, the administrator instructs them to proceed with the remaining questions on their own. Younger subjects are often concerned about correct spelling and grammar, so the administrator may wish to emphasize that their *thinking* is what matters; perfect grammar and spelling are of lesser importance. However, the administrator should carefully inspect completed questionnaires for intelligibility. Administering the SRM-SF to young subjects (e.g., fourth graders) takes approximately 40 minutes. This procedure may also be necessary for older subjects who have reading problems. One-on-one oral administration is also an option, particularly for young children. The first author, John Gibbs, successfully administered the SRM-SF to his then 6-year-old son (although coaxing, follow-up questions, and subject payment in the amount of 25¢ were necessary).

Administrator Activities During
Administration of the SRM-SF

For most subject populations, there is not much the administrator needs to do while subjects are working on the SRM-SF. If subjects ask the meaning of a word in the questionnaire, give a simple and straightforward dictionary definition, without special interpretation. Requested spellings of words can be written directly on the subject's questionnaire for the subject to copy in writing a response. With elementary-school subjects, it is advisable to walk around among the subjects as an encouragement for them to remain task-oriented. While doing so, it is easy to make sure that subjects are, in fact, writing responses down.

Administrator Activities as Respondents
Turn in Their Questionnaires

As each questionnaire is turned in, the administrator should quickly inspect the responses for possible deficiencies listed below. This quick inspection allows the administrator to identify and remediate potentially unscorable questionnaires, resulting in an acceptable attrition rate (preferably below 10%).

If a questionnaire has one of the following deficiencies the subject should be asked to work further:

1. Question unanswered. If all of the lines following a question are blank, the subject should be asked to respond to the question.

2. Illegible writing. Subjects should be asked to re-write the response so that it is legible.

Because of the desirability of this inspection, two administrators may be necessary for group sizes larger than 30. If an administrator is working with fewer than 20 subjects, there may be enough time to examine the item responses in more detail. In this case, the administrator may be able to identify item responses with more subtle scoring difficulties (see "Unscorable Response Units," described later).

SELF-TRAINING

Self-training in SRM-SF scoring is not accomplished overnight; the process requires at least 30 hours of study and practice. Although one could conceivably complete self-training in one week, it is more usual--and advisable--to distribute the work over four to eight weeks. This time-span is comparable to that required in assessment training for other inferential measures in developmental psychology, such as the widely used Loevinger and Wessler Sentence Completion Test (1970).

The three phases of self-training are: overall familiarization; scoring practice by question (exercises provided in Appendix B); and scoring practice of questionnaires (exercises provided in Appendix C). The most important aspect of self-training is your self-improvement through study of the answer key annotations, especially the annotations of those items you rated inappropriately. The absolute percentage of response units correctly scored is of secondary importance, although a persistently high error rate (over 50%) should be cause for concern. Check to make sure that your percentage correct is generally improving as you work through the question and questionnaire exercises. Attaining competence in use of the SRM-SF will also entail study of the latter sections of this chapter, which deal with rules for calculating questionnaire score, designation of Moral Type status, and guidelines for interrater reliability.

Phase 1: Overall Familiarization

The first phase of self-training is to review chapter 1, which presents summaries of the moral judgment stages and their aspects; to examine the format of the SRM-SF questionnaire (Appendix A); and to survey the reference manual chapters (chapters 4 through 8).

Responses to the SRM-SF questions are scored by consulting the appropriate chapter in the reference manual. Questions 1 through 4 address contract and truth values and are scored using the criteria provided in chapter 4 ("Contract and Truth"). Similarly, questions 5 and 6 pertain to chapter 5 ("Affiliation"), questions 7 and 8 pertain to chapter 6 ("Life"), questions 9 and 10 pertain to chapter 7 ("Property and Law"), and question 11 pertains to chapter 8 ("Legal Justice"). (For quick and easy reference, you may wish to attach a colored and labeled index tab to the first page of each reference manual chapter.)

The basic idea of SRM-SF scoring is to assess the developmental level of questionnaire responses in accordance with the criteria in the reference manual. Each chapter of the reference manual follows a standard format. First, there is an opening discussion of moral judgment development in the context of that chapter's sociomoral value (e.g., contract and truth). Second are *montages*, that is, summary representations of moral judgment stages or transitional levels used to make a preliminary estimate of the developmental level of the response. Third are *criterion justifications* (CJs). CJs are skeletal forms of stage-significant sociomoral reflection used to make the final rating of the response. Once you have become familiar with chapter 1, the questionnaire, and the reference manual format, you should practice scoring by question (Phase 2), and, finally, entire questionnaires (Phase 3).

Phase 2: Scoring Practice by Question (Appendix B)

This phase of SRM-SF self-training involves massed practice in scoring each SRM-SF question. Appendix B contains practice exercises and annotated answer keys for each of the 11 SRM-SF questions. Each exercise is made up of 25 typical responses, taken word-for-word from actual data. These sample responses were judged to be of average-to-challenging difficulty and to be heuristic for developing assessment skill. You should work through each question exercise in accordance with the procedure described.

Turn to Appendix B and consider the first exercise response to question 1: Keeping promises to friends is important because "in this way you demonstrate you can be trusted." During Phase 2, you will learn to estimate the developmental level of this response, to evaluate the accuracy of your estimate, and to document your final stage rating.

Step 1. Familiarization with the Reference Manual Chapter

Your practice scoring should begin with a review of the reference manual chapter used in scoring each exercise response. This will familiarize you with important stage-related themes, distinctions, and justifications. Because the first four question exercises are scored using chapter 4, this chapter—especially the opening discussion and the montages—should be studied first. You should then read the first exercise response to question 1.

Step 2. Preliminary Estimate of Developmental Level

Compare the exercise response with the montage in the reference chapter. The montages provide global impressions of the stages of sociomoral reflection pertinent to the response. You may find that the montage includes a moral justification that seems similar to the exercise justification with which you are working. In such a case, it is easy to make a preliminary rating of the stage (or transitional level) of a scorable idea. (Even when such a justification is not present, however, it should be possible to make a preliminary rating based on a global impression.)

For the first exercise response, the pertinent chapter is chapter 4, "Contract and Truth." The response that justifies promise-keeping as a way to "demonstrate you can be trusted," relates most closely to the Stage 3 montage (note the justification in the montage to "**showing** that you care and **can** be trusted"). Hence, your preliminary estimate of the stage level of the response is Stage 3.

Step 3. Confirmation or Adjustment of the Preliminary Estimate

The next step is to confirm or adjust your estimated rating by examining the CJs in the pertinent reference chapter. Although the montages permit a preliminary estimate, they are insufficiently detailed to support a confident assessment of stage level (indeed, the CJs were constructed precisely because it was not possible to make the montage representation exhaustive).

CJs in a given chapter represent particular stage aspects; variations in content are indicated by lower-case letters. For example, in the Contract and Truth chapter, Stage 4:Aspect 1a (which begins "**Society** is based on trust . . .") is a CJ. Close matches between questionnaire justifications and CJs occur frequently, because the CJs were derived from a fine-grained, theoretically based analysis of more than 20 years of longitudinal and cross-sectional data (including MJI data of Colby et al., 1987, SRM data of Gibbs & Widaman, 1982, and pilot SRM-SF data used in Basinger, 1990).

Not all features of the CJs are equally important in the matching process. Portions of the CJ that are in boldface are crucial in determining the stage significance of the CJ; their essence must be in the questionnaire response if a match to the CJ is to be accomplished. On the other hand, portions of the CJ that are in parentheses, although helpful in understanding the CJ's meaning, need not appear in the response for a match to occur. As you seek to infer the optimal conceptual match, stay as close as possible to the denotative meaning of the response. Be careful not to read into a response meaning that may not have been intended.

To check your estimate, turn to the pages in the reference chapter providing the pertinent CJs for your estimated developmental level. Within each stage, CJs are organized by aspect (see chapter 1). CJs representing Moral Type B sociomoral reflection (see chapter 1) are so designated in brackets. Find the CJ at the estimated developmental level that best matches the response idea. In the example, the bracketed [4] following the Stage 3 montage reference to "**showing** that you care and **can** be trusted" indicates that this criterion justification is subsumed under Stage 3: Aspect 4 (Prosocial Intentions). The particular CJ that relates to the response is 4b, especially the phrase, "it shows you **can** be trusted."

To decide whether this CJ provides the best match, you should investigate CJs at other (usually adjacent) developmental levels which also appear to relate to the response idea. You may have noticed references to such CJs during your inspection of the montages. Most CJs include a note suggesting other developmental levels or aspects that should be reviewed. In the present example, the note suggests that the rater should compare the Stage 3 CJ "especially with Transition 2/3:Aspect 2a, 5b, and 6a, and with Transition 3/4:Aspect 8a." Inspect the lower-level CJs first. Transition 2/3:Aspect 2a will be seen not to be relevant in this case, because its content features caring rather than trust. Transition 2/3:Aspect 5b suggests promise-keeping is important because "that person will trust you (again)"; and Transition 2/3:Aspect 6a suggests that, otherwise "word will get around that you don't keep your promises." Both of these Transition 2/3 CJs are concerned to some extent with the advantages to the self of keeping a promise; neither expresses a Stage 3 concern with whether you **can** be trusted (as opposed to whether you *will* be trusted). Hence, these CJs do not provide as good a match as did the Stage 3 CJ. Now consider the higher level comparison, Transition 3/4:Aspect 8a: "(in order) to show that you are . . . **trustworthy**." The boldfaced term "trustworthy" connotes a character attribute that is not necessarily implied by the simpler "can be trusted."

Notice that "compare especially" notes are also provided for both the Transition 2/3 and the Transition 3/4 CJs. Using these notes, one might investigate possible matches at Stage 2 and Stage 4. Some responses do require investigation beyond adjacent levels (see "Complexities in Scoring" later). However, in the present example, the match at Stage 3 seems so clear that investigation beyond the adjacent (Transition 2/3 and Transition 3/4) levels is almost certainly unnecessary.

Step 4. Citation

As a result of the evaluative process of Step 3, you should be able to specify a stage and CJ that best fit the response unit. Note the stage and CJ on a work sheet. In the example, you would record Stage 3:Aspect 4b, which in the answer keys we denote as 3:4b.

Follow the four steps just described until all 25 responses of the first exercise have been rated. Then check the accuracy of your ratings by referring to the answer key. If you think you have performed well, you may be disappointed. We have rarely seen a perfect performance. Most of our self-trained raters (see chapter 2) achieved no better than two-thirds correct on the first exercise. At this point in self-training the important concern should be with how much you learn from errors, not with your percentage of correct citations. All of our self-trained raters showed progressive improvement on subsequent exercises, especially during Phase 3 of self-training (on the Appendix C questionnaires).

The notes associated with the keyed answers provide explanations of common mistakes made in scoring that question. You should read them even if your answer agrees with the key, because it is always possible that you were right for the wrong reason. It is also important for you to read and study the next section, which provides guidance in dealing with certain complexities you will encounter. Only after coming to understand why the keyed citations indicate the best match should you move on to the next exercise. After working through all eleven question exercises, you will be ready to begin Phase 3 of self-training.

Complexities in Scoring

In the course of your work with the self-training exercises, certain scoring complexities will arise. The following sections will discuss how to deal with multiple-unit or ambiguous responses, and how to identify unscorable responses.

Multiple Response Units

A response to a given question may yield more than one scorable idea or unit of justification. Consider, for example, the following justification for the importance of keeping a promise to a friend (question 1): "You keep the promise to the friend so others will like you and you need friends." This response encompasses two related but distinct scorable units: (a) that keeping promises will lead to one's being liked, and (b) that one will thereby satisfy the need for friends. During your self-training you should score each scorable unit that you find.

Although many response ideas or units are expressed in just a few words, occasionally an idea will encompass several sentences. There is no easy way to define the boundaries of a moral justification unit. Indeed, you will encounter training exercises where the boundaries of the idea are unclear: One rater may perceive and score two justification units where another rater perceives a single encompassing unit. Fortunately, the specification of the unit is ordinarily not a problem; prospective scorers typically come to perceive unit size in the same way, as they familiarize themselves with stage aspects (chapter 1) and work through the training materials. Even in those instances where the size of the unit is open to individual judgment, the scoring of the question as a whole is seldom affected because only the highest developmental level is used to establish the rating for each question in the protocol (see "Practical Scoring" section).

Ambiguous Response Units

You will often encounter an ambiguous response, that is, a justification idea that seems to match CJs at multiple levels. If the response idea spans two or more levels, that is, if the idea seems to match equally well with CJs at two, three, or more different levels, the following rules apply (you will encounter examples of such responses while working through the exercises):

Rule 1. If a response unit matches equally well with CJs at two adjacent developmental levels (e.g., CJs at Stage 3 and Transition 3/4), score the justification at the higher of the two levels (in this case, Transition 3/4).

Rule 2. If a response unit matches equally well with CJs disparate by three developmental levels (e.g., CJs at Transition 2/3 and Transition 3/4), score the justification at the intermediate level (in the example, Stage 3).

Rule 3. If a response unit matches equally well with CJs that are disparate by more than three developmental levels (e.g., CJs at Transition 2/3 and Stage 4), designate the response as unscorable.

Scoring "Same as Above" Responses

If a subject—ignoring a request in the instructions—refers to a previous response, for example, by writing "same as above," assign to the "same as above" response the same score as that assigned to the previous response, provided that the "same as above" response seems appropriate to the question.

Irregular Citations

Occasionally, an otherwise unscorable response can be matched to a CJ in another chapter. Scoring a response unit using such a match is called an irregular citation. Irregular sources for evaluation should be considered only after you have concluded that none of the CJs in the usually appropriate chapter support an accurate assessment of the response ideas. Although allowance for irregular use of the manual maximizes its applicability, an over-readiness to resort to irregular sources will tend to reduce the reliability of the measurement.

Unscorable Response Units

Occasionally a response will be unscorable, not because it is excessively ambiguous, but rather because it does not really provide a moral justification, that is, it does not support the evaluation to which it refers (e.g., the importance of promise-keeping). These pseudo-justifications usually can be classified into one of the following categories. In the course of the discussion, we suggest ways in which test administrators can encourage respondents to provide scorable material, if there is time to scan questionnaires as they are turned in.

1. Repeat evaluations. These are responses that simply affirm the value contained in the evaluation, but add no real content. The subject who justifies a moral evaluation by writing "because it's just very important" or "because sometimes it's important and sometimes it isn't," should be asked to explain *why* it's very important or sometimes not important. A subject who writes a justification like "because you should help," or "because judges should not only throw criminals in jail but keep them there" should be asked to write why you should help, or why judges should keep criminals in jail. However, you must be careful. A response like "You should always help your parents," at first seems to be a repeat evaluation, but it contains an absolute rule or maxim, and thus would be scorable as Stage 1. Because certain Stage 1 criterion justifications are only subtly distinguishable from repeat evaluations, check the Stage 1 CJs before dismissing a response as a repeat evaluation.

2. Tautologies. Tautologous responses are similar to repeat evaluations. One respondent justified the importance of parents' keeping their promises to their children by writing "Saying that you can do something and then saying you can't is like breaking a promise." This response merely defines breaking a promise, a word already used in the question; the response has added nothing new. However, a tautology often gives an *impression* of significance until analyzed. For example, a common tautology is the attempt to justify promise-keeping with the assertion, "A promise is a promise." A substantive meaning might have been intended. Perhaps the subject wanted to say that "one should be true to one's word," which would be scored at Transition 3/4. However, we cannot be sure. The literal meaning adds no content, so the response should be regarded as unscorable. A subject who writes a tautologous response should be asked to write down what he or she thinks it means to say that.

3. Fragments. Fragments are grossly incomplete responses, like a sentence containing a subject but no predicate ("because a promise is"). Fragments are usually the result of haste and seem most often to afflict younger subjects' performances. A subject who writes a fragment should be encouraged to complete the sentence. If one is cautious not to embellish or inject meaning,

one can sometimes render a fragment intelligible and possibly matchable to a CJ. For example, one may supplement or complete a sentence with a word or phrase that the respondent clearly intended but inadvertently omitted (hence the references to "completions" in the self-training appendices).

4. Word Salads. Word salads are jumbled combinations of fragments. After indicating that helping a friend is "not important," one respondent wrote: "A isn't important to him afraid is to do nice thing for him not bad thing." The words are tossed together so randomly that we cannot be confident about any interpretation of the intended meaning. In some cases, however, a recomposition of the material (with care to avoid any misrepresentation) can establish a coherent idea.

5. Disclosures or Anecdotes. Occasionally, the rater will encounter a "justification" that consists of a personal disclosure, reference to a past event in the respondent's life, or an anecdote. To justify the importance of helping one's parents, a respondent wrote, "because my mother is blind." In such cases, subjects should be asked to supplement their answers by saying why, *in general*, they think it is important for people to help their parents. Responses that are less particularly or personally historical may be scorable: "Because my mother needs my help," although still personally referenced, is matchable enough to be marginally scored as Transition 2/3.

6. Comments. Writers of repeat evaluations, tautologies, fragments, word salads, or disclosures probably think that they have provided a meaningful justification. Some respondents, however, deliberately offer a criticism of the question rather than give a justification. One respondent wrote, after evaluating that it is "important" for judges to send lawbreakers to jail: "Sentence does not give enough detail to flatly agree or disagree." Nor does such a response "give enough detail" to be scorable! In such cases, subjects should be thanked for their comment but also asked to provide a reason for their moral evaluation.

7. Disavowals. A response is considered unscorable—even if perfectly matchable to a CJ—if it is disavowed by the respondent. One subject evaluated helping others as important, then wrote: "but if it's only because of things another person will do for you, that's not important at all." Although the respondent rejects the Stage 2 concern with instrumental advantages, the respondent does not actually justify the evaluation. Without the disavowal ("*only* because of things . . . that's not important at all"), the response would be scored at Stage 2. The disavowal implies a higher-stage level of reasoning but provides no specification of which stage or transitional level is intended. Because this example could be completed with reasoning at any level from Transition 2/3 to Stage 4, it is unscorable by Rule 3.

Phase 3: Scoring Practice of Questionnaires (Appendix C)

After you have completed extensive massed practice on each of the 11 questions, you should begin scoring questionnaires. Twenty-five sample questionnaires, copied word-for-word from data sources, are provided in Appendix C, along with annotated answer keys. You should work carefully through this material in a fashion similar to that of the Phase 2 sequence: Familiarize yourself with the data, estimate ratings, evaluate the estimate, and specify a citation. Duplicate 25 copies of the rating form (Appendix A) for use in recording your assessments. Then, after each questionnaire exercise, check your answers with the key so that you can learn from your successes and failures. As part of this work you will be learning to compute overall questionnaire ratings.

The steps for scoring questionnaires are essentially the same as were those for question scoring. This four-step sequence is applied to the 11 questions of each questionnaire.

Step 1. Familiarization and Screening

The first step is to read through the subject's entire response to the question. As you read the response, try to gain some sense of the ideas involved, that is, of possible scorable units. Attend particularly to response units which seem to represent high level and Moral Type B reasoning (see "Practical Scoring" section). You may also be able to identify obviously unscorable units that need not be considered further (review Unscorable Response Units, discussed earlier). Also, refresh your memory of the relevant portions of the reference manual by looking through the chapter containing the discussion, montages, and CJs for the question at hand.

Step 2. Estimate Ratings of Response Units

For self-training, it is useful to estimate the moral stage represented by each unit in the response. You can make each estimate on the basis of a thorough inspection of the montages.

Step 3. Evaluate Estimates

As in the previous phase of work, you must confirm or adjust your preliminary estimated ratings. Refer to the specific CJs pertinent to that estimate, as well as those at other levels that may actually provide a closer fit to the response idea (in cases of equal fit, the original estimate must be adjusted in accordance with Rules 1, 2 or 3).

Step 4. Citation

On a copy of the rating form (Appendix A) next to each question: (a) Cite the developmental rating and associated aspect of each scorable justification you found in the response (enter a "U" for an unscorable response); (b) underline the highest developmental level among the specified ratings; (c) write a note if Rule 1 or Rule 2 was used to identify the highest level; and (d) circle any CJ designated as Moral Type B and record the Type B component.

This general procedure is then applied to each of the remaining questions in each questionnaire. As you work through the 25 practice questionnaires in Appendix C, you should monitor not only your percentage of correct ratings among the questions, but also your overall SRMS score on the questionnaires. You should determine whether you are tending to: (a) score responses at an inappropriately high or low level, (b) commit the "false positive" error of scoring responses that are in fact unscorable, or (c) commit the "false negative" error of designating as unscorable responses that are in fact scorable. An adverse trend or tendency should be cause for more careful scrutiny in your use of the manual. If you consistently obtain SRMS scores more than 0.20 points discrepant from the answer key SRMS score, review the materials in chapter 1, the present chapter, and the reference chapters. Then re-do the exercises in the appendices.

PROTOCOL SCORING

Rules For Calculating Questionnaire Ratings

After scoring all 11 items in the questionnaire you will have as many as 11 underlined ratings, representing the highest developmental level found in each of the scorable items. Next, summary scores are calculated. The primary summary score in SRM-SF assessment is the Sociomoral Reflection Maturity Score (SRMS), which is simply the mean of the item ratings.

Calculating the SRMS entails four steps that are best conveyed through an illustration. Suppose that we have established the following set of highest level question ratings for a questionnaire (citations and same or lower level ratings excluded):

1. Contract: Friends	3	
2. Contract: Anyone	2/3	
3. Contract: Children	3/4	(Moral Type B, Conscience)
4. Truth	3	
5. Affiliation: Parents	3/4	
6. Affiliation: Friends	3	

7. Life: Stranger	2/3	
8. Life: Self	3/4	(3—Moral Type B, Fundamental
9. Property	4	Valuing)
10. Law	3	
11. Legal Justice	U	

Overall questionnaire scores are computed by following these steps:

1. Make sure that at least 7 questions have yielded scorable responses. Questionnaires yielding fewer than 7 scorable responses do not result in reliable protocol scores, and should be discarded from analysis. In the example, 10 out of the 11 responses were scorable (the Legal Justice response was "U," unscorable).

2. Replace all transitional scores with a numerical value midway between the stages represented in the transition. Transition 1/2 should be replaced by 1.5, Transition 2/3 by 2.5, and Transition 3/4 by 3.5.

3. Calculate the arithmetic mean, which constitutes the SRMS. In our example, the SRMS is 3.15 (the total, 31.5, divided by the 10 scores). The SRMS can range from 1.00 (a questionnaire yielding exclusively Stage 1 ratings) to 4.00 (a questionnaire yielding exclusively Stage 4 ratings). The SRMS represents the index best suited for most research purposes. It is wise to form an impressionistic estimate of the appropriate SRMS level by inspection of the item ratings. In the example, inspection would suggest that the SRMS should be somewhat above 3, corroborating the computation. For data-analytic purposes it is helpful to multiply the SRMS by 100, yielding a range of scores from 100 to 400.

4. Assign a Global Stage status to the questionnaire, which represents the developmental vicinity in which an SRMS is located. Global Stage is a ten-level scale that, in terms of SRMS scores, is represented as follows: 1.00–1.25 = Stage 1; 1.26–1.49 = Transition 1(2); 1.50–1.74 = Transition 2(1); 1.75–2.25 = Stage 2; 2.26–2.49 = Transition 2(3); 2.50–2.74 = Transition 3(2); 2.75–3.25 = Stage 3; 3.26–3.49 = Transition 3(4); 3.50–3.74 = Transition 4(3); and 3.75–4.00 = Stage 4. The transitional levels are named by the more prominent or major stage first, with the minor stage indicated in parentheses. The global rating for the SRMS given in the example above would be Stage 3. These point boundaries for Global Stage replicate those used for Global Stage in the Sociomoral Reflection Measure, from which the SRM-SF was derived. In addition to Global Stage, other summary stage indices (for example, modal stage, frequency profile of stage usage across the items, standard deviation of the variance in item stage levels, and Moral Type) may be used for some research purposes. Moral

philosophical discourse may be noted, but in fact is rarely seen, among responses to the Sociomoral Reflection Questionnaire–Short Form.

Moral Type Scoring

As just noted, some researchers may be interested in distinguishing Moral Type B from Moral Type A subjects. To accomplish Moral Type identification, the researcher must supplement the scoring procedure just described. In particular, the scorer must investigate and cite all Moral Type B components evident among the questionnaire responses. In our example, Moral Type B components are associated with questions 3 and 8. Note that the component associated with question 8 derives not from the highest level rating but instead from another unit in the response, a common occurrence in Moral Type Scoring.

Moral Type identifications are then recorded in the upper right-hand corner of the rating form (see Appendix A). If any item response evidences a Type B component, a 1 should be placed in the appropriate space. In the example, Fundamental Valuing was involved in the Life/Self (question 8) response; hence, place a 1 in the Fundamental Valuing space. Similarly, in accordance with the question 3 information, a 1 should be placed in the Conscience space.

A protocol is designated as Moral Type B if the protocol responses have yielded at least two of the three Type B components (Balancing, Fundamental Valuing, and Conscience). The sample protocol, then, would be regarded as Moral Type B. Alternatively, moral ideality can be interpreted quantitatively as a continuum or scale from 0 to 3.

Evaluation of Interrater Reliability

An essential part of any research project using a production measure is attainment of satisfactory interrater reliability. Upon completion of the self-training exercises and initiation of scoring work in connection with a research project, you should check your scoring reliability with another rater, using protocols from the sample entailed in your project or a related one. If either you or the other rater is inexperienced, it is advisable to begin by scoring a few questionnaires independently and then identifying and discussing scoring discrepancies. Attaining criterion interrater reliability may necessitate several rounds of such discussion.

At least two prospective raters who have worked through the SRM-SF self-training materials should independently score 20 to 30 questionnaires selected randomly from their research data. The questionnaire ratings should then be compared to determine interrater reliability. In our judgment, minimal standards for acceptable interrater reliability are as follows:

SRMS correlation: $r = .80$

Mean absolute SRMS discrepancy: 0.20 points

Global Stage agreement within 1 interval [e.g., 3 vs. 3(4)]: 80%

Exact Global Stage agreement: 50%

Practical Scoring of the SRM-SF

After self-training, the scoring process can be simplified in three ways. First, you will be scoring only the most mature-level unit in the response, because only the highest level of sociomoral reflection per question contributes to the questionnaire score. The highest level can sometimes be found by elimination, that is, by excluding clearly lower level material from consideration. Response units that are estimated as being at the *same* level should also be rated, however, because many of the distinctions across adjacent levels are rather subtle, and an under-evaluative error in one's estimate of supposedly same-level material is entirely possible. Second, although specifying citations insures against perfunctory scoring, the pro forma act of finding and recording the citation number may not be worth the time and effort if you are quite certain of a match. Third, because one gains considerable familiarity with the developmental distinctions during self-training, use of comparison notes can be less exhaustive during regular scoring than during self-training.

Reference Manual

Chapter 4

Contract and Truth

Changes in the development of sociomoral reflection can be discerned in the context of promise-keeping (contracts), as well as the broader context of reasoning in support of telling the truth. This chapter provides criteria for assessing the developmental maturity of moral justifications for the importance of these values. Justifications pertaining to contracts or promises are found in connection with moral evaluation responses to questions 1 (keeping promises to friends), 2 (keeping promises even to someone you hardly know), and 3 (parents keeping promises to their children). Truth justifications are found in response to question 4 (telling the truth).

Many of the justifications for keeping promises focus on the consequences that would ensue if promises were not kept. The conceptualization of the "consequences," of course, changes qualitatively by stage. The Stage 1 conceptualization of "friend" as a readily attachable and detachable label is evident in the predicted consequence that the person to whom you break your promise "won't be your friend again"; consequences at Stage 1 also tend to be physical: the friend will "cry," or "beat you up." By Stage 2, the consequences have become more instrumental and calculative: The promise should be kept because "you may want that person to like you or need that person to do you a favor," because "friends are hard to find," or because "you could run into the same person again." The Transition 2/3 concern that you could "lose a friend" raises the hint of a more intrinsic concern with the friendship involved. By Stage 3, then, the concern is with consequences to the (actual or potential) relationship. At Stage 3, friendship is no longer understood superficially as at Stage 1 or instrumentally as at Stage 2; one becomes emotionally invested in a friend (a friend "becomes a part of you"), and one would experience empathic guilt if, by breaking the promise, the friend's feelings were hurt and the relationship thereby undermined.

Higher levels address broader functional consequences. Promise-keeping or truthfulness as a generalized practice generates desirable results ("If everyone kept their word there would be more understanding"—Transition 3/4), or may be functionally necessary ("Children have to be able to trust their parents"—Transition 3/4). Finally, the functional necessity of contracts and truth as a generalized practice is explicitly linked at Stage 4 to social systems ("you wouldn't want to live in a society where you couldn't trust anyone") or to system-related respect for oneself as one who accepts social responsibility and honors commitments ("otherwise you have degraded yourself"). Regarding social systems, the essential role of consistent promise-keeping or truth for social order may be pointed out ("If people break promises whenever they wish there would be anarchy").

Some interesting qualitative age trends can be discerned with respect to perceived emotional consequences. At Stage 1, feelings are generally referred to in terms of their overt manifestations as inevitable physical consequences (e.g., if you don't keep a promise the other person "will cry"). Transition 1/2 marks either inevitable but covert appeals ("**will** be sad") or probabilistic but overt appeals ("**might** cry"). Stage 2 typically designates calculations concerning contingent and covert emotional consequences ("**might** be **sad** or **might** be **mad** at you"). At Transition 2/3, the emotional consequences specified are the other person's "disappointment" (either in not getting what he or she wanted—Stage 2, or in you as a person—Stage 3) and possible reluctance to trust you in the future. These justifications become more clearly empathic and mutualistic at Stage 3 (your hurting the other person's "feelings" or the relationship). Also, instead of whether the person will "trust you" (trust as a verb, possibly pragmatically intended—Transition 2/3), the Stage 3 appeal is to whether the person will **have trust in** you (an invested state of trust as a noun, or a condition of entrusted confidence). Finally, the concern with adverse consequences at Stage 2 evolves toward a concern with social impression at Transition 2/3 (a "bad reputation"), a concern that clearly relates to the prosocial personality at Stage 3 ("so that others will think of you as a good person").

At higher levels, references to emotion are more self-directed and conscience-oriented. There is no reference to conscience per se at Stage 1 or Stage 2. When conscience first emerges, at Transition 2/3, it seems to be construed as a kind of external annoyance (your conscience would **bother** you, keep **hounding** you, etc.). By Stage 3, this nuisance connotation has dropped out (it would simply be "on your conscience"; or more positively, keeping a promise would "make you feel good **inside**"). Transition 3/4 and Stage 4 entail justifications that more clearly construe conscience as integral to one's self-definition. The appeal at Transition 3/4 is to "your **own** well-being," "your **personal** satisfaction," or "your **sense of** well-being." At Stage 4, maintaining a consistent standard in one's social interaction makes possible fully integral, stable self-attributions such as "integrity," "dignity," "honor," or "self-respect."

Concern with the consequences of breaking promises may also be action-oriented. As noted, consequences at Stage 1 are inevitable and physicalistic: an anticipation of getting "punished" or "beaten up" on the one hand, or a "treat" on the other. By Stage 2, the concern is mainly with advantages or disadvantages: whether the person will "keep a promise to you" if you keep your promise, or conversely, with whether the person will "start a fight" if you don't. In the case of someone you hardly know, keeping a promise may be "not important" because of the lack of advantages ("That would be stupid to keep the promise, if they'll never know"). Stage 2, Transition 2/3, and Stage 3 are generally concerned with action consequences in terms of reciprocity of actions. At Stage 2, this reciprocity is manifested as a simple exchange (whether the person will "return the favor" or has already done a favor for you). Instead of the future tense ("will"), Transition 2/3 uses the future subjunctive mood to imply a more hypothetical reciprocity: whether the other person **would** keep a promise to you, or whether you **would want** a promise to you broken. The prescriptive ideal of the hypothetical reciprocity becomes explicit at Stage 3: "You **would hope** the other person would keep a promise to you." The emphasis is also on mutual expectations, not preference: Instead of "you **would want** . . ." (Transition 2/3), the consideration may be that "you (would) **expect** the other person to keep the promise to you" (Stage 3).

References to other people or friends in general rather than to another particular person or "your friend" are more typical beyond Stage 3. The concern with action consequences at Transition 3/4 and Stage 4 is in terms of functional necessities for interaction beyond that of a particular dyadic relationship. Transition 3/4 moves beyond relatively simple Stage 3 appeals to "the relationship" or "trust" to a suggestion that "a relationship is **based** on trust" or that "a friend **has to be able** to depend on you." The implication is that keeping promises serves as a required foundation for viable relationships. By Stage 4, the point is made that "**society** is based on trust," and that without kept contracts and truth "social interaction would be meaningless."

MONTAGES

Keeping promises or telling the truth is important because:

The Immature Level

Stage 1: Unilateral and Physicalistic

"You should **always** keep your promise [3]. It's your friend [2], and it wouldn't be **nice** to break your promise to your friend [4]; then he wouldn't play with you [5] or be your friend any more [4]. Besides, you shouldn't be a tattletale or tell a lie [4]. If you don't keep the promise, the other person **will** cry or beat you up, or your parent will punish you [5]." But it's not important "if the other person didn't do what his parents **told** him [1]. And if it's a stranger, it's not important because you should never talk to strangers [3]—they will tell you to do something bad [5]."

Transition 1/2

"This friend might be your **best** friend. If you don't keep your promise, you **will** get in **trouble**. It **will** make your friend sad, or they **will** be angry and **might** beat you up or even kill you, or at least not play with you. Also, they might tell on you. If it's a child, they might run away and get lost or kidnapped [2]." But it's not important because "the parent can break a promise [1]."

Stage 2: Exchanging and Instrumental

"Your friend has probably helped you and may return the favor if you help him [1]. Besides, you may like your friend, and your friend wants you to keep this promise [4]. After all, you need a friend and this could be your **only** friend [5]. Lies catch up with you sooner or later, and once they do you'll be in **worse** trouble [6] because your friend won't like you and might even get mad at you [6]. If it's a child, the parents want the children to keep their promises, so the parents should keep theirs [1]. Children are equal to parents, and children can't break promises, so parents shouldn't, either [2]. The child needs the promise kept [5]. If the parents break their promises, their children won't want to keep promises, either [6]." But it's not important because "if you hardly know them, then you can do what you want [3] since it won't matter anyway-they'll never know [6]."

Transition 2/3

"You **would want** your friends or children to keep promises to you [1]. They trust you and are counting on you, and **need** your **help** [4]. You shouldn't let them down, especially if it's something **personal** [3] and you love them or like them **a lot** [2], or they're a **good** friend [5]. If you're not friends yet, you could **become friends** [5]. After all, you want to **gain** friends, not **lose** them [5]. Once you start lying, it's hard to stop [6]. And once you start breaking promises you get a bad reputation [6]. Besides, you wouldn't feel good about it, so you'd only be hurting yourself [7]. Furthermore, your children would no longer believe you [5]." But it's not important because "you don't **even** know the person, and he is not important **to you** [5]."

The Mature Level

Stage 3: Mutual and Prosocial

"Your friend **has** faith **in** you. If it's someone you hardly know, you may start a good relationship or friendship [1] by **showing** that you care and **can** be trusted [4]. Then you **know** you have someone you can trust. Besides, you would **expect** them to keep promises to you [1]. The other person would feel hurt if you broke the promise [2], although a **true** friend would understand [1]. In general, though, keeping promises is what friends are for [3], and having a friend to share feelings with means a lot [1]. And even if it's not a friend, honesty is still the best policy and it's just common courtesy [3]. It's selfish to break promises [4]. You wouldn't be much of a friend, and once you make a bad impression people won't think much of you [4]. Also, you just don't feel good **inside** about yourself [6]. If it's a child and the parents don't keep promises, the children will **lose** trust and stop believing **in** their parents [1]. Promises mean a lot to children. If they are let down by **their own parents**, they will **think** that their parents don't love them [2]. Keeping promises will **show** the children that the parents do love them [4]. After all, children are people, too, and shouldn't be lied to [5]. If that keeps happening, the children will start to think dishonesty is all right [4]."

Transition 3/4

"Friendships are **based** on trust and honesty, and that's how friendships **develop**. After all, **people need to be able to** depend on you [1]. That way there would be better communication or harmony in the world, or mutual respect in the family [2]. After all, your word is your bond [7], and you should develop character in order to keep others' respect [8], not to mention your own **sense of** well-being or self-esteem [10]. It does **depend** on the **circumstances**, however. In the **case** of a child [5], the child is still developing and looks up to the parent for guidance; the parent should be a good influence so that the child **learns** honesty, is **taught** responsibility, and becomes trustworthy [8]. Not **breaking** or **destroying** that trust [1] is a way of respecting the child [9] and showing what **type** of person you are [8]."

Stage 4: Systemic and Standard

"**Society** is based on trust, and keeping promises is **necessary** for the sake of order [1]. Honesty is a standard everyone can accept, and you wouldn't want to live in a society where you couldn't trust anyone [2]. After all, promises have **intrinsic** value, and a relationship is **meaningless** if there is no trust [2].

A promise is a commitment or responsibility and a matter of honor [3], and whether you keep it reflects dependability or reliability and integrity [4]. People **must** be consistent and not break promises whenever they feel like it [5], at least partly for the sake of self-respect and one's integrity [7]. In the case of a child, parents have an **obligation** to keep their word [3] and to provide an example of **character** for the sake of the child's achievement of self-sufficiency and development as an individual [4] with a **sense of** responsibility [7]. Parents must **earn** their children's respect [6], both for the sake of the parents' self-respect [7], and so that the child will have a **sense of** self-worth [4]."

CRITERION JUSTIFICATIONS

Keeping promises or telling the truth is important because:

The Immature Level

Stage 1: Unilateral and Physicalistic

Responses that seem to relate to Stage 1 criterion justifications, but entail significant qualifications or elaborations, are not scorable at Stage 1.

1:1 Unilateral Authority

"You're **told** to do it"; or it's not important "**if** the other person didn't do what his parents told him (to do)."

1:2 Status

"It's your friend"; or it's not important because "it's a stranger." *Note:* "He's your friend so you should help him" and other such elaborated reasons are unscorable. Also, "we're friends" is unscorable.

1:3 Rules

(a) "You should **always** keep or follow your promises, **everyone** should keep their promises, people should **always** tell the truth, parents should or can **never** break promises, or you're **never** supposed to tell (on someone)." *Note:* Compare especially with Stage 3:Aspect 3b. Similar-sounding but qualified or elaborated justifications, such as "you should always keep promises or else don't make them," are not scorable. "Parents shouldn't break promises" and "a promise should not be broken" are unscorable.

(b) "You should always be nice to strangers"; or it's not important because "you should never talk to strangers."

1:4 Labels

(a) "It's a promise, or you made a promise." *Note:* Elaborated versions, for example, "you have made a promise and you should now keep it," are unscorable at Stage 1.

(b) "You shouldn't be a tattletale; or (otherwise) you'd be lying or a liar, you'd be bad, it's a lie, or it is bad, not nice, or a sin." *Note:* Compare especially with Transition 1/2:Aspect 2b.

(c) "(Otherwise) they **won't** be your friend, or the person would never be your friend (again)." *Note:* Compare especially with Transition 1/2:Aspect 2a.

1:5 Physical Consequences

"(Then) you or the other person **will** get a candy or treat; (otherwise) your friend **would** not play with you or give you something you ask for, **won't** talk to you, or **will** cry; the other person **will** kidnap you, beat you up, kill you, do something bad to you, or tell you to do something bad; or you **will** be punished." *Note:* Compare especially with Transition 1/2:Aspect 2b,c.

Transition 1/2

1/2:1 Unilateral Authority/Needs

It's important but "parents can break a promise; or they're just kids (so it's all right for parents to break their promise)." *Note:* Compare especially with Stage 2:Aspect 5b.

1/2:2 Labels/Physical Consequences/Advantages

(a) "He might be your **best** friend; or (otherwise) he **might** not be your friend any more." *Note:* Compare especially with Stage 1:Aspect 4c and with Stage 2:Aspect 6b.

(b) "You or the other person **might** get a candy or treat; (otherwise) you **will** make the child sad or unhappy; they **will** be sad, **might** cry, **could** run away, or **could** get lost or kidnapped; or the person **will** or **would** get mad or angry." *Note:* Compare especially with Stage 1:Aspect 5, Stage 2:Aspect 6b, and Transition 2/3:Aspect 3a.

(c) "(Otherwise) you will or would be found out or punished; the friend **will** or **would** get you in trouble or tell on you; the friend **might** beat you up, kill you, do something bad to you, or call you a liar, or not play with you; the parent **might punish** you; or (important) **if** they won't tell on you (when you've done something bad)." *Note:* Compare especially with Stage 1:Aspect 5 and with Stage 2:Aspects 4c and 6c,d.

Stage 2: Exchanging and Instrumental

2:1 Exchanges

(a) "Your friend (may have) done favors for you"; or it's not important because "the person (you hardly know) has done nothing for you."

(b) "The friend will return the favor or keep a promise to you; they would keep a promise to you **the next time**; or (otherwise) they may do the same thing to you, or may get even." *Note:* Compare especially with Transition 2/3:Aspect 1a. Although "**return** the favor" is scored under Exchanges, "do you a favor" would be scored under Advantages (Aspect 6). In general, Stage 2 justifications emphasizing a quid pro quo "return" of benefits in kind are scored under Exchanges, whereas more general anticipations of possible future benefits are scored under Advantages.

(c) "The parents want children to keep their promises (so the parents should keep theirs); or if you want your friend to keep a promise to you, you should keep a promise to your friend." *Note:* Compare especially with Transition 2/3:Aspect 1a.

(d) "If you make it, you keep it." *Note:* Explicitly prescriptive or elaborated versions, such as "If you make a promise, then you should keep it," are unscorable.

2:2 Equalities

(a) "Strangers need promises kept, too." *Note:* Compare especially with Stage 3:Aspect 5b. If there is only the need element expressed, score under Stage 2:Aspect 5 (Needs).

(b) "Children are equal (to their parents); parents should keep promises just like anyone else; if the parents don't keep their promises, why should the children?; or children can't break promises, so parents shouldn't either." *Note:* Compare especially with Stage 3:Aspect 5b. "It is important for anyone to keep his or her promise" is unscorable.

2:3 Freedoms

(a) "It's their business (and not for others to know about)." *Note:* Compare especially with Transition 2/3:Aspect 3b.

(b) "(Otherwise) the other person may not get to do something (he wants to do)"; or it's not important because "if you hardly know them then you can do what you want." *Note:* Compare especially with Transition 2/3:Aspect 3a.

2:4 Preferences

(a) "You (may) like your friend or not want him to get in trouble; **if** you want to (have this friend); **if** you like to tell the truth"; or it's not important because "if you hardly know them, then who cares?" *Note:* Compare especially with Transition 2/3:Aspect 2a.

(b) "That person may not want anyone to know (their secret), wants you to keep the promise, wants the child to tell the truth, or may not want you to tell (anyone)." *Note:* "You're not supposed to tell" is unscorable.

(c) "No one wants to be (found out to be) a liar or person who doesn't keep promises." *Note:* Compare especially with Transition 1/2:Aspect 2c and with Transition 2/3:Aspect 6a.

(d) "Then the children will want to keep their promises to their friends." *Note:* Compare especially with Stage 3:Aspect 4c.

2:5 Needs

(a) "You need a friend or need to tell a secret; this might be your **only** friend; friends are hard to find; everyone needs a friend; you may **need** the person (to do something for you some day); (otherwise) you won't have any friends"; or it's not important because "you can get another friend, or you may not need this person." *Note:* Compare especially with Transition 2/3:Aspect 5a.

(b) "Friends **need** promises kept; they may **need** what you promised them; or but parents can break promises **if they need to**." *Note:* Compare especially with Transition 1/2:Aspect 1 and with Transition 2/3:Aspect 4a.

2:6 Advantages

(a) "They may cheat you or may be lying to you; you could run into that person again; (then) the friend will do you a favor or help you out (when you have a problem); (otherwise) they might not keep telling you secrets"; or (it's not important if you hardly know the person because) "you don't know what you're getting into."

(b) "Others will like you; friends don't like liars; then the children will like the parents more; (otherwise) they **might** be sad, **might** get mad at you, or won't want you for a friend; or you might not like each other any more." *Note:* Compare especially with Transition 1/2:Aspect 2a,b and with Transition 2/3:Aspects 3a, 5a, and 6a. "(Otherwise) the children would rebel" is unscorable.

(c) "It may get the person off your back; (otherwise) you might risk danger; or there might be fights." *Note:* Compare especially with Transition 1/2:Aspect 2c and with Transition 2/3:Aspect 5c. "(Otherwise) there would be arguments" and "you would suffer the consequences" are unscorable.

(d) "Lies (always) catch up to you **(sooner or later)**; you **could** get in (a lot of) trouble; you would get in **more** trouble; you (might just) get in **worse** trouble; (otherwise) you would **eventually** or **probably** be caught; you might be, or would worry about being, found out; you would keep thinking that they might tell; or **if you know** they won't tell on you, or if they can keep a secret." *Note:* Compare especially with Transition 1/2:Aspect 2c and with Transition 2/3:Aspects 6b and 7b.

(e) "(Otherwise) you will keep lying, or lie again and again." *Note:* Compare especially with Transition 2/3:Aspect 6b. "(Otherwise) you may get into a bad habit" is unscorable.

(f) (It is not important because) "if you hardly know the person then why do it?; that would be stupid (for someone you hardly know to ask you to keep a promise); it won't matter; you won't see them again; or the other person will never know or might forget anyway."

Transition 2/3

2/3:1 Exchanges/Relationships

(a) "They **would** keep a promise to you; you **wouldn't want** someone to break a promise to you; I **wouldn't want** it done to me; or the parents **wouldn't** like it (if the children were to break their promises to them)"—Moral Type B, Balancing. *Note:* Compare especially with Stage 2:Aspect 1b,c and with Stage 3:Aspect 1d.

(b) "(Otherwise) you wouldn't trust each other"—Moral Type B, Balancing. *Note:* Compare especially with Stage 3:Aspect 1d.

2/3:2 Preferences/Prosocial Intentions

(a) "You may like the person **a lot**; you may love or care about that person; that person may love you"; or it's not important because "most people don't care." *Note:* Compare especially with Stage 2:Aspect 4a and with Stage 3:Aspect 4b.

(b) "You don't or wouldn't want to be around someone who lies."

2/3:3 Preferences/Freedoms/Empathic Role-Taking

(a) "Children look forward (to parents keeping their promise)"; or "(otherwise) the child is let down, is disappointed, will feel bad, or will **get upset** or **get** hurt." *Note:* Compare especially with Transition 1/2:Aspect 2b, with Stage 2:Aspects 3b and 6b, and with Stage 3:Aspect 2a.

(b) "It might be personal." *Note:* Compare especially with Stage 2:Aspect 3a.

2/3:4 Needs/Empathic Role-Taking

(a) "That person depends on, relies on, or is counting on you; they **need** (your) **help**, may need it (kept) **badly**, or it could be important to them; the other person (has) trusted or trusts you (enough to tell you something); they believe you or are trusting you; or (otherwise) their plans would be **ruined** or wouldn't work out." *Note:* Compare especially with Stage 2:Aspect 5b and with Stage 3:Aspect 2b.

(b) It's important but "if someone could **get** hurt, you should tell; or (unless) breaking the promise helps the other person." *Note:* Compare especially with Stage 2:Aspect 5b and with Stage 3:Aspect 2a. "If it is something serious" is unscorable.

2/3:5 Advantages/Empathic Role-Taking/Relationships

(a) "That person could **become** your friend, you may **become** friends, you'd be a better friend; you may make a friend; friends are **important to have**; if it is a **good** friend; (so that) you will keep your friends or make new friends; (otherwise) you could **lose** a friend; people will turn against you; the child would become resentful; others won't want to be around you (if you lie)"; or not important because "you don't **even** or **really** know the person; you shouldn't keep a promise to **just** anyone; or they are not important or special **to you**." *Note:* Compare especially with Stage 2:Aspects 5a and 6b and with Stage 3:Aspects 1a,c. "If you can't keep a promise, then you're not a friend" and "(because otherwise) you won't be friends" is unscorable. Also, "they are not important" and "you don't know them" are unscorable.

(b) "That person will trust you (again); or (otherwise) others won't believe you (any more), children will no longer believe or trust their parents, children don't forget, children will stop relying on their parents or counting on them (for help), or others will think you are lying." *Note:* Compare especially with Stage 3:Aspects 1a,b and 4b.

(c) It's important "(unless) you could be hurt (by keeping the promise)." *Note:* Compare especially with Stage 2:Aspect 6c and with Stage 3:Aspect 1b. Being "hurt" with reference to the self is classified as Transition 2/3 because it can be intended pragmatically.

2/3:6 Advantages/Prosocial Intentions

(a) "(Otherwise) they may start rumors (about you); you will get a bad reputation; or the word will get around that you don't keep your promises." *Note:* Compare especially with Stage 2:Aspects 4c and 6b, and with Stage 3:Aspect 4b.

(b) "It's easier; it's hard to stop lying (once you start); or lies (only) lead to more lies (to cover up the first ones)." *Note:* Compare especially with Stage 2:Aspect 6d,e.

2/3:7 Advantages/Intrapersonal Approval

(a) "It makes you feel good or better; (it's) for your own good; (otherwise) your conscience would **bother** you or keep **hounding** you, you would feel bad or sorry, you will regret it, you won't like yourself (very much); or you're only hurting yourself"—Moral Type B, Conscience. *Note:* Compare especially with Stage 3:Aspect 6.

(b) "(Otherwise) it could be embarrassing (if your lie is found out)." *Note:* Compare especially with Stage 2:Aspect 6d.

The Mature Level

Stage 3: Mutual and Prosocial

3:1 Relationships

(a) "A friendship should be sincere; if you are a **real, true, or close** friend; it would be a chance to get to know that person better or have a better relationship; for the sake of the friendship or relationship; to gain or keep the other person's trust or faith (in you); (then) the family will be closer; (in order) to start a good relationship; (then) they will want to get to know you better, or there won't be hard feelings; (otherwise) the friendship may be hurt, you won't feel as close, you would lose trust (in each other), the children will **lose** trust or faith, feel betrayed, or be misled, or the children would stop believing **in** or confiding **in** their parents"; or it's not important to keep a promise to someone you hardly know because "there would be no relationship." *Note:* Compare especially with Transition 2/3:Aspect 5a,b,c and with Transition 3/4:Aspect 1a,b. "You need their trust [unelaborated]" is unscorable.

(b) "It **shows** others that you have faith in them; (so that) they'll **know** or **feel** they can trust you; (then) you'll have someone you can **relate to**; or you'll **know** you have someone you can trust or confide in." *Note:* Compare especially with Transition 2/3:Aspect 5b.

(c) "A friend becomes a part of you, or **means** a lot (to you); you look to your friends for (emotional) support; friends share feelings; or (because) friendships are an important part of your life." *Note:* Compare especially with Transition 2/3:Aspect 5a and with Stage 4:Aspect 2c.

(d) "You should treat others the way you would want them to treat you; you should put yourself in their place; friends **should** trust each other; parents would expect their children to keep their promises (so the parents should keep theirs); how would the parents feel (if their children did that to them?); friends **would want you to treat them the way you** (would) **want** them to treat you; you **would hope** the other person would keep a promise to you, or (would) **expect** your friend to keep a promise to you; (otherwise) we **can't expect** our children to keep their promises to us; or **(but)** a (true) friend would understand or wouldn't mind (if you had to break the promise)"—Moral Type B, Balancing. *Note:* Compare especially with Transition 2/3:Aspect 1a,b.

(e) "**I know, think, or realize** that my friends are willing to help me."

3:2 Empathic Role-Taking

(a) "Promises **mean** a lot or are everything to children; (then) children have trust or faith in their parents; a child may be too young to understand (when a promise has to be broken); (otherwise) the child may be **deeply** disappointed; broken promises are heartbreaking, hurt (a child), or (can) cause (emotional) stress, pain, or (feelings of) insecurity; (then) they are let down **by their own parents** or by ones who should love them; if you can keep the promise without hurting someone or affecting that person's life; the person could **feel** let down, feel unwanted, or feels unimportant, not trusted, taken for granted, or unappreciated; the children will **think** that their parents don't love them; your friend will think you're (just) using him or don't care (about him); it is **upsetting** (to the other person when you tell a lie); (but) the truth can be painful; or (unless) it is a white lie (said to avoid hurting someone's feelings), or the other person is using that promise to hurt someone." *Note:* Compare especially with Transition 2/3:Aspects 3a and 4b, and with Transition 3/4:Aspects 1b and 8c. "Hurt" on Contract and Truth questions almost always connotes socioemotional hurt and so is generally rated Stage 3 (cf. Transition 2/3 rating on Property and Law). "Then the children will **say** their parents don't love them" is unscorable.

(b) "That person has trusted you **with their feelings** or **trusted you with something important to them**; or you should **realize** that the other person trusted you." *Note:* Compare especially with Transition 2/3:Aspect 4a.

(c) "The other person may need to understand your (changed) circumstances, or take the situation into consideration; or (important but) parents are (only) human." *Note:* Compare especially with Transition 3/4:Aspect 5.

3:3 Normative Expectations

(a) "That's what friends are for, that's what friendship is all about; or one should be loyal or faithful to one's friend."

(b) "The friend would be or is expecting you (to keep the promise); it's **expected** (that you'll keep your promise); children are **expected** or **supposed** to show respect for their parents; people deserve to hear the truth (from you); or it's a common courtesy or only proper." *Note:* Compare especially with Stage 1:Aspect 3a and with Transition 3/4:Aspect 2b.

(c) "Honesty is the best policy."

3:4 Prosocial Intentions

(a) "You think less of people who break promises, or (otherwise) it is selfish, inconsiderate, insincere, faithless, shameful, or cruel, or you are not much of a friend." *Note:* Compare especially with Transition 2/3:Aspect 6a and with Transition 3/4:Aspect 8a. "(Otherwise) it is mean or horrible" is unscorable.

(b) "It **shows** that the parents love or care for their children; it **shows** others that you care; it shows you **can** be trusted or depended on; (then) others will **think of you** as a good person, or will **know** what you're really like; (in order) to make or leave a good impression; (otherwise) you'd worry about what people thought of you, or people would get a bad image or opinion of you; it **shows** you don't (really) care about the other person or are dishonest; or it will be harder for others to trust you." *Note:* Compare especially with Transition 2/3:Aspects 2a, 5b, and 6a, and with Transition 3/4:Aspect 8a. Judgments that are not explicitly interpersonal, such as "breaking a promise is terrible," are not scorable. Also, "(so that) you can say you are honest" is unscorable.

(c) "(Otherwise) the children will be dishonest or will think dishonesty is all right." *Note:* Compare especially with Stage 2:Aspect 4d and with Transition 3/4:Aspect 8c.

(d) It's important but "you shouldn't make a promise just to get rid, or take advantage, of a person."

3:5 Generalized Caring

(a) "Promises are precious or priceless"—Moral Type B, Fundamental Valuing. *Note:* Compare especially with Stage 4:Aspect 2c.

(b) "Children are people, too (and shouldn't be lied to), or the stranger is just as important (as anyone else)"—Moral Type B, Fundamental Valuing. *Note:* Compare especially with Stage 2:Aspect 2a,b, and with Transition 3/4:Aspect 9.

(c) "It may be life-threatening or a matter of life or death"—Moral Type B, Fundamental Valuing. *Note:* Compare especially with Stage 4:Aspect 2c.

3:6 Intrapersonal Approval

"It makes you feel good **inside**; so that you would have a clear conscience; or (otherwise) it would be on your mind, you'd have to live with it, you would feel rotten, terrible, ashamed, bad **about yourself**, or guilty, or you could have emotional problems or become depressed"—Moral Type B, Conscience. *Note:* Compare especially with Transition 2/3:Aspect 7a and with Transition 3/4:Aspect 10a,b.

Transition 3/4

3/4:1 Relationships/Societal Requirements

(a) **"Relationships** are **based** or **built** on trust, honesty, truth, or caring; **friendship** is **made up** of promises; (in order) to **establish, build,** or **develop** honesty, openness, or the relationship; to **make** better relationships; to build **stronger** or make **more dependable** relationships; or (otherwise) you **break** or **destroy** the trust (that is the basis for the relationship)." *Note:* Compare especially with Stage 3:Aspect 1a and with Stage 4:Aspect 1a. "Trust is important in life" is unscorable.

(b) "People **should be able** to (have) trust (in) you; parents **must show** that they can be trusted; children **have to be able to** trust their parents, **need** to feel or know that they can trust their parents, or **need** to have a sense of security; or parents **need** to have their children's trust or confidence." *Note:* Compare especially with Stage 3:Aspects 1a and 2a. "Your word is important" is unscorable.

(c) "People **need to** or **have to** depend on or **be able to** trust **each other"**—Moral Type B, Balancing. *Note:* Compare especially with Stage 4:Aspect 1b.

3/4:2 Relationships/Basic Rights or Values

(a) "If everyone kept their word, there would be more openness, better communication or understanding, or greater harmony; (in order) to lessen (the amount of) deceit, injustice, or corruption in the world; this may make the family stronger; or for the sake of smoother relationships or (open) communication (between parents and children)." *Note:* Compare especially with Stage 4:Aspect 1a.

(b) "People or one's parents deserve respect; **out of** respect (for the other person); (because) of one's respect (for that friend's trust); or you should respect their faith in you." *Note:* Compare especially with Stage 3:Aspect 3b and with Stage 4:Aspects 2a and 6. "You should respect your parents" is unscorable.

(c) "People should respect one another"—Moral Type B, Balancing.

3/4:3 Relationships/Responsibility

"There is or should be a **bond** of trust or confidence (even if you aren't close); or the trust **binds** or will **tie** you together."

3/4:4 Empathic Role-Taking/Basic Rights or Values

"It makes life less stressful, or it can have an effect beyond the person you made the promise to."

3/4:5 Empathic Role-Taking/Procedural Equity

It's important "in most **cases; except** in certain **situations; (but)** it **depends** on the **circumstances** or **situation; priorities** or (new) **circumstances** (can) change (the conditions of the promise), or parents have many responsibilities (and sometimes cannot keep a promise)." *Note:* Compare especially with Stage 3:Aspect 2c. "It depends on the promise," "it depends on the kind of friend," "sometimes you can't keep the promise," "occasionally things come up," and "you can't fulfill all your promises" are unscorable.

3/4:6 Normative Expectations/Societal Requirements

"There are already too many people (in society) who don't tell the truth."

3/4:7 Normative Expectations/Responsibility

"Your word is or should be your bond; (if you make a promise then) you are obligated (to keep it); or you are responsible (for carrying out that promise)." *Note:* Compare especially with Stage 4:Aspects 3a and 4a. "A promise is a promise" is unscorable.

3/4:8 Prosocial Intentions/Character

(a) "Your word should be reliable; (in order) to show that you are **respectable, responsible, dependable, or trustworthy**; to gain, build, or keep respect; to show **virtue, or the type of person you are;** (otherwise) it's irresponsible or shows that you are unreliable; parents will lose their children's respect; or you will lose others' respect." *Note:* Compare especially with Stage 3:Aspect 4a,b and with Stage 4:Aspects 3a, 4a, 5, and 6. "I try to be as responsible as I can" and "(otherwise) you lose credibility" are unscorable.

(b) "Your word is or represents you; you are (only) as good as your word; you should live up to your word; or (otherwise) your word means nothing or is worthless." *Note:* "You gave your word," "that's your word," "you should try to keep your word," "it's good to keep your word," and "a promise is a promise" are unscorable.

(c) "It **develops** or **builds** your values; the child is still young or developing, or his or her character is still forming; the child looks up to the parent (for guidance); the parents should be trustworthy, **dependable**, or a good guide, model, example, teacher, or influence; the parents should **teach** values so that the child will **learn** honesty, trust, or to respect promises or truth, or so that the parent can be relied on; (so that) the child will be **taught** responsibility; (otherwise) the child would **become** dishonest or hypocritical or **grow** to distrust others; or the parents would be **teaching** a double standard, or **teaching** that parents can lie but children can't." *Note:* Compare especially with Stage 3:Aspects 2a and 4c, and with Stage 4:Aspect 4b. "(Because) parents should practice what they preach," "it will teach the child to keep promises," "children get their attitudes from their parents," "(otherwise) the children will lie or won't learn to keep their promises," and "(otherwise) the child will grow up doing the same thing to others" are unscorable.

(d) "If you don't keep a promise to a stranger, then you won't be able to keep a promise to someone close to you, either."

(e) "The truth provides a guideline for people to follow (through life)."

(f) It's important but "that **depends on** one's **morals**"—Moral Type B, Conscience (Relativism of Personal Values).

3/4:9 Generalized Caring/Basic Rights or Values

"The parent should treat the child as a person or human being; parents should respect their children; you should treat the child no less seriously than you treat an adult; or the child should have a voice in family affairs"—Moral Type B, Fundamental Valuing. *Note:* Compare especially with Stage 3:Aspect 5b.

3/4:10 Intrapersonal Approval/Standards of Conscience

(a) "Then you (know you) can trust yourself; you should be true to yourself or honest with yourself; I pride myself in keeping my word; (otherwise) you would lose faith in yourself; (you are not only lying to the other person but) you are (also) lying to, cheating, or deceiving yourself; or you (feel) disappointed (in) yourself or feel that you have let yourself down"—Moral Type B, Conscience. *Note:* Compare especially with Stage 3:Aspect 6 and with Stage 4:Aspect 7a.

(b) It's important "for the sake of your **own** well-being, your **sense of** well-being, **personal** satisfaction, self-esteem, or self-concept"—Moral Type B, Conscience. *Note:* Compare especially with Stage 3:Aspect 6 and with Stage 4:Aspect 7a. Simple references to "well-being" or "satisfaction" are unscorable.

Stage 4: Systemic and Standard

4:1 Societal Requirements

(a) "**Society** is based on trust or promises; promises must be kept for the sake of society or order; trust, honesty, respect, or truth is **necessary** for or **essential** to the economy, government, social stability, social survival, social vitality, or human development; trust is a method of interaction, dealings, or functioning; (solid) relationships or friendships **require** truth; (otherwise) what kind of world would it be (without trust)?; or social interaction or relationships could not function or wouldn't exist." *Note:* Compare especially with Transition 3/4:Aspects 1a and 2a. On these "Contract and Truth" questions, "order" is rated Stage 4 because it almost always has a societal connotation (cf. Transition 3/4 rating in chapters 5-8).

(b) "It promotes interdependence which is important for society"—Moral Type B, Balancing. *Note:* Compare especially with Transition 3/4:Aspect 1c.

4:2 Basic Rights or Values

(a) "**Everyone** has the **right** to be respected or to have a promise (to them) kept; it affirms the worth of the other person; or (otherwise) it is a **violation** of trust." *Note:* Compare especially with Transition 3/4:Aspect 2b.

(b) "Honesty is a standard everyone can accept."

(c) "Promises are **sacred**, or have **intrinsic** value; (unless) breaking the promise can be justified by a greater good for human life or society; or (otherwise) social interaction or relationships would be **meaningless**"—Moral Type B, Fundamental Valuing. *Note:* Compare especially with Stage 3: Aspects 1c and 5a,c.

(d) "Trusting relationships reflect favorably upon society; (otherwise) you wouldn't want to live in a society where you couldn't trust anyone; or you are or would be a parasite (upon society)."

4:3 Responsibility

(a) "It is a commitment, responsibility, duty, obligation, matter of honor, pledge, vow, or statement of faith." *Note:* Compare especially with Transition 3/4:Aspects 7 and 8a. "It's my duty because I need him some day" is unscorable.

(b) "It is a pact, contract, or agreement, or (otherwise) it is a breach of trust"—Moral Type B, Balancing.

(c) "That **must** be accepted as a part of parenthood, friendships, or relationships." *Note:* "Parents should keep their word" is unscorable.

4:4 Character

(a) "It reflects, is a sign of, is a part of, or shows **character**, responsibility, integrity, or **dependability**; it is a serious statement about yourself or your moral standards; it shows self-respect or that one is a responsible **member of society**; or (otherwise) it shows a lack of **reliability** or **maturity**." *Note:* Compare especially with Transition 3/4:Aspects 7 and 8a.

(b) "Parents should provide a model of integrity or honor, or an example of character or **responsibility**; for the sake of the child's future integrity or development as a (responsible) individual; (so that) the child understands the importance of **reliability** or **consistency**; or in order to instill a **set of** values (to live by)." *Note:* Compare especially with Transition 3/4:Aspect 8c.

4:5 Consistent Practices

"People **must** not break promises whenever they (happen to) feel like it; for the sake of **consistency**, **reliability**, or **dependability**; or if people break their promises **whenever** they wish, there would be anarchy." *Note:* Compare especially with Transition 3/4:Aspect 8a.

4:6 Procedural Equity

"Parents should **earn** or **must deserve** their children's respect or trust, or should not abuse their authority or misuse their power; (in order) to show that you are worthy of your friend's trust; or (otherwise) the parent is not worthy of the child's respect"—Moral Type B, Balancing. *Note:* Compare especially with Transition 3/4:Aspects 2b and 8a.

4:7 Standards of Conscience

(a) "It is a **personal** oath; for the sake of self-respect, or one's integrity, dignity, honor, consistency, or sense of self-worth; or (otherwise) you have

degraded or **debased** yourself"—Moral Type B, Conscience. *Note:* Compare especially with Transition 3/4:Aspect 10a,b.

(b) "(Then) the child will have a **sense of** responsibility or personal value."

Chapter 5

Affiliation

The questions relating to affiliation concern justifications for helping parents (question 5) and friends (question 6). These justifications imply certain conceptualizations of relationships. At Stage 1, relationships are often conceptualized in terms of physical status (e.g., children should obey parents because parents are bigger). Stage 2 conceptualizes the relationship in more pragmatic terms, focusing on the possible advantages that can ensue from exchanges satisfying the respective needs and preferences of the individuals involved. Friendships are appreciated for their quasi-economic value as possibly scarce commodities (the person to be helped "might be his **only** friend," or, more generally, "friends are hard to replace"). In general, pragmatic exchanges characterize the Stage 2 conception of friendship.

Exchanges at Transition 2/3 are less pragmatic and more hypothetical, for example, "your friend **would** help you." It is not until Stage 3, however, that the mutual and truly interpersonal perspective comes to the fore. The appeal is not simply to love as an affiliative motive (e.g., "you love your parent," Transition 2/3) but rather to love as an enveloping sentiment (e.g., "you would help **out of** love"), which should be interpersonally expressed (e.g., "to **show** that you love them"). Also, "good" friend tends to be supplanted by "close" friend, an explicitly relationship-oriented term (the reference here is not likely to be to physical proximity).

Affiliation reasoning addressed specifically to the parent-child question may refer to the obligations of a child to a parent. At Stage 1 the conceptualization of "obligation" is absolutistic ("you should **always** obey your parents") and physicalistic ("they are bigger so they can tell you what to do"; "if you don't do it they can spank you"). In contrast, Stage 2 reasoning is much less accepting of hierarchical obligations and, indeed, is thoroughly pragmatic ("the parents shouldn't boss the children around"; "the children shouldn't have to help if they don't want to, but if they don't the parents won't to extra things for them"). Obligatory prescriptions return at Stage 3, in the form of normative expectations and prosocial intentions ("you are **supposed to** show respect for your parents and should help them **out of** love"). Furthermore, the phenomenological orientation of obligation is for the first time clearly internal: "if you help you will feel proud, and if you don't

you'll have it on your conscience that you could have helped and didn't."
Stage 4 may relate the obligation to help parents to the functioning of the
family as a social system ("it contributes to the family **unit**"). Furthermore,
there are explicit appeals to the child's acceptance of responsibility, future
character, and self-respect. Stage 4 reasoning may also entail a Moral Type
B concern, however, that parents must **earn** or be worthy of their children's
respect through fair conduct.

MONTAGES

Helping one's parent or friend is important because:

The Immature Level

Stage 1: Unilateral and Physicalistic

"It's your parents—they're big and grown up [2] so they can tell you what to
do and you should **always** obey them [3]. That's a nice and good thing to do
[4], and besides, if you don't do it they'll yell and you'll get spanked [5]".

Transition 1/2

"Children should do what their parents tell them to do [1]. If you don't do it,
they **would** get mad and you **might** get punished [3]. It might be your **best**
friend [2]."

Stage 2: Exchanging and Instrumental

"Your parent or friend has done things you, and may return the favor [1].
Besides, you may want to keep your parents happy [6], or may like to help
this friend [4]. He may be your **only** friend and you may not get another one
like that again [5]. Furthermore, you may need your friend's help some day,
and if you help him he may do you a favor some time. If you don't help
parents, they won't do extra things for you [6]. On the other hand, parents
are not the boss of children [2], and children don't have to help if they don't
want to [3]. After all, there are lots of things parents can do by themselves
and don't need you for [5]."

Transition 2/3

"Your parent or friend **has helped** or **helps** you a lot, and you **would want**
to be helped [1]. This may be a **good** friend of yours that you may want to

keep and not lose [2]. Certainly a good friend would help [4], because you'd feel sorry for them [3]. You love your parents or may like your friend a lot, and shouldn't just let your friend die [5]. After all, they need your help [6], and friends need each other [1]. Friends are special [7], and if you don't help your friend your conscience will bother you [8]."

The Mature Level

Stage 3: Mutual and Prosocial

"It could be a close or true friend, and you would certainly expect your friend to help you. After all, you should follow the Golden Rule [1]. Regarding parents, helping them out lets them know how loved and appreciated they are [2]. It's the least you can do, after you realize how much they've sacrificed for you [1]. Besides, it's only natural that children should honor their parents; in other words, it's expected that children show respect [3]. Furthermore, you should help them out of love [4], because you care about them so much and they're a part of you after all you've shared together [1]. Think of helping your parents or friend as a gift of love [4], especially if they are in need [2] or a life is at stake [5]. If you help your parents can think well of you [4] and you will feel proud [6]; but if you don't then you're not much of a friend [4] and you'll have it on your conscience that you could have helped and didn't [6]."

Transition 3/4

"Friendship is based on trust and love; you have to be able to cooperate and depend on one another [1]. In families, each member needs to do his or her share because it should be a team effort [1] for the sake of the whole family [2]. Helping your friend or parent will promote harmony and communication [2], and strengthen the relationship as well as the common bond between you [1]. Whether you help or not does depend on the circumstances [4], but usually it is important to help do your share and show that you are responsible [5]. You should help out of respect [2], and because you should care about your fellow human beings [6]. Helping one's parents is a good way to be taught responsibility [7], and to develop one's self-esteem [9]. It also means, perhaps, following your convictions [8]."

Stage 4: Systemic and Standard

"Cooperation is required for a working friendship [1]. After all, it contributes to the family unit, and even to society [2]. If a life is involved, remember that life is **sacred** [2]. The child has perhaps made a commitment, and should feel a responsibility toward the family [3]. It is through helping out that the child's **character** will develop [4]. In general, it is important to be **consistent** in helping others [5]. But on the other hand, parents **must** deserve their children's respect and **earn** their trust [6]. If the parents are worthy, the child should help for the sake of self-respect and in order to develop a **sense of** responsibility [7]."

CRITERION JUSTIFICATIONS

Helping one's parent or friend is important because:

The Immature Level

Stage 1: Unilateral and Physicalistic

Responses that seem to relate to Stage 1 criterion justifications, but entail significant qualifications or elaborations, are not scorable at Stage 1.

1:1 Unilateral Authority

"Your parents can tell you to do things, can tell you to help someone, or told you to help others." *Note:* Compare especially with Transition 1/2:Aspect 1.

1:2 Status

(a) "It's your parent or friend." *Note:* Any elaborated version of this justification, for example, "They're your parents and you should respect them," should not be scored at Stage 1 (some elaborations may be scorable at a higher level). "If it's your friend" is unscorable.

(b) "Your friend might be an important person, or might own a lot of furniture; or your parent is big, grown up, or the oldest."

1:3 Rules

"You should **always** or must **always** obey or help your parents or family." *Note:* Compare especially with Stage 3:Aspect 3a. Vaguely elaborated versions of this justification, for example, "You should help in any way you can," are unscorable. Other elaborations may be scorable at a higher level.

1:4 Labels

"It's nice, or so that you are good (to your parents)." *Note:* Compare especially with Stage 3:Aspect 4a.

1:5 Physical Consequences

"(Otherwise) the child will get spanked or punished, or the parents **would** yell (at the child)." *Note:* Compare especially with Transition 1/2:Aspect 3.

Transition 1/2

1/2:1 Unilateral Authority/Preferences

"Children should do what their parents tell or want them to do." *Note:* Compare especially with Stage 1:Aspect 1.

1/2:2 Labels/Advantages

(a) "The friend may be your **best** friend."

(b) "Your parent will be happy; or (otherwise) you **will** be **sad** (if your friend dies)." *Note:* Compare especially with Stage 2:Aspect 6a,b.

(c) "(Otherwise) they **will** get **mad** or **angry**." *Note:* Compare especially with Stage 2:Aspect 6b.

1/2:3 Physical Consequences/Advantages

"The child **might** or **could** get a prize; or (otherwise) the child **might** get punished, **might** get sent to their room, or **will** get in trouble." *Note:* Compare especially with Stage 1:Aspect 5.

Stage 2: Exchanging and Instrumental

2:1 Exchanges

(a) "Your friend might have done you favors, or might return the favor; your parents do or have done things for you, or your parents helped you or **gave** you things; parents pay for their children or give them things; or you should help them **back**, or you want others to do for you the same things you do for them." *Note:* Compare especially with Transition 2/3:Aspect 1a. "You owe your parents a lot" is unscorable.

(b) "If the parents help the children, then the children should help the parents; parents help children so children help parents; or the children want the parents to help *them* (**so** they should help their parents)." *Note:* Compare especially with Transition 2/3:Aspect 1b.

2:2 Equalities

It's important but "children are equal to their parents, or the parents are not the boss or shouldn't boss you around."

2:3 Freedoms

"Children **don't** always get to do what they want; or (**but**) children don't have to help if they don't want to." *Note:* "You can't always do whatever you want" is unscorable.

2:4 Preferences

(a) "You like your friend (enough); it's fun; children (should) want to help their parents; if you want or like to help them; if you (really) want to have this friend or save them." *Note:* Compare especially with Transition 2/3:Aspect 5a. "Children should help their parents" is unscorable.

(b) "The parent wants you to help or to do things for them, or the friend wants to live."

2:5 Needs

(a) "Your friend is bad off, needs you, may be sick, or needs to get better; your parents work or may need money; or (**but**) parents don't need you to do lots of things." *Note:* Compare especially with Transition 2/3:Aspects 3 and 6. "It helps them get done faster" and "it makes their work easier" are unscorable.

(b) "(If the friend dies) you might not get a friend like that again; this might be your only friend; you need your parents (to take care of you); your parents may be all you have; or friends are hard to find or replace." *Note:* Compare especially with Transition 2/3:Aspects 2 and 7a.

2:6 Advantages

(a) "Your friend **may** or **will** help you (some time); you may need their help (some day), want a favor (later), want your parents to help you (when you get older), or want to keep your parent happy; (then) your parents will thank you or let you have fun; (otherwise) parents won't do extra things or anything for their children; or there might be a fight or you **could** get in **trouble**." *Note:* Compare especially with Transition 1/2:Aspect 2b and with Transition 2/3:Aspect 1a.

(b) "Then your parents will (still) like you or talk to you, or (otherwise) **might** get mad (at you for not helping)." *Note:* Compare especially with Transition 1/2:Aspect 2b,c.

(c) It's not important because "You may get stuck with (doing) the whole job (by yourself)."

Transition 2/3

2/3:1 Exchanges/Relationships

(a) "Your friend **helps** you; the parents help or **have** helped you, took care of you, supported you, brought you up, do or give (up) **a lot, try to** help their children, or do or give **what they can**; helping your friend is helping both of you; if it weren't for your parents, you wouldn't even be here; they are there for you so you should be there for them; children should thank their parents"; or it's not important "**if** they aren't appreciative (when you help them)." *Note:* Compare especially with Stage 2:Aspects 1a and 6a, and Stage 3:Aspect 1a,b,c. Self-attributed characterizations, for example, "I will do anything I can for people," are unscorable. "You owe it to them" is also unscorable.

(b) "Your friend **would** (probably) help you; the children **would want** their parents to help them (so they should help their parents, or you could be in their situation (and need help)"—Moral Type B, Balancing. *Note:* Compare especially with Stage 2:Aspect 1b and with Stage 3:Aspect 1c.

(c) "Friends (should) help or count on each other, or need each other"—Moral Type B, Balancing. *Note:* Compare especially with Stage 3:Aspect 3b and with Transition 3/4:Aspect 1b.

2/3:2 Preferences/Needs/Relationships

"You may want to **keep** your friend or don't want to **lose** your friend; if it is a **good** friend." *Note:* Compare especially with Stage 2:Aspect 5b and Stage 3:Aspect 1a.

2/3:3 Preferences/Empathic Role-taking

"You'd feel sorry for them." *Note:* Compare especially with Stage 2:Aspect 5a and with Stage 3:Aspects 2a,b and 4a.

2/3:4 Preferences/Normative Expectations

"A **good** friend would help." *Note:* Compare especially with Stage 3:Aspects 1a and 4a.

2/3:5 Preferences/Prosocial Intentions

(a) "You **love** your parent (a lot), or shouldn't **just** let your friend die; if you know your friend well enough, if you like them **a lot**." *Note:* Compare especially with Stage 2:Aspect 4a and Stage 3:Aspects 2b and 4a. "You shouldn't let your friend die" is unscorable.

(b) It's important "**if** you or they have a **good** reason or cause."

2/3:6 Needs/Empathic Role-Taking

"They need (your) **help**, may have had a hard day, worked hard all day, can't do it all (by themselves), need a rest, are older, need it **badly**, **really** need to get better, or will (then) cheer up or feel better or good; or it is important **for him or her**; or (otherwise) they might **get** hurt." *Note:* Compare especially with Stage 2:Aspect 5a and Stage 3:Aspect 2a. "You need to help them" and most self-attributed characterizations (e.g., "I would not let them get hurt") are unscorable. Also, "they need help" is unscorable if stated in response to question 6 (which explicitly includes the phrase "need help" in the question). "You should always help a friend in need" is unscorable.

2/3:7 Needs/Relationships

(a) "Having a friend is great; (best) friends are special; **good** friends are hard to come by; or (while helping) children can spend more time with their parents." *Note:* Compare especially with Stage 2:Aspect 5b and Stage 3:Aspect 1a.

(b) "(Then) they will trust, love, or care about you; or the friend would be grateful or appreciative."

2/3:8 Advantages/Intrapersonal Approval

"It makes you feel good or better; (otherwise) your conscience will **bother** or **keep hounding** you; or you're only hurting yourself"—Moral Type B, Conscience. *Note:* Compare especially with Stage 3:Aspect 6.

The Mature Level

Stage 3: Mutual and Prosocial

3:1 Relationships

(a) "You would be or feel close; your parent is a **loved** one; if you are a **real, true,** or **close** friend; your friend would **mean** so much to you; a friend is like a part of you, or they have shared their life with you; it's for the sake of the relationship, faith, trust, or love; it brings the family (members) closer, or would be a way to get to know your parents better; (otherwise) there is little or no relationship, or it would spoil the relationship"; or it's important but "it depends on how **close** the relationship or friend is; or a true friend would not put you on the spot (by asking you to do such a thing)." *Note:* Compare especially with Transition 2/3:Aspects 1a, 2, 4, and 7a, and with Transition 3/4:Aspect 1a. "It is for your parent" is unscorable.

(b) "Parents sacrifice (for the children or the relationship), go out of their way (for the children), are always helping (their children), do or have given so much, have cared for you, have been there for you, have always shown kindness, or **would** do or give anything they could (for you); the children should **realize, think of, look at,** or **remember** how much their parents do or have done for them; it's the least you can do; you should be there for them; or the children should **be thankful, appreciative, or grateful,** or should return the kindness (shown by their parents)." *Note:* Compare especially with Transition 2/3:Aspects 1a,b and 5a.

(c) "You would **expect** them to help you, **would hope** the other person would help you (so you should help them); you **know in your heart** that they would help you; you should take (into account) their point of view, love them the way they love you, or follow the Golden Rule; we should love one another; or how would the children feel if the parents didn't help them?"—Moral Type B, Balancing. *Note:* Compare especially with Transition 2/3:Aspect 1a,b. "You should follow the Golden Rule" is only marginally scorable. Do not score if the respondent merely writes "because of the Golden Rule," because the developmental significance could be Stage 1 (Unilateral Authority).

3:2 Empathic Role-Taking

(a) "Your parents or friend may be in a bad situation, suffering, going through hard times, burdened, **in** (great) need, or under (a lot of) stress; when a friend hurts, you hurt; or parents are (only) human (and may need a lot of help)." *Note:* Compare especially with Transition 2/3:Aspects 3 and 6.

(b) "You don't or wouldn't want to **see,** or shouldn't just **watch,** your parent or friend in pain." *Note:* Compare especially with Transition 2/3:Aspects 3 and 5. "You should always help a friend in need" is unscorable.

(c) "The parents need to know that their children care enough to help; the parents will enjoy their children's company; (otherwise) the parents may feel hurt or exploited; (so that) the parents know they are loved or appreciated, will feel secure (knowing their children are there for them), or will see that the children love them; the parents can feel proud (of their children); or your friend will feel close to you."

(d) It's important but "the parents shouldn't expect too much from a young child."

3:3 Normative Expectations

(a) "Your parent would expect you to help; children should be loyal to their parents; children should honor or are **supposed to** show respect for their parents; or children are part of the family." *Note:* Compare especially with Stage 1:Aspect 3 and with Transition 3/4:Aspects 2b and 7b. "Children should help, too," "you're helping part of the family," "you should respect your parents," and "your parents expect it from you" are unscorable.

(b) "That's what friends are for, a friend should always be there to help, or friends are supposed to help one another." *Note:* Compare especially with Transition 2/3:Aspect 1c and Transition 3/4:Aspect 1b.

(c) "The parents may **deserve** help."

(d) "It is the human thing to do, it's (only) natural, or it is (a matter of) common decency." *Note:* Compare especially with Transition 3/4:Aspect 6.

3:4 Prosocial Intentions

(a) It's important because "of your emotions or feelings; you care about or love them **so** much; children should (be ready or willing to) sacrifice, shouldn't be selfish or lazy, **should** love their parents, or should give **out of** love; it's a gift or act of love; it would be nice **of** the children (to help their parents out); you **should** care or be sympathetic, **should realize** that they need help, would give of yourself, or would care **deeply** about your friend; if you (really and truly) love them then you **should** help them; or (otherwise) you're not much of a friend or not a **true** friend." *Note:* Compare especially with Stage 1:Aspect 4, with Transition 2/3:Aspects 3 and 5a, and with Transition 3/4:Aspect 7.

(b) It's important "(in order) to show that you love them or think they're important; or to **show** your friend that you don't want to lose him or her."

(c) "(Then) their parents will think well of them."

3:5 Generalized Caring

"He or she is a human being, life is precious, **everyone's** life is important, it's a (matter of a) person's or human life, a life is at stake, or it's a life-or-death situation"—Moral Type B, Fundamental Valuing. *Note:* Compare especially with Transition 3/4:Aspect 6. "It's a life," "it's important," and "it's a person" are unscorable.

3:6 Intrapersonal Approval

"Then the children will feel better **about themselves**; so that one can have peace of mind or feel good **inside**; the children will feel proud (of what they can do for their parents); or (otherwise) you would feel guilty, have it on your conscience, or couldn't live with yourself"—Moral Type B, Conscience. *Note:* Compare especially with Transition 2/3:Aspect 8.

Transition 3/4

3/4:1 Relationships/Societal Requirements

(a) "Friendship is **based** on trust, honesty, love, or caring; the friend **should or needs to be able** to trust or depend on you; you may have **built** up a good relationship (with your parents); it helps **establish** a good (working) relationship (with your parents); or (in order to) **develop** trust." *Note:* Compare especially with Stage 3:Aspect 1d and with Stage 4:Aspect 1d.

(b) "We are (all) in this world together (and should help one another); friends should be able to depend on one another; friendship is a common **bond** of helping each other; **everyone in the family** or **each family member** should (be willing to) help out, or do their share; it's a team effort; or it develops (a feeling of) teamwork, cooperation, or interdependence"—Moral Type B, Balancing. *Note:* Compare especially with Transition 2/3:Aspect 1c, with Stage 3:Aspect 3b, and with Stage 4:Aspects 1a,d and 2a. "A family should stick together" is unscorable.

3/4:2 Relationships/Basic Rights or Values

(a) "This may make the family stronger; it is for the **whole** or **entire** family; for the sake of harmony or smoother relationships; or for the sake of (open) communication (between parents and children)." *Note:* "Then they'll get along better" and "it's for the family" are unscorable.

(b) "Your parents deserve respect; out of respect; your friend should be respected; or (in order) to show respect." *Note:* Compare especially with Stage 3:Aspect 3a and with Stage 4:Aspect 6. "You should respect your parents" is unscorable.

(c) "Friends or parents and children should respect one another"—Moral Type B, Balancing.

3/4:3 Relationships/Responsibility

"Your parents took on a big responsibility (in bringing you into the world), and maybe they need help now." *Note:* Compare especially with Stage 4:Aspect 3.

3/4:4 Empathic Role-Taking/Procedural Equity

It's important but "it **depends** on, or you should **consider**, the **circumstances, case, situation,** or **level of friendship.**"

3/4:5 Normative Expectations/Responsibility

(a) "Children must or should **learn** how to work with others, how to share or respect others, that they can't always do what they want, that they **must** sacrifice sometimes, or that they **cannot** expect everything to (just) be handed to them." *Note:* Compare especially with Stage 4:Aspects 1a and 2a. "The children should help, too," "the children will grow up to be helpful," "they are family," and "you can't always do what you want" are unscorable.

(b) "The parent's word should be law, or the parent is the head of the household."

3/4:6 Prosocial Intentions/Basic Rights or Values

"You should have **humane** feelings or should have compassion for **another** human being or your **fellow** human beings; you should care about humanity; or (so that) there will be more love in the world." *Note:* Compare especially with Stage 3:Aspects 3d and 5.

3/4:7 Prosocial Intentions/Character

(a) "(Then) the child is **taught** responsibility; or so that the children will **learn** to be dependable, to sacrifice, or to share." *Note:* Compare especially with Stage 3:Aspect 4a and with Stage 4:Aspects 3 and 4. "(So that) child will learn to help or do their job better" and "they are trying to teach you something" are unscorable.

(b) "That shows the children are **responsible** or **dedicated** (to their parents); or (so that) the parent will realize how **responsible** the children are." *Note:* Compare especially with Stage 3:Aspect 3a and with Stage 4:Aspect 4.

3/4:8 Prosocial Intentions/Standards of Conscience

It's important but "one should follow one's conscience or convictions"—Moral Type B, Conscience (Relativism of Personal Values). *Note:* "But it depends on what they need" is unscorable.

3/4:9 Intrapersonal Approval/Standards of Conscience

"It helps the child's self-esteem or personal satisfaction, or it develops the child's self-concept"—Moral Type B, Conscience. *Note:* Compare especially with Stage 3:Aspect 6 and Stage 4:Aspects 4 and 7.

Stage 4: Systemic and Standard

4:1 Societal Requirements

(a) "The family **must** come before individual desires, or a family **must** pull together." *Note:* Compare especially with Transition 3/4:Aspects 1b and 5a. "Family comes first" and "the family should come before anything else" are unscorable.

(b) "The child must understand priorities, different levels of importance, or exceptional circumstances."

(c) "You have to have a head of the family, or someone has to be in charge."

(d) "A friendship **requires** or **must** be based on **cooperation** or **respect** for one another; or you **cannot** have a relationship if you don't **trust each other**"—Moral Type B, Balancing. *Note:* Compare especially with Transition 3/4:Aspect 1a,b.

4:2 Basic Rights or Values

(a) "That is what a family is all about; children should or must **contribute** (to the family); it's for the sake of the **common good, society,** the family **unit,** family unity, solidarity, functioning, the general welfare, or survival." *Note:* Compare with Transition 3/4:Aspects 1b and 5a. "Then the family will be helped" is unscorable.

(b) "Life is **sacred,** or (otherwise) you are demeaning **human worth**"—Moral Type B, Fundamental Valuing.

4:3 Responsibility

"The parent has (accepted) the responsibility or authority, is the child's provider or guardian, or is legally entitled or in charge; the child is a minor or is still living at home; (because) of one's commitment, responsibility, duty, or obligation; children have an obligation, or should feel or take responsibility (towards the needs of the family); it gives children a responsibility (when they take care of their parents)." *Note:* Compare especially with Transition 3/4:Aspects 3 and 7a. "It's my responsibility to help in my family" and "you are obligated to help because some day you may need them" are unscorable.

4:4 Character

"It shows **character, dependability, integrity,** or **responsibility**; for the sake of the child's (development of) character; or so that the child will have or develop a sense of the work ethic or accomplishment (through helping his or her parents)." *Note:* "(So that) the child will form good work habits" is unscorable. Compare especially with Transition 3/4:Aspects 5b, 7a,b, and 9.

4:5 Consistent Practices

It's important "for the sake of **consistency.**"

4:6 Procedural Equity

It's important but "parents should **earn** or **must deserve** their children's respect"—Moral Type B, Balancing. *Note:* Compare especially with Transition 3/4:Aspect 2b.

4:7 Standards of Conscience

It's important "for the sake of one's self-respect or integrity, sense of self-worth, or sense of personal value; in order to instill a **sense of** responsibility or personal value"—Moral Type B, Conscience. *Note:* Compare especially with Transition 3/4:Aspect 9.

Chapter 6

Life

In this chapter, justification for the normative value of life is addressed in terms of saving a stranger's life (question 7) or living even when one does not want to live (question 8). Life may be conceptualized as having value for the person, for others or society, or for God. At Stage 1, life's value for the person tends to be confounded with physical or material attributes (e.g., a life is valuable if the person "owns a lot of furniture"). At Stage 2, life is valued as long as it offers practical or hedonistic advantages and opportunities (you could still "do things" or "have fun"), and because the alternative would mean a deprivation of these opportunities (you wouldn't know "how things would have turned out" or "what would have happened"). At Stage 3, one may emphasize a more intrinsic enjoyment and appreciation of life. This "appreciation" is related at Transition 3/4 to the "perspectives" which individuals may have on life; accordingly, Transition 3/4 usually supports the importance of living even when you don't want to because "your views may change." Transition 3/4 may also involve going beyond the Stage 3 disapproval of self-pity to prescribing a need for "courage" or "will"; these attributes are expressive of prosocial considerations, but may also reflect a concern with character (Stage 4).

In sociomoral development, life's value is increasingly conceptualized in relation to other people or to society. At Stage 2, there is the suggestion that one's life has value in relation to others' preferences (other people "want you to live") or needs ("other people still need you"). At Stage 3, needs may still be referred to, but in a context suggestive of mutual role-taking ("you **should realize** that others still need you"). Also, the concern for others becomes more directly empathic at Stage 3, for example, "**loved ones** would suffer." Finally, at Stage 4, the value of life is often related to **society**: life, even if not desired, remains a "responsibility" or an "obligation" because "we all have a role to play in society," for the sake of society's "survival" or "progress."

One special developmental theme refers to the valuing of life in religious terms. At Stage 1, God is conceived as a unilateral authority who directly acts in the world to cause life and death (e.g., "We should live until God kills us"). By Stage 2, there is the suggestion that one should accommodate to the life-affirming preferences or interests attributed to God ("God wants people to live"). At Stage 3, life is valued as "precious" in light of its status as a "gift," which we in our relationship with God should "appreciate." Transition 3/4 marks the extension of God beyond the mutualistic context to a conception of God as the prime authority whose jurisdiction over questions of life and death must be respected: "We cannot question God," or "we should not take it upon ourselves to decide life's worth." Finally, respect for life as intrinsically worthy of reverence is indicated in the Stage 4 reference to human life as "sacred."

THE MONTAGES

Saving a stranger's life or living even when you don't want to is important because:

The Immature Level

Stage 1: Unilateral and Physicalistic

"The stranger might be an important person [2], and you should save him to be nice [4]. Besides, God put us here, and we should live until God kills us [3]; God doesn't like it if you kill yourself [1]." But it's not important because "you should never go near strangers [3] unless you are a fireman or a doctor [4], because the stranger will grab you or do something bad to you [5]."

Transition 1/2

(Otherwise) "there won't be many people left [1], and if you die you **will** make other people **sad** [2]." But it's not important because "you could get into **trouble** [1], or the stranger **could** grab you or do something bad to you [1]."

Stage 2: Exchanging and Instrumental

"The stranger may reward you or save your life some day if you help [1]. Everyone has just one life and should have the chance to live [2]. The stranger probably wants to live [4], and will probably thank you by doing you a favor. In fact, you may need the stranger some day [5]. Even if you don't want to live, you can still do things and have fun for a long time [6], and other people may want you to live [4]. After all, someone might still need you [5]. If you die you won't find out what would have happened if you had lived longer [6]." But it's not important because "you shouldn't stick your nose into the stranger's business. Whatever the problem, it's his problem, not yours [3]. Besides, for all you know the stranger is just faking in order to trick you [6]. Even if he isn't, why help someone you don't know? [6]. Also, you may want to die [4], and you don't have to live if you don't want to [3]."

Transition 2/3

"The stranger **would** do it for you [1]. He needs **your help** [5], and could **become** a friend once you save him [6]. Besides, if no one saves anyone, the world would get to be a lonely place [6]. Others love you and don't want **to lose** you because they would **miss** you [2]. Also, there may be children who need to be **cared for** [5]. She still has reasons to live, and **deep down** she **really** wants to [3]. After all, you should enjoy life **while you can** [6]. Besides, things can change [3] and you could become happy later [3]; you don't know what God has in store for you [5]." But it's not important because "the stranger is not as important **to you** as your friend. After all, you don't **even** know the stranger [6]."

The Mature Level

Stage 3: Mutual and Prosocial

"Life is precious [5], and people **deserve** to live [3]. It is horrible to watch someone **in** pain suffer [2], so saving the stranger is the **human** thing to do; it would be selfish not to help [4] in a life-or-death situation [5]. After all, if you help you can feel good about yourself—and if you don't it will be on your conscience [6]. Life is a gift we should appreciate [1]. Besides, we should be concerned about the feelings of loved ones and not hurt them [4]. We should enjoy life [4] and if we try we can find some purpose to live for or some hope for a **full** life [3]. You shouldn't just feel sorry for yourself [4]." But it's not important because "you wouldn't feel attached or close to the stranger [1]. Besides, you can only do so much [4]."

Transition 3/4

"We are all human beings, and should have compassion for a **fellow** human being [6]. Also, we have no right to play God and make a decision to kill ourselves [3], and should not abuse life [7]. You can make it if you have the courage; if you just quit, it's a cop-out [4]. After all, everyone has something to offer and can help others [6]. Besides, your views about the value of life may change [6]." But it's not important because "it **depends** on the **situation**, of course, on whether the suffering is physical or emotional [2]. Each person should follow his or her own judgment [6]. You have no **bond** of friendship with the stranger [1]."

Stage 4: Systemic and Standard

"People **must** help **each other** for the sake of society [1]. Life is sacred, and everyone can make a contribution [2]. Anyone can be useful and productive, because we all have a role to play in society [2]. People **must** feel responsible for others [3]. You must save the stranger's life, because you can't measure the value of another person's life [5]. If you don't save even a stranger's life, you could scarcely respect yourself [7] and life loses its meaning [2]." But it's not important "if under severe circumstances, the individual chooses to die with dignity [4]."

CRITERION JUSTIFICATIONS

Saving a stranger's life or living even when you don't want to is important because:

The Immature Level

Stage 1: Unilateral and Physicalistic

Responses that seem to relate to Stage 1 criterion justifications, but entail significant qualifications or elaborations, are not scorable at Stage 1.

1:1 Unilateral Authority

(a) "God doesn't like it (if you kill yourself)."
(b) "God put you here or made you come here." *Note:* Compare especially with Transition 2/3:Aspect 4. "You were created" is unscorable.

1:2 Status

"The stranger might be an important person; if the stranger is someone important; or the stranger could be famous (later)." *Note:* "But it depends on who the stranger is" is unscorable.

1:3 Rules

(a) "We should live until God kills us or takes us off the earth." *Note:* Compare especially with Transition 2/3:Aspect 4 and with Transition 3/4:Aspect 3. "God made us to live" and "we should die when God wants us to" are unscorable.

(b) It's not important because "you should never go near a stranger, or should not help strangers."

1:4 Labels

(a) "It is always nice to help someone; (it's important) to be good or nice; or (if) it is someone nice."

(b) "(Otherwise) it's a sin (not to want to live)." *Note:* "In a way it's a sin to commit suicide" is unscorable.

(c) It's not important unless "You are a fire fighter, policeman, or doctor."

1:5 Physical Consequences

"You will get a **treat** (if you save the stranger)"; or it's not important because "the stranger will grab, kill, or do something bad to you."
Note: Compare especially with Transition 1/2:Aspect 1a,b.

Transition 1/2

1/2:1 Physical Consequences/Advantages

(a) "You **could** or **might** get a **treat**; (otherwise) you **would** be **blamed** (if the stranger dies);" or it's not important because "you **will** get in **trouble** (if the stranger dies anyway)." *Note:* Compare especially with Stage 1:Aspect 5 and with Stage 2:Aspect 6c.

(b) It's not important because "The stranger **could grab**, **kill**, or do **something bad** to you, **could** be **bad** or a **killer**, or **will hurt** you." *Note:* Compare especially with Stage 1:Aspect 5 and with Stage 2:Aspect 6c. "It may not be safe" is unscorable.

(c) "(Otherwise) there would be no one or not many people left." *Note:* "It may not be safe" is unscorable.

1/2:2 Labels/Physical Consequences/Advantages

"You **will make** other people sad or they **will** be sad (if you die); (then) your friend can't play with you; or (otherwise) other people **will** be **mad** (if you let someone die)." *Note:* Compare especially with Stage 2:Aspect 6d.

Stage 2: Exchanging and Instrumental

2:1 Exchanges

"The stranger may return the favor, could reward you, or might save your life (some day)." *Note:* Compare especially with Transition 2/3:Aspect 1. Although "**return** the favor" is scored under Exchanges, "do you a favor" would be scored under Advantages (Aspect 6). In general, Stage 2 justifications emphasizing a quid pro quo "return" of benefits in kind are scored under Exchanges, whereas more general anticipations of possible future benefits are scored under Advantages.

2:2 Equalities

"Everyone should have a chance to live, or just has one life; or the stranger needs to live, **too**." *Note:* Similar but elaborated justifications, for example, "you just have one life and should realize how important life is," are not scorable at Stage 2. "The stranger needs to live" is scorable under Needs (see Aspect 5). "Everyone has the right to live," "everyone is equal," and "you shouldn't take the chance of letting them die" are unscorable.

2:3 Freedoms

"You shouldn't butt in or stick your nose into someone else's business; it's their life or problem (not yours); they can do what they want with their life; or if you don't want to live, you don't have to." *Note:* Compare especially with Transition 3/4:Aspect 7b. Similar but elaborated justifications are not scorable at Stage 2. Also, "It's the person's choice," "whether someone lives or dies should not be someone else's choice," "you can't make someone stay alive if they don't want to," and "you shouldn't be forced to live (if you don't want to)" are unscorable.

2:4 Preferences

(a) "People (should) want to live; the stranger (is a person who) wants to live; (if I were the stranger,) I would want to live; that would be stupid (to want to die); or no one wants to go through pain or die"; or (it's not important) "if you want to get rid of the pain; or (because) the stranger may want to die." *Note:* Compare especially with Transition 2/3:Aspect 3 and with Transition 3/4:Aspect 4.

(b) "Someone might like you or want you to live; you don't or wouldn't want anyone to die"; or it's not important because "you may not like the stranger; or I don't care (about strangers)."
Note: Compare especially with Transition 2/3:Aspect 2a. "We should die when God wants us to" is unscorable.

2:5 Needs

"The stranger needs to live; you need to live (even if you don't want to); you might need that stranger (to help you some day); but you may need to get rid of your pain, or someone might need you." *Note:* Compare especially with Transition 2/3:Aspect 5a.

2:6 Advantages

(a) "Everyone would like you (for saving the stranger's life); or the stranger will thank you, might do you a favor (some day), or might do lots of things (for you)."

(b) "You (still) have many things you can do; you can (still) have fun or (still) have good times (ahead of you); you only live once; you may (otherwise) have a long life or live longer; life is the best thing you know; you don't know that death is better; you may find out later that it wasn't worth it (to kill yourself); you'd never know what you would have gotten (in the future)." *Note:* Compare especially with Transition 2/3:Aspects 2b and 3 and with Stage 3:Aspect 3b.

(c) It's not important because "why help (someone you don't know)?; that would be stupid (to help someone you don't know); you shouldn't take the risk; you could get hurt; or the stranger could be a **crook**, faking, or tricking you." *Note:* Compare especially with Transition 1/2:Aspect 1a,b. "You don't know whether it's safe" is unscorable. "Getting hurt" is rated Transition 2/3 in chapter 4, where the pragmatic context is less clear.

(d) "Others **may be sad** (if you die); or other people **may** get **mad** (at you if you let someone die)." *Note:* Compare especially with Transition 1/2:Aspect 2 and with Transition 2/3:Aspect 2a.

Transition 2/3

2/3:1 Exchanges/Relationships

"The stranger **would** do it for you, you could be in that situation (some day), I **would want** the stranger to help me"; or it's not important because "the stranger (probably) **wouldn't** do it for you"—Moral Type B, Balancing. *Note:* Compare especially with Stage 2:Aspect 1 and with Stage 3:Aspect 1a.

2/3:2 Preferences/Relationships

(a) "Someone (probably) **loves** the stranger; someone might love you; or others may love or care about you, might miss you or worry, or don't want to **lose** you." *Note:* Compare especially with Stage 2:Aspects 4b and 6d and with Stage 3:Aspects 2b and 4b.

(b) "There may (still) be (some) people you care about"; or it's not important because "most people wouldn't care." *Note:* Compare especially with Stage 2:Aspect 6b.

2/3:3 Preferences/Advantages/Prosocial Intentions

"You **really** (still) want to live; you just think you want to die; **deep down** you want to live; you may (still) have a few reasons to live; you could become happy or glad you're alive (later), get over it, or see the good things in life; you may find life gets better (later) or things can change; or you could still have a wonderful life." *Note:* Compare especially with Stage 2:Aspects 4a and 6b, and with Stage 3:Aspect 3b,c. "You may change your mind" and "there is always a tomorrow" are unscorable.

2/3:4 Preferences/Normative Expectations

"You don't know what God wants or has in store for you; or there is a **place** (on earth) for everyone." *Note:* Compare especially with Stage 1:Aspects 1b and 3a, with Stage 3:Aspect 3b, with Transition 3/4:Aspect 3, and with Stage 4:Aspect 2b. "(Because) you were created" is unscorable.

2/3:5 Needs/Empathic Role-Taking

(a) "Everyone needs help or needs someone to talk to; the stranger needs **your help** or needs someone to help; the stranger may be going through a lot of pain; there may be children who need to be taken **care of**"; or it's not important because "God will help the stranger." *Note:* Compare especially with Stage 2:Aspect 5 and with Stage 3:Aspects 2c and 4b.

(b) "Maybe the stranger never hurt anybody (and so should be saved)." *Note:* Although generally "hurt" is rated Stage 3 in this chapter, the use of "hurt" with reference to the stranger is scored Transition 2/3 (because the meaning of "hurt" in this context is less clearly socioemotional).

2/3:6 Advantages/Relationships

(a) "The stranger would be grateful, could **become** a friend, or you could become **good** friends;" or it's not important because "the stranger is not as important **to you** (as your wife or friend), or you don't **even** or **really** know the stranger. *Note:* Compare especially with Stage 3:Aspect 1c. "You could be friends," "the stranger is not important," and "you don't know the stranger" are unscorable.

(b) "You should enjoy life **while you can**." *Note:* Compare especially with Stage 3:Aspect 4c.

(c) "(Otherwise) you would be alone, or the world would be a lonely place."

2/3:7 Advantages/Prosocial Intentions

"(Otherwise) people would start rumors (that you don't help others)."

2/3:8 Advantages/Intrapersonal Disapproval

"Then you would feel good; or (otherwise) it would hurt you or you'd feel bad (if you didn't save the stranger)"—Moral Type B, Conscience. *Note:* Compare especially with Stage 3:Aspect 6.

The Mature Level

Stage 3: Mutual and Prosocial

3:1 Relationships

(a) "How would you feel if you were dying (and someone wouldn't help you?); what if you were the stranger?; you **would hope** that the stranger would save your life, or **would expect** the stranger to save your life; we should care about one another; or you **should** do what you would want others to do for you"—Moral Type B, Balancing. *Note:* Compare especially with Transition 2/3:Aspect 1.

(b) "Life is a gift; we should appreciate God's love; or we should be **thankful** for (the) life (God gave us)."

(c) "A loved one is a part of you; or you could become **close** or **true** friends;" but it's not important for a stranger because "You wouldn't feel attached to, would have no feelings for, or would not be close to a stranger; the stranger doesn't **mean** as much to him; or the stranger's **loved ones** should care for him." *Note:* Compare especially with Transition 2/3:Aspect 6a.

3:2 Empathic Role-Taking

(a) "You wouldn't want to **watch** someone die; or it's horrible to see someone suffer."

(b) **"Loved ones** or your family would suffer, you would hurt others who love you, or it would be upsetting (to loved ones)." *Note:* Compare especially with Transition 2/3:Aspect 2a. "Hurting others" is rated Stage 3 with reference to the value of life because in this context it generally connotes *emotional* hurt. "The stranger probably has a family, too" is unscorable.

(c) "They are **in** need or **in** pain; or (important unless) they are suffering too much." *Note:* Compare especially with Transition 2/3:Aspect 5a.

3:3 Normative Expectations

(a) "People deserve to live." *Note:* "Some people may deserve to die" is unscorable.

(b) "There is still some **purpose** (for you to live) or some hope; each person has something to live for; you have a lot to live for; or you can still live a **full** life." *Note:* Compare especially with Transition 2/3:Aspects 3 and 4, with Transition 3/4:Aspect 6a,b, and with Stage 4:Aspect 2b. "You should enjoy life" is unscorable.

(c) "You may be too upset, depressed, or confused (to realize that life may be better later on); you may need to talk to someone **you trust**; you may **feel** different, become less bitter, or accept your condition (later); or you may not realize what you're doing." *Note:* Compare especially with Transition 2/3:Aspect 3, and with Transition 3/4:Aspects 4 and 6b. "You may need psychological counseling" is unscorable.

3:4 Prosocial Intentions

(a) "It is the **human** or compassionate thing to do; to show your love for them; (otherwise) you're not much of a person;" or it's not important because "you can only do so much."

(b) "You should be concerned about (the feelings of) others, shouldn't have to think twice (about saving them), or shouldn't hurt people (who love you); you are important to **loved ones**; **you should realize** that there are people who love or need you; suicide is selfish; or you shouldn't (just) feel sorry for yourself, or feel ashamed." *Note:* Compare especially with Transition 2/3:Aspects 2a, 3, and 5a.

(c) "You should enjoy life (as best you can)." *Note:* Compare especially with Transition 2/3:Aspects 3 and 6b.

3:5 Generalized Caring

(a) "You should care for everyone; you shouldn't just care about your friends; it is **still** a person or a human life; this is a life-or-death or life-threatening situation; or **even** a stranger is a person"—Moral Type B, Fundamental Valuing. *Note:* Compare especially with Transition 3/4:Aspect 6a. "It's important to help anyone," "it's a life," "a life is a life," "it's a person," "people are human," "someone is dying," and "it's not right for anyone to die" are unscorable.

(b) "Life is precious, priceless, invaluable, beautiful, a privilege, or more important than money or possession; or life should be treasured"—Moral Type B, Fundamental Valuing. *Note:* Compare especially with Stage 4:Aspects 2a and 5. "A life is worth living," "saving a life is important," and "saving someone is special" are unscorable.

3:6 Intrapersonal Approval

"You would feel good **inside**, or would feel good or better about yourself; you would feel good thinking or knowing that you helped someone or did what you could; or (otherwise) you would feel guilty, feel terrible, regret it, have it on your conscience, have an empty feeling inside, blame yourself, or not be able to live with yourself"—Moral Type B, Conscience. *Note:* Compare especially with Transition 2/3:Aspect 8 and with Stage 4:Aspect 7a. "You would feel responsible (for the stranger's death)" is scorable as Transition 3/4:Aspect 5a.

Transition 3/4

3/4:1 Relationships/Responsibility

It's not important because "there is no **bond** of friendship (with the stranger)."

3/4:2 Empathic Role-Taking/Procedural Equity

It's important but "it **depends on the situation, case, or circumstances**; or it depends on whether the suffering is physical or emotional, or from serious ailments or (just) dissatisfaction with life"—Moral Type B, Balancing. *Note:* Compare especially with Stage 4:Aspect 4. "But it depends on the person" and "a person may have a disease" are unscorable.

3/4:3 Normative Expectations/Basic Rights or Values

"We shouldn't play God or try to make decisions of life and death; we cannot question God, or should have faith in God's wisdom; whether one lives or dies should be God's decision; it isn't up to the individual; we should not take it upon ourselves to decide life's worth; we have no right to kill ourselves; or we cannot control life." *Note:* Compare especially with Transition 2/3:Aspect 4. "God will always see you through," "everyone has a right to live," "God made us to live," and "we should die when God wants us to" are unscorable.

3/4:4 Prosocial Intentions/Character

"You shouldn't end your life just because of emotional stress, depression, or personal problems; you must have the courage or should have the will (to live or keep on going); you have to learn to bounce back; or (otherwise) it's a cop-out or irrational." *Note:* Compare especially with Stage 2:Aspect 4a and with Stage 3:Aspect 3c. "Suicide won't solve your problems" is unscorable.

3/4:5 Prosocial Intentions/Responsibility

(a) "You should or would feel responsible; or it's **irresponsible** (not to save the stranger)." *Note:* Compare especially with Stage 4:Aspect 3a. It's not important because "it isn't your responsibility" is unscorable.

(b) "You may have **goals** to **achieve**."

3/4:6 Generalized Caring/Basic Rights or Values

(a) "We are all human beings; you should have compassion for a **fellow** or **another** human being; you should be (a) humanitarian or should care about society or humanity; everyone has something to offer, has potential, or can help others (in some way); you can still have an impact or effect (on others); a life shouldn't be wasted; life should be developed (to the utmost); helping one another is the way the world should be; or we should respect or not abuse life"—Moral Type B, Fundamental Valuing. *Note:* Compare especially with Stage 3:Aspects 3b and 5a, and with Stage 4:Aspects 1b and 2b. "We should help each other" is unscorable.

(b) "You should see the positive aspects of life; (you should realize that) unhappiness is a part of life; you can still lead a **fulfilling** life; your outlook or views (about the value of life) may change; you may (come to) see life differently." *Note:* Compare especially with Stage 3:Aspect 3b,c.

3/4:7 Intrapersonal Approval/Standards of Conscience

(a) "A person should follow his or her own judgment"—Moral Type B, Conscience (Relativism of Personal Values).

(b) It's important but "people should be allowed or have the right to decide whether to end their own lives, or should be in control of their life; you should respect their right or **personal** choice (regarding suicide in extreme circumstances); or in the final analysis it is the individual's decision." *Note:* Compare especially with Stage 2:Aspect 3. "It's their life," "it's their choice," and "you can't make them change their mind" are unscorable.

Stage 4: Systemic and Standard

4:1 Societal Requirements

(a) "(To save a life) is a higher law, or **must** take priority."

(b) "People **must** help **each other** (if society is to survive); we are interdependent; or the world won't survive or society cannot function if no one cares for anyone"—Moral Type B, Balancing. *Note:* Compare especially with Transition 3/4:Aspect 6a.

4:2 Basic Rights or Values

(a) "Life is sacred"—Moral Type B, Fundamental Valuing. *Note:* Compare especially with Stage 3:Aspect 5b.

(b) "Everyone has something to offer **society**, has a role to play in **society**, or can make a contribution; you can still lead a **productive** life or be **useful** to **society**; it is through each person's life or contribution that there will be advances or progress; it is for the sake of society; life has no meaning if you don't give to others;" or it's not important "if the (terminally ill, dying) person decides not to be a burden on society." *Note:* Compare especially with Transition 2/3:Aspect 4, with Stage 3:Aspect 3b, and with Transition 3/4:Aspect 6a.

4:3 Responsibility

(a) "One has a responsibility, obligation, or commitment to any human being; people **must** feel responsible for others or should sense a duty to (help) others; or we all have an obligation or responsibilities (to society or to serve life)." *Note:* Compare especially with Transition 3/4:Aspect 5a. "It's your duty" is unscorable.

(b) "We should (choose to) accept (the) responsibility (of doing the best we can in life), or (**but**) one must accept responsibility for one's actions or life."

4:4 Character

It's important but "under severe or extreme circumstances, the individual may choose to die with dignity; or forcing continued life may violate the personhood of the individual." *Note:* Compare especially with Transition 3/4:Aspect 2.

4:5 Consistent Practices

"Who is to say that the life of one is 'worth' more than the life of another?; or you can't measure the value of another person's life." *Note:* Compare especially with Stage 3:Aspect 5b.

4:6 Procedural Equity

This aspect is not typically in evidence with regard to the life value.

4:7 Standards of Conscience

(a) It's important "for the sake of (one's) self-respect"—Moral Type B, Conscience. *Note:* Compare especially with Stage 3:Aspect 6.

(b) It's important but "one should not compromise one's integrity"—Moral Type B, Conscience.

Chapter 7

Property and Law

Justifications for obeying the law and not stealing frequently appeal to the consequences of breaking the law for the group, the self, or others, and to the functions served by laws. One of the main lines of development pertains to consequences for the group. At Transition 1/2, the group consequence is conceptualized in terms of physical—but also possibly instrumental—disadvantages ("there would be nothing left to steal, no money"; "everyone would be in jail"). At Stage 2, the instrumental nature of the disadvantages is more clear (e.g., "people will be getting away with things"). A Stage 3 rating refers to the potential confusion from widespread violations of normative interpersonal expectations ("things would fall apart"; "there would chaos"; "it would be crazy").

The concern at higher levels is with the need for order in social functioning. Transition 3/4 marks the simple appeal to "order," "control," or the prevention of "lawlessness" (the appeal for "order" could concern either conformity with interpersonal normative expectations—Stage 3, or stability in societal functioning—Stage 4). At Stage 4, there is a direct suggestion that laws keep "**society** in order," that is, make a stable social system possible.

Justifications referring to consequences can also refer to consequences for the self. At immature levels, these consequences are externally oriented. At Stage 1, the external consequences are presented as physical and inevitable ("you will be caught, found out, killed, put in the hospital, or sent to jail"). At Transition 1/2, the external consequences are physical or inevitable but not both (e.g., "you **might** be caught, **may** get spanked, **will** get in trouble, or **will end up** in jail"). By Stage 2 the punitive connotations have disappeared, and the "consequences" are construed as benefits or liabilities resulting from the calculations of a self-interested individual (you should obey the law "so you can get further in life," because otherwise "you're taking a risk," or because the person you steal from "might get mad at you"). If the usually punitive term "trouble" is used, it is found at Stage 2 in the context of prudential calculation (obeying the law is important "**if you know** you would get caught or in trouble") or pragmatic liabilities (stealing "just causes trouble").

At higher levels, the referents for self-consequences become more internal. At Transition 2/3, the self's conscience (seen as a somewhat extrinsic, adversarial agent) would "bother" you if you steal. By Stage 3, the consideration is more intrinsic (your having stolen would be "on your mind"). The corresponding Stage 4 consideration implies not simply a self-disapproval but also a set of internal standards that one must live up to in order to judge oneself worthy of "self-respect."

Somewhat specific to the property question (#9) is a concern with the importance of working rather than stealing. At Stage 2, this concern is expressed in the form of an appeal to the concrete rights or freedoms of persons who may have "worked for their things." At the next higher levels, more empathic concerns may be implied ("they worked **hard** for their things"—Transition 2/3) or directly expressed ("they sacrificed or worked **so hard** for their things"—Stage 3). There is also the Stage 3 expectation that we "should work for **our** things" or "shouldn't take advantage of others." The broader and possibly societal concern with the loss of a "motivation to work" is designated Transition 3/4; discriminatively Stage 4 is the specific concern that widespread theft could destroy the "incentives needed for a prosperous society."

It is interesting to trace the development of perspective-taking in justifications for the importance of property and law. At Stage 2, moral reciprocity is understood in terms of instrumental exchanges and applies to the importance of obeying the law in terms either positive ("the laws will help you if you help them") or negative ("if you break a law and get caught, then you pay for it"). Transition 2/3 marks a perspective-taking that, although still instrumentally oriented, is more hypothetical ("you **wouldn't want** someone to take your things"). By Stage 3 the appeal is oriented to mutualities of feelings and expectation ("how would you feel if . . .?"; you would "expect" or "hope" that the other person wouldn't take your things). At more advanced levels, the perspective-taking relates interpersonal concerns and circumstances to the functions of the larger social whole. On the one hand, society must be responsive to the individual. Specifically, there is an appeal to the need for flexibility and responsiveness to individual circumstances in the case-by-case application of the laws ("laws **cannot** take into account every circumstance"— Stage 4). On the other hand, the individual must be responsive to society. Instead of the Stage 2 acceptance of "paying" if you happen to "get caught," the Stage 4 acceptance of consequences prescribes an inner acknowledgement of the legitimacy of those consequences even at the outset of acts of civil disobedience (one must be "**prepared** to accept the consequences").

MONTAGES

Obeying the law or not stealing is important because:

The Immature Level

Stage 1: Unilateral and Physicalistic

"The law is there for you to follow [1]. You should **always** obey the law and should never take other people's things [3], which could cost a lot of money [2]. Stealing is a bad thing to do, and you're not nice if you steal. You should obey the law to be good [4]. If you steal, then those people **will** steal your things. You **will** be found out and **put** in jail [5]."

Transition 1/2

"Other people's things are theirs; those things don't belong to you [1], and if you steal they **will** get **mad** [3] and call you a criminal [2]. You **will** get in trouble and **go** to jail, or could even get killed. Meanwhile, murderers would be walking the streets killing people, there would be nothing left to steal, and there would be no one left to obey the law [3]."

Stage 2: Exchanging and Instrumental

"The laws will help you if you help them [1]. If you don't steal, others shouldn't either [2]. If you do break a law, you **have to pay** for it [1]. Besides, you **don't want** people to steal your things [1]. No one wants to go to jail, even if it is for someone you **like** [4]. Stealing gets you nowhere, and **if you are caught** you will get in trouble or may even get hurt [6]. The person you steal from might get mad at you [6], because that person worked for [3] and may need what you took [5]. People would be killing and getting away with things [6]." But it is not important because "maybe the other person stole from you, so why shouldn't you steal back [1]? Besides, you may need it [5]."

Transition 2/3

"You **wouldn't want** people to steal your things [1], and you want others to trust you [7]. Besides, the other person may have worked **hard** for what he had [3], and it could be something they care about [6]. If people break the law, someone you **love** might go to jail [5], someone could be hurt [8], the world would be unsafe, a mess, and full of crime [9], and your conscience would **bother** you [10]. So you shouldn't steal unless you need it **badly** [6]."

The Mature Level

Stage 3: Mutual and Prosocial

"Then the world would be happier [1]. After all, how would you feel if someone took your things [1]? You would **expect** others not to steal from you, and you lose the trust of others if you steal from them [1]. You should realize that people often work **so hard** and feel sentimentally attached to their property, and it causes a hardship when you steal something that means a lot to them [2]. You can understand how the person would feel [2]. Furthermore, the laws protect **people**, and it's a matter of common decency not to steal [3]. If there were no laws and everyone stole, the world would be crazy, the country would fall apart, and there would be chaos [3]. We **should** work for and deserve **our** things [3], and it is selfish, dishonest, and despicable to take advantage of others [4]. Earning money instead of just stealing gives you a feeling of pride [6], that people **can** trust you [4]. Remember, you're only hurting yourself by stealing [6]."

Transition 3/4

"Laws make life more harmonious [1]. Obeying the law shows your trustworthiness [9]. If you stop following the guidelines provided by laws, you would lose others' respect [9]. Admittedly, laws aren't always fair [3]. It does depend to some extent on the circumstances, and there can be exceptions for special cases [3]. But laws are important for the sake of not only order [4], but also harmony and justice [1]. Laws are made for the people, and if people don't follow them there would be no **point** in having them [5]. For example, the motivation to work and earn money would be lost [7], and there would be no respect for one another's property [5]. The laws should serve as a guide to encourage self-control and greater awareness of right and wrong [9], so that people can live together in peace and avoid anarchy [4]. You have no right to take something just because you **think** you need it [8]. Of course, you should act according to your values and make your **own** decision [10], but then you should be **willing** to accept the penalty [6]."

Stage 4: Systemic and Standard

"Laws **make possible** order in society [1]. Without the agreement [3] and sacred trust [2] represented by laws, there could be no organization, smooth functioning, or predictability [1]. The law is for the common good and **protects** people's **rights**, including the right to property [2]. If stealing is widespread, there is no incentive for people to be productive or invent things that help the quality of life for humanity [2]. Besides, you have a **responsibility** [3] to **respect** others' **rights** to property [2]. This is one of the obligations that go along with the privileges of living in society [3]. If you do steal, you have to be **prepared** to accept responsibility for your actions, especially since stealing violates God's law as well as human law [3] and the rights of others [2]. That way you won't violate your conscience [7] and lose your self-respect and integrity [6]. After all, we must have some system; people **cannot** break the law whenever they feel justified, because any theft can be rationalized [5]. Nonetheless, laws **cannot** always be fair or appropriate for every particular circumstance; you do **have to** judge each case individually [6]. Sometimes, one must follow one's own **internal laws** [7]."

CRITERION JUSTIFICATIONS

The Immature Level

Stage 1: Unilateral and Physicalistic

Responses that seem to relate to Stage 1 criterion justifications, but entail significant qualifications or elaborations, are not scorable at Stage 1.

1:1 Unilateral Authority

"The law is (there) for you to follow, the law tells you what to do, the Bible says Don't steal, or the law was put here by God." *Note:* "'Thou shalt not steal' is one of God's commandments," "the laws are made to be followed," and "it is Biblically wrong" are unscorable.

1:2 Status

"It may be (really) expensive or cost a lot of money."

1:3 Rules

(a) "You should **always** or are **always** supposed to obey the law; you must obey or have to follow the law; or no one should steal or break the law." *Note:* "You should obey the law no matter what" and "you are supposed to obey the law" are unscorable.

(b) "You should **never** take other people's things, or you should ask your parents first." *Note:* "It isn't fair to take other people's things" and "if you want or need something you should ask" are unscorable.

1:4 Labels

"It's the law; stealing is bad; or it's a sin; (in order) to be good; or (otherwise) it's not nice or that's stealing." *Note:* Compare especially with Transition 3/4:Aspect 5c. "Stealing is a crime, wrong, or goes against the law" is unscorable. Also, elaborated or qualified assertions, for example, "stealing is bad, even if for a good cause," are not scorable at Stage 1. (The example is scorable at Transition 2/3.)

1:5 Physical Consequences

"(Otherwise) you **will** be caught, injured, killed, found out, **sent** to jail, **put** in jail, or **put** in the hospital; or they **will** steal your things." *Note:* Compare especially with Transition 1/2:Aspect 3a.

Transition 1/2

1/2:1 Labels/Freedoms

(a) "It isn't yours or doesn't belong to you, or it's theirs." *Note:* "It's not for you to take" is unscorable. Any elaborations, for example, "It's not rightfully yours" and "if it isn't yours, leave it alone" are unscorable at Stage 1 or Transition 1/2. (The latter example is scorable at Stage 2.)

(b) It's important unless "they have something that's yours."

1/2:2 Labels/Advantages

"(Otherwise) he will or might be called a criminal or a thief." *Note:* Compare especially with Stage 2:Aspect 6b and Transition 2/3:Aspect 8b.

1/2:3 Physical Consequences/Advantages

(a) "(Then) you **won't** get in trouble or be blamed; (otherwise) they **will** be mad, or **might** steal your things or get you; you **might** be caught or found out, or **would** get punished, **go** to jail, or end up in jail; or you **could** be killed, injured, made sick, or **be put in** or **sent to** jail or the hospital." *Note:* Compare especially with Stage 1:Aspect 5 and Stage 2:Aspects 1b, 4a, and 6b,d.

(b) "(Otherwise) everyone will be stealing or killing, there would be murderers (walking the streets), or there would be trouble; there would be nothing left to steal, or no money; everyone would be in jail, or there would be no one left to obey the law." *Note:* Compare especially with Stage 2:Aspect 6b,c. "(Because then) people will do what they want" and "(because otherwise) there would be a lot of consequences" are unscorable.

Stage 2: Exchanging and Instrumental

2:1 Exchanges

(a) "The laws will help you if you help them."

(b) "You **don't want** your things stolen; if you don't steal from others, they won't or shouldn't steal from you; or (otherwise) they might get even." *Note:* Compare especially with Transition 1/2:Aspect 3a and with Transition 2/3:Aspect 1.

(c) "If you didn't buy it, don't take it; it's not yours so don't touch it; or if it isn't yours, leave it alone." *Note:* Similar responses missing a simple, concrete if/then quality (e.g., "You shouldn't take things that don't belong to you") are unscorable.

(d) "If you don't follow the law you go to jail; if you can't do the time, don't do the crime; once you break the law you **must** pay the price; (otherwise) you **have to** pay (for your crime); or (**but**) you can steal if you can take it (when they get even)." *Note:* Compare especially with Transition 3/4:Aspect 6. "If you break the law you should be punished or should go to jail" and "you should pay the consequences" are unscorable.

(e) It's important but "if somebody is stealing from you, you can or should steal back or get even."

(f) It's important unless "somebody is too stupid to watch their things."

2:2 Equalities

"I don't steal so they shouldn't either."

2:3 Freedoms

(a) "They may have worked for or earned their things, or paid for what they have; or they can do whatever they want (with their property)." *Note:* Compare especially with Transition 2/3:Aspect 3.

(b) "You should stay out of someone else's space or keep out of their business."

2:4 Preferences

(a) "You wouldn't want to get in trouble or go to jail, you don't want to spend your life in prison; no one wants to go to jail, or I don't want to be in jail." *Note:* Compare especially with Transition 1/2:Aspect 3a.

(b) "They want their things or don't like their things stolen." *Note:* Compare especially with Transition 2/3:Aspect 6a

(c) "(Otherwise) someone you **like** might go to jail, or (**unless**) it is for someone you **like**." *Note:* Compare especially with Transition 2/3:Aspect 5.

2:5 Needs

(a) "You might not need to (steal or break the law); or (unless) you need it." *Note:* Elaborated versions of this response are not scorable at Stage 2.

(b) "They may need it."

2:6 Advantages

(a) "Stealing gets you nowhere or isn't worth it; or (so that) you can get further in life or do things."

(b) "You would (probably) be found out **sooner or later**; you **could** get into (a lot of) trouble, go to jail or end up in jail; you would get a (criminal) record; there would be hassles; **you** could get hurt or hurt yourself; you're taking a risk; **if** you are **caught** you will get in trouble; it's important if "you **know** or **think** that you will get caught or in trouble; if you are afraid or worried (all the time about getting caught); (**but**) it depends on whether it's for a friend who is worth going to jail for; (**unless**) you can get away with it." *Note:* Compare especially with Transition 1/2:Aspects 2 and 3a, and with Transition 2/3:Aspect 8a.

(c) "(Otherwise) people will be getting away with things." *Note:* Compare especially with Transition 1/2:Aspect 3b. "(Because otherwise) everyone will be doing all kinds of things" is unscorable.

(d) "(Otherwise) they will not like you, or could get mad at you." *Note:* Compare especially with Transition 1/2:Aspect 3a.

Transition 2/3

2/3:1 Exchanges/Relationships

"You **wouldn't want** people to steal your things; or I **wouldn't like** it or **want** it done to me"—Moral Type B, Balancing. *Note:* Compare especially with Stage 2:Aspect 1b and with Stage 3:Aspect 1a.

2/3:2 Equalities/Normative Expectations

"No one is special (enough to be allowed to break the law)."

2/3:3 Freedoms/Empathic Role-Taking

"The other person (may have) worked **hard** or **long** (for what he has), or had a purpose (for it)." *Note:* Compare especially with Stage 2:Aspect 3a and with Stage 3:Aspect 2a.

2/3:4 Freedoms/Normative Expectations

"It **isn't fair** to take what they worked for or earned." *Note:* Compare especially with Stage 3:Aspect 3a.

2/3:5 Preferences/Prosocial Intentions

"Someone you **love** might go to jail; or **(unless)** it is for someone you **love**." *Note:* Compare especially with Stage 2:Aspect 4c and Stage 3:Aspect 2b.

2/3:6 Needs/Empathic Role-Taking

(a) It's important because "that **could** have been all that person has (in the world), or could be very valuable, special, or important to them; or they care about their things, or may like this thing **a lot**." *Note:* Compare especially with Transition 2/3:Aspect 4b and with Stage 3:Aspect 2a.

(b) It's important unless "you **really** need it or need it **badly**."

2/3:7 Advantages/Preferences/Relationships

"Others are trusting you; you want others to trust you (the next time); or (so that) others **will** trust or believe you again." *Note:* Compare especially with Stage 3:Aspects 1c and 4a.

2/3:8 Advantages/Prosocial Intentions/Empathic Role-Taking

(a) "(Otherwise) you could hurt or harm someone; **(unless)** it wouldn't hurt anyone, or you could help someone (by breaking the law)." *Note:* Compare especially with Stage 2:Aspect 6b, with Stage 3:Aspects 2a and 3c, and with Transition 3/4:Aspect 2.

(b) "(Otherwise) you would get a bad reputation." *Note:* Compare especially with Transition 1/2:Aspect 2 and with Stage 3:Aspect 4b.

2/3:9 Advantages/Normative Expectations

(a) "If everyone obeyed the law things would be nicer; (so that) things would be peaceful, or in order to make things better; the laws (were made to) make things safer; or (otherwise) people would or might be hurt; things would be a mess, wreck, or would be in bad shape; there would be crime or constant battles, the world wouldn't be worth living in, or it would be hard to live or get along in the world." *Note:* Compare especially with Stage 3:Aspects 1b and 3c, and with Transition 3/4:Aspect 2. "(Because) the laws were made for a reason" and "(because otherwise) there would be war or problems" are unscorable.

(b) "(Otherwise eventually) **people would think** that you don't get caught (if you steal)."

2/3:10 Advantages/Intrapersonal Approval

(a) "(Otherwise) your conscience will or would **bother** you; you will or would regret it; or you are hurting yourself"—Moral Type B, Conscience. *Note:* Compare especially with Stage 3:Aspect 6.

(b) "(Otherwise) it would be embarrassing (if you are caught)." *Note:* Compare especially with Stage 3:Aspect 6.

The Mature Level

Stage 3: Mutual and Prosocial

3:1 Relationships

(a) "**We should treat others the way we would like to be treated**; you would **expect** others not to steal from you; others would **expect** the same from you; or (otherwise) how would you feel?"—Moral Type B, Balancing. *Note:* Compare especially with Transition 2/3:Aspect 1.

(b) "(Then) the **world** would be nicer or happier; or (otherwise) **life** would be unhappy." *Note:* Compare especially with Transition 2/3:Aspect 9a and with Transition 3/4:Aspect 4a. "(Then) people would be happier" and "there would be a better quality of life" are unscorable.

(c) "(Otherwise) you lose (the) trust (of other people), or others won't believe **in** you (any more)." *Note:* Compare especially with Transition 2/3:Aspect 7 and Transition 3/4:Aspect 1b.

3:2 Empathic Role-Taking

(a) It's important because "of the hardship stealing causes; you should understand their feelings; they feel attached to or sentimental over their things; people work **very hard** (for what they have in life); their things are so special or **mean** a lot to them; they (may) have worked **so hard** for their things; or (otherwise) the person stolen from will **lose faith** or **trust** in other people." *Note:* Compare especially with Transition 2/3:Aspects 3, 6a, and 8a, and with Transition 3/4:Aspect 2.

(b) It's important but "you may (have to steal or break the law) for a **loved one**." *Note:* Compare especially with Transition 2/3:Aspect 5.

3:3 Normative Expectations

(a) "We **should** work for or deserve **our** things; we don't deserve to be stolen from; or people should be able to **enjoy** their things (and not have them stolen)." *Note:* Compare especially with Transition 2/3:Aspect 4.

(b) "It is common **decency** or **courtesy** (not to steal from others)."

(c) "The laws protect **us** or **people**, or are for our own good; (otherwise) the world would be confusing or would go crazy; the country would be in havoc, would be a disaster, or would fall apart; the world would be a terrible place to live; there would be chaos or (great) distress; or **innocent** people could get hurt." *Note:* Compare especially with Transition 2/3:Aspect 8a and 9a, and with Transition 3/4:Aspects 4a and 5a. "(Otherwise) everyone will be doing all kinds of things" is unscorable. The reference to "hurt" is rated Stage 3 in other chapters, where it can be assumed to refer to socioemotional hurt.

3:4 Prosocial Intentions

(a) "(Then) you **can** be trusted; or people **can** depend on you." *Note:* Compare especially with Transition 2/3:Aspect 7 and with Transition 3/4:Aspects 1b and 9a.

(b) "(Then) you will or can be (seen as) a better person or good citizen; or (otherwise) you would be **looked down on** (by others)." *Note:* Compare especially with Transition 2/3:Aspect 8b and with Transition 3/4:Aspect 9a.

(c) "It is selfish, dishonest, cruel, callous, or despicable to steal; you shouldn't take advantage of others, or want what others have; or just because you don't (always) get what you want is no reason to take it; (unless) you are acting **out of** love or for a **loved one**." *Note:* Compare especially with Transition 3/4:Aspect 5b and 8b. "(Because) stealing is mean" is unscorable.

3:5 Generalized Caring

It's important unless "a human life is at stake"—Moral Type B, Fundamental Valuing.

3:6 Intrapersonal Approval

"(Then) you can be proud or have a good feeling **inside**; or (otherwise) you are **only** hurting yourself, you will feel guilty, or it will be on your mind"—Moral Type B, Conscience. *Note:* Compare especially with Transition 2/3:Aspect 10a,b, and with Transition 3/4:Aspect 11.

Transition 3/4

3/4:1 Relationships/Basic Rights or Values

(a) "Laws promote harmony or justice."
(b) "(Then) you will or can be trusted **in society** or **in the community.**"
Note: Compare especially with Stage 3:Aspects 1c and 4a.

3/4:2 Empathic Role-Taking/Basic Rights/Values

"Breaking the law affects others; the welfare of people is at stake; or stealing hurts everyone or all of us (through higher prices or by destroying trust)." *Note:* Compare especially with Stage 3:Aspect 2a and with Transition 2/3:Aspects 8a and 9a.

3/4:3 Empathic Role-Taking/Procedural Equity

(a) It's important but "there can be special **cases or situations**; or it **depends on** the **circumstances.**" *Note:* "But it depends," "but sometimes it's best to steal," and "but sometimes there are exceptions" are unscorable.
(b) It's important but "laws aren't perfect or always fair; or some laws have flaws." *Note:* "Some laws are dumb" is unscorable.

3/4:4 Normative Expectations/Societal Requirements

(a) "We need to maintain a code of ethics; (otherwise) things would get out of hand; (so that) there is order (in society) or we **can live in peace** or **security**; or to prevent lawlessness, disruption, or anarchy." *Note:* Compare especially with Stage 3:Aspects 1b and 3c and with Stage 4:Aspect 1a. "(Because otherwise) there would be no law," "(because otherwise) the world would be dangerous," or "(because otherwise) there would be war" are unscorable.
(b) "We need to work together (in society); or others must do their part, too"—Moral Type B, Balancing. *Note:* Compare especially with Stage 4:Aspect 3b.

3/4:5 Normative Expectations/Basic Rights or Values

(a) "Laws are made by the people or the majority; laws are made or designed for the people or the public; laws were made to help us or for our benefit; or (otherwise) lawbreaking would have harmful effects (on people)." *Note:* Compare especially with Stage 3:Aspect 3c and with Stage 4:Aspect 2a. "(Because) laws are for our own good," "laws are there to help us," and "laws are made to be followed" are unscorable.

(b) "The **law, property, or people** should be respected; or (otherwise) it is an invasion or violation." *Note:* Compare especially with Stage 3:Aspect 4c and with Stage 4:Aspects 1c,d and 2d. "It is morally wrong" is unscorable.

(c) "Stealing is wrong in the eyes of the law or society, or is a violation of morality." *Note:* Compare especially with Stage 1:Aspect 4.

(d) "What would the world be like if there were no laws; or (otherwise) there would be no point in having laws, laws wouldn't have to be enforced if they weren't important, or there would be exploitation of the weak by the strong." *Note:* "That's what laws are for" and "(otherwise) there would be no laws" are unscorable.

3/4:6 Normative Expectations/Responsibility

It's important unless "you are **willing** to accept the risk or penalty; people have good judgment or know how far they should go (in breaking the law)." *Note:* Compare especially with Stage 2:Aspect 1d and with Stage 4:Aspect 3d. "If you get caught, you should pay the consequences," "you will have to pay the consequences," and "there are consequences if you steal" are unscorable.

3/4:7 Normative Expectations/Character

"People should or must learn the value or importance of work; or (otherwise) people would not be motivated to work or earn money."

3/4:8 Prosocial Intentions/Basic Rights or Values

(a) "You have no right to take something just because you may **think** you need it." *Note:* Compare especially with Stage 4:Aspect 5a.

(b) "(Otherwise) there would be no caring, we would be uncivilized, or people would just be looking out for themselves." *Note:* Compare especially with Stage 3:Aspect 4c.

3/4:9 Prosocial Intentions/Character

(a) "Stealing is copping out (instead of earning something honestly); (in order) to show that you are trustworthy, a good citizen, civilized, or respectable in society; or (otherwise) you would lose others' respect." *Note:* Compare especially with Stage 3:Aspect 4a,b and with Stage 4:Aspect 4. "(Because otherwise) you couldn't trust anybody" is unscorable.

(b) "The laws should be a guide, provide direction, or keep order in our lives; people should not just do what they want to or feel like (all the time); people cannot always have what they want, or must have patience; people need self-control or should not act impulsively; or (otherwise) people will steal even if they don't have to, get out of control, think that stealing is O.K., or lose sight of right and wrong." *Note:* Compare especially with Stage 4:Aspect 2b. "(Because then) people will do what they want" and "people need to learn to be honest" are unscorable.

3/4:10 Prosocial Intentions/Standards of Conscience

(a) It's important but "one should act according to one's values; it **depends** on your morals; you must make your **own** decision, or **may feel** that you must break the law"—Relativism of Personal Values. *Note:* Compare especially with Stage 4:Aspects 3c and 7.

(b) It's important but "there may be a moral **issue** (involved)." *Note:* Compare especially with Stage 4:Aspect 3c. "Somebody's rights may be involved" is unscorable.

3/4:11 Intrapersonal Approval/Standards of Conscience

It's important "for the sake of self-esteem; or (otherwise) you're only cheating or deceiving yourself, or would develop a poor self-image"—Moral Type B, Conscience. *Note:* Compare especially with Stage 3:Aspect 6 and with Stage 4:Aspect 7.

Stage 4: Systemic and Standard

4:1 Societal Requirements

(a) "**Society** or **civilization** needs or is based on laws, or **must** have order; (in order) to keep **society** together or things in order, or to **make possible** order or stability (in society); the law is the backbone or basis of society; (otherwise) there would be no structure, organization, or predictability; society could not work smoothly or function; the **system** would break down; **society** would not survive; or there would be no society." *Note:* Compare especially with Transition 3/4:Aspect 4a.

(b) "Honesty, character, or self-control is important for **society**."

(c) "Property (rights) or the law **must** be protected or respected." *Note:* Compare especially with Transition 3/4:Aspect 5b.

(d) "We **must** respect one another's rights or property"—Moral Type B, Balancing. *Note:* Compare especially with Transition 3/4:Aspect 5b.

4:2 Basic Rights or Values

(a) "Laws are made to help (protect or build) **society, civilization**, or productivity; for the common good, quality of life, or the advancement of **society**; thieves are a burden on **society**; or (but) sometimes the law must be broken for the **good of the whole** or **humanity**." *Note:* Compare especially with Transition 3/4:Aspect 5a.

(b) "Stealing is against the morality that humanity or society has set up (for itself); or (otherwise) society would have no boundaries (for right and wrong)." *Note:* Compare especially with Transition 3/4:Aspect 9b.

(c) "(Otherwise) you have broken a **sacred** trust"—Moral Type B, Fundamental Valuing.

(d) "It is a (basic) **human** right (to own property); property is a right everyone **should** have; the law **protects** people's **rights**; you should **respect** the **rights** of others; or stealing **violates, trespasses against, or infringes upon** another person's **rights** or **dignity**." *Note:* Compare especially with Transition 3/4:Aspect 5b. "Everyone has a right to their property" is unscorable.

(e) "(Otherwise eventually) the (personal) incentive needed for a productive society would be destroyed."

4:3 Responsibility

(a) "You have a **responsibility** to respect another's property; or (because of) one's duty (as a citizen)."

(b) "One has obligations as well as privileges (in society); you must accept the restrictions along with the benefits of laws; the law is an agreement." (Type B, Balancing) *Note:* Compare especially with Transition 3/4:Aspect 4b.

(c) "Stealing violates God's law **as well as** human law; laws **are based on** God's law or common morality; (important if) the law is in accordance with God's law; or (but) there are times when civil disobedience is necessary." *Note:* Compare especially with Transition 3/4:Aspect 10a,b.

(d) It's important unless "you are **prepared** to accept the consequences, or will accept **responsibility** or be held accountable (for your actions); or (not important) as long as one realizes or understands the legal implications." *Note:* Compare especially with Transition 3/4:Aspect 6.

4:4 Character

"It is a sign of self-respect, integrity, or responsibility"—Moral Type B, Conscience. *Note:* Compare especially with Transition 3/4:Aspect 9a.

4:5 Consistent Practices

(a) "People **cannot** or **must not** break the law for emotional reasons or whenever they disagree or feel justified; we must have some system even if some don't agree; people's standards are inconsistent, or there are too many individual beliefs or subjective values; theft can be rationalized by anyone who steals; or (because otherwise) there would be people taking the law into their own hands." *Note:* Compare especially with Transition 3/4:Aspect 8a.

"The law is the law" and "there should be no exceptions to the law" are unscorable.

(b) "Changes can be made **within the system, through** the **proper channels,** or by an orderly process."

4:6 Procedural Equity

(a) It's important but "the law **cannot** always be fair, appropriate, or right (for every specific situation); laws **cannot** take into account every case or circumstance, or **cannot** be more than simplistic rules; or you **cannot** generalize, or each case **must** be judged individually"—Moral Type B, Balancing.

(b) It's important if "the law is the result of a democratic process; or (**but**) some laws are made for the good of the few or reflect a tyranny of the majority"—Moral Type B, Balancing.

4:7 Standards of Conscience

It's important "for the sake of (one's) self-respect, integrity, inner order, or **sense of** (personal) responsibility; (unless) the law **violates** one's conscience; (because otherwise) you are debasing yourself; or (but) one **must** (also) follow one's **internal laws** or **higher values**"—Moral Type B, Conscience. *Note:* Compare especially with Transition 3/4:Aspects 10a and 11.

Chapter 8

Legal Justice

Legal justice value provides a good context for tracing the development of justificatory themes such as deterrence and role responsibilities. Deterrence is not evident among Stage 1 justifications, which emphasize retributive reasons for punishment. At Transition 1/2, respondents justify punishment as important so that the lawbreaker "won't do it again," which may (a) presume that punishment automatically or "immanently" (Piaget, 1932/1965) brings forth this outcome (Stage 1), but (b) may also already reflect a concern with pragmatic deterrence (Stage 2); hence, the Transition 1/2 rating. Where "do it again" is elaborated in a way suggestive of a concern with bad behavior as a practical **habit** ("will **keep** on doing the **same** thing" or "will do it **over and over**") or with the possibility—but not inevitability—of recidivism ("**might** do it again"), the rating is Stage 2. Transition 2/3 marks an implicit expectation that the punishment will be educational (e.g., that the lawbreaker "will **know** not to do it again"), although the concern here could still be externally oriented (i.e., he will know he is likely to be caught). Another Transition 2/3 suggestion is that without punishment the lawbreaker "would steal again for someone he **knows** or **loves**," either for the sake of a future exchange (Stage 2) or for the sake of a relationship (Stage 3). Stage 3 ratings are assigned where the act's basis in a loving relationship is more clear (e.g., "otherwise he might steal again **out of** love or for a **loved one**"), or where the concern is to prevent widespread violations of normative expectations ("otherwise there would be chaos").

At higher developmental levels, the concern is with judicial practices such that one must consider the effect of a precedent established by an individual case for other cases and society. At Transition 3/4, this concern is already discernible ("people would break the law and use this **case** as an excuse"). Stage 4 marks a discriminatively clear expression of this justification, for example, "The laws have to be consistently enforced to avoid setting a dangerous precedent." Similarly, at Transition 3/4 there is a concern that "people should not break the law whenever they feel **dissatisfied**," either because such dissatisfaction is antisocial (Stage 3) or because such dissatisfaction is a subjective and therefore unjustifiable reason for breaking the law (Stage 4). By Stage 4, this idea has crystallized into an appeal to the potential for widespread subjectivity and rationalization that could develop once excuses for lawbreaking are permitted ("People cannot break the law whenever they feel **justified**" or "**exceptions** would lead to chaos"). Also, the related concern with "order" at Transition 3/4 is specifically related to the functioning of society at Stage 4 ("to keep society in order").

Justifications for punishment by appeal to role expectations or obligations may refer either to the judge or to the lawbreaker. Stage 1 conceptions of the judge's role are constraint-oriented ("The judge has to send people to jail; it's a rule"), sometimes backed up by an appeal to punitive consequences ("If the lawbreaker isn't punished, the judge **will** be **put** in jail"—Stage 1). At Stage 2, the concern becomes contingent and prudential ("If the lawbreaker isn't punished, the judge **might** get into **trouble**"). At Stage 3, one finds an appeal to normative expectations or rightful conduct for a judge ("That is what is expected of judges" or "judges are supposed to give the sentences people **deserve**"). Higher levels relate role expectations for the judge to the framework of law and society. Transition 3/4 asserts that "a judge's job is to uphold the law." By Stage 4, the appeal is explicitly to the judge's **responsibility**, to his or her having accepted the **position** or having "**sworn** to uphold the law," and to the necessity for impartial judgment ("The judge **must not** be influenced by his feelings or biases").

Sending lawbreakers to jail may also be justified by appeals to the sentencing as an obligatory consequence of the lawbreaker's wrongdoing. At Stage 1, the concern is simply with the transgressive act itself as constituting a self-evident reason for punishment ("He did something wrong"). By Stage 2, the lawbreaker's transgression is construed as a voluntary act that is not necessarily objectionable but that entailed a risk which should be accepted by the lawbreaker (e.g., "He was taking a risk"). Accepting punishment as part of an implicit "deal" is expressed in the cliche sometimes heard among correctional inmates: "If you can't do the time, don't do the crime." The general idea of punishment as an outcome that the lawbreaker should accept is also found at higher levels. At Stage 3, the appeal is to the lawbreaker's presumed prior awareness of moral wrongdoing ("He **knew** it was **wrong**"). At Transition 3/4, there may be a direct prescriptive suggestion that the lawbreaker "**should** accept the consequences" or "**should** be willing to pay the penalty," as well as a justification of punishment "as an example to people that if you break the law you must pay the penalty." By Stage 4, the prescription regarding the lawbreaker has become specifically obligatory ("He **must** accept the consequences"), emphasizing the conscious and deliberate nature of the decision to break the law (he broke the law "of his own free will" or "because of his convictions"). Stage 4 justifications for punishment may emphasize the idea of a balanced obligation to society ("The sentence may show people that there are responsibilities as well as rights").

Considerations addressed to the lawbreaker's actions, personality, or character may be used as justifications for either punishment or leniency. The developing justification for punishment in terms of this theme assumes that jail will be ameliorative for the lawbreaker (or for lawbreakers in general) in some way. At Transition 1/2, punishment is often evaluated as very important because it is felt that a stiff jail sentence will "teach him a lesson" and "set him straight." There seems to be a simple assumption that a punishment that is severe enough will inevitably or automatically cause expiation and correction (Stage 1), but there may also be a quid pro quo retaliatory element (Stage 2). At Transition 2/3, the appeal instead is to instilling "regret" in the sense of either a conclusion that wrongdoing isn't worth the risk (Stage 2) or a remorse for antisocial conduct (Stage 3). Stage 3 thinking indicates an expectation of personality reform (they can **realize** they've done **wrong**"). Transition 3/4 is assigned where the concern with prosocial reform also implies a possible concern with promoting a potential for productiveness or societal contribution (jail may be important "if that way the person may be rehabilitated"). Stage 4 ratings are reserved for discriminatively clear expressions of this thought ("If they can learn to become productive, or to contribute to society").

References to the lawbreaker's actions, feelings, or character may also be entailed in justifications for leniency. At Stage 1, the justification may consist simply of a reference to an unqualified positive label ("Maybe the lawbreaker is **nice**"). At Stage 2, the action may be excused on pragmatic grounds ("Maybe he needed to break the law"), whereas a Stage 3 response may make an empathic role-taking appeal ("Perhaps he has already suffered enough"). The Relativism of Personal Values sometimes entailed in Transition 3/4 (see chapter 1) marks suggestions that perhaps the lawbreaker "**felt** that what he did was **right**" or "was doing what he **thought** was **right**." Stage 4 may relate the lawbreaker's actions to the dictates of a **higher** law, but may also evaluate the impact of those actions upon society (perhaps the lawbreaker "is not a threat to society").

Justifications for leniency reflect a progression in social role-taking. Stage 2 features pragmatic role-taking ("The judge might have done it, too"), which at Transition 2/3 becomes possibly empathic ("The judge might feel sorry for the lawbreaker"). Role-taking at Stage 3 entails a discriminatively empathic expression (the judge "would understand" or "should have a heart"), and by Stage 4, leniency through role-taking is recommended as an option within the framework of the judicial function ("the judicial system should be flexible" or "the judge can use discretion").

A related development takes place in terms of the appeal for leniency on the basis of motive or circumstance. A Transition 2/3 rating is given to the suggestion that the judicial decision depends on the reasons or motives for wrongdoing: The suggestion that the lawbreaker may have had a "good" reason may connote a motive that is pragmatic (Stage 2) or prosocial (Stage 3). The suggestion that the sentence "**depends** on the **circumstances**" is rated

Transition 3/4 because there is an implication of a concern with considerations of judicial practice and precedent. Stage 4 marks an obligatory prescription to make an equitable exception in some cases ("The judge **must** recognize special circumstances") or a suggestion that the laws, as they are applied, need to be fine-tuned ("The law **cannot** always apply appropriately").

THE MONTAGES

It is important for judges to send lawbreakers to jail because:

The Immature Level

Stage 1: Unilateral and Physicalistic

"They did something bad [4]. The judge has to send people to jail; it's a rule [3] that bad people get locked up [5]. After all, maybe he killed an important person [2]. If the lawbreaker isn't sent to jail, the judge will go to jail [5]." But it is not important because "maybe he is nice [4]."

Transition 1/2

"Then they won't do it again [1]. Besides, punishment could teach them a lesson and set them straight [2]. After all, if the lawbreaker isn't sent to jail, the judge **will** get in **trouble**, and there would be more stealing and mugging, and a lot of murderers walking the streets and killing people [3]."

Stage 2: Exchanging and Instrumental

"They broke the law and were taking a risk—they were caught, so now they go to jail [1]. If the lawbreaker isn't sent to jail, he'll think he can get away with it [5] and will **keep** doing the **same** things, **again and again** [6]. But it is not important because "he wanted to do it [4] and may have needed to [5]."

Transition 2/3

"It will make them regret it, so they'll **know** not to do it again and may **learn** from their mistake [1]. After all, he should have known better [1]. He should go to jail like any other lawbreaker [2] who has hurt someone [6], because otherwise it wouldn't be fair to other lawbreakers; if he isn't punished, then others would have to be let free [2]. Laws do make things safer so people don't have to be as afraid [6]." But it is not important because "he may have had a **good** reason [5]—perhaps he was only trying to help someone [3], and feels sorry for what he did [4]."

The Mature Level

Stage 3: Mutual and Prosocial

"(Otherwise) life would be unhappy [1]. Judges are supposed to give the sentence people **deserve** [3] so that **innocent** people are protected [3]. There is no **excuse** for wrongdoing, and **hard** criminals shouldn't get off easy—if they do, there will be chaos [3]. Also, the lawbreaker must have **known** that what he did was **wrong** [4]. But it is not important because "the lawbreaker might have been under great strain [2] and had good intentions [4]. He may have suffered quite a bit already [6]."

Transition 3/4

"The laws **must** be enforced if there is to be order and an effective deterrent [2]. The lawbreaker **should** accept the consequences, and should be punished **as an example** that if you break the law you must pay the penalty [3]. Otherwise, without the laws as a guideline people wouldn't think twice about breaking the law [3] and there would be anarchy [2]. So the judge shouldn't play favorites [4]—it's the judge's job to uphold the law [3]. If a lawbreaker isn't punished, people could use **that case** as an excuse to break the law and will steal whenever they feel **dissatisfied** [4]. Besides, the judge and the law should be respected. Jail may be the place for rehabilitation [3]." But it is not important because "the sentence should **depend** on the **circumstances** of the particular case [1], and in this case the lawbreaker may have **felt** that what he was doing was **right** [6]."

Stage 4: Systemic and Standard

"Laws are needed to **protect society** and **must** be enforced for **society's sake** even if a particular law is unfair [1]. Laws were created to **protect rights** and help society [2]. Besides, the judge has **sworn** to uphold the law and has the **responsibility** to enforce it [3]. The lawbreaker **must** accept the consequences and be held accountable [3]. After all, if you live in society, you must be willing to accept its restrictions [3]. The laws have to be consistent [5]. People cannot break the law whenever they feel **justified**, and **exceptions** will only lead to chaos--society couldn't function then in an orderly fashion [5]. The judge **must** go by the law rather than his feelings [5]." But it is not important because "the lawbreaker may have made contributions to society

[2]. The judge **must** recognize extreme circumstances, since the law does not always apply appropriately [6]. The judge should use discretion and temper justice with mercy [6], especially since the lawbreaker may have been responding to a **higher** law [7]. In the long run, society must find better solutions than prison [6]."

CRITERION JUSTIFICATIONS

It is important for judges to send lawbreakers to jail because:

The Immature Level

Stage 1: Unilateral and Physicalistic

Responses that seem to relate to Stage 1 criterion justifications, but entail significant qualifications or elaborations, are not scorable at Stage 1.

1:1 Unilateral Authority

"It says 'don't steal' in the Bible, or maybe he didn't get permission (to take something)."

1:2 Status

"Maybe they killed an important person"; or (it's not important because) "maybe they saved an important person."

1:3 Rules

"The judge has to (send people to jail); judges should never let people go free; it's a rule; or you're **always** supposed to obey the law." *Note:* Compare especially with Stage 3:Aspect 3a. "The judge has a job to do" is unscorable.

1:4 Labels

"He did something bad or wrong, he could have killed someone, or he could be a murderer; (then) bad people won't kill; he may have stolen something, taken something that wasn't his"; or (it's not important because) "the lawbreaker was **nice**." *Note:* "He broke the law" is unscorable.

1:5 Physical Consequences

"(Then) bad people are locked up; maybe he killed somebody, so the judge should kill him; or (otherwise) the judge **would** get **put** in jail." *Note:* Compare especially with Transition 1/2:Aspect 3a.

Transition 1/2

1/2:1 Labels/Advantages

"(Then) they **won't** do it again, or **won't** steal any more; or (because otherwise) he **will** do it again, **will** do the same thing, **will** do something else, or **might** kill someone." *Note:* Compare especially with Stage 2:Aspect 6a.

1/2:2 Physical Consequences/Exchanges

"Punishment or jail will or could set him straight; (it will) teach him a lesson; (then) the lawbreaker will learn **never** to break the law again"; or (it's not important because) "he may have already learned his lesson." *Note:* Compare especially with Stage 2:Aspect 5b. "So the lawbreaker will learn that breaking the law is prohibited" is unscorable.

1/2:3 Physical Consequence/Advantages

(a) "The judge **will** or **would** get in **trouble, could** get **punished**, or **would go** to jail." *Note:* Compare especially with Stage 1:Aspect 5 and with Stage 2:Aspect 6b.

(b) "(Otherwise) everybody will be free or will be doing it; others will do it; there would be more stealing, mugging, or killing; there would be (a lot of) murderers or criminals (walking the streets); they could steal your things; or not many people would be alive." *Note:* Compare especially with Stage 2:Aspects 2a and 6a and with Transition 2/3:Aspect 6.

Stage 2: Exchanging and Instrumental

2:1 Exchanges

"If you are caught or mess up you go to jail; so they'll get what's coming to them; the lawbreaker took a chance or risk; if you take it, you pay; or if you can't do the time, don't do the crime." *Note:* Compare especially with Transition 2/3:Aspect 1b and with Transition 3/4:Aspect 3d. "That is the price you pay," "if you break the law you should be punished," and "it was his decision or choice" are unscorable.

2:2 Equalities

(a) It's not important because "if they don't follow the law, why should I?" *Note:* Compare especially with Transition 1/2:Aspect 3b and with Transition 2/3:Aspect 2.

(b) It's important but "the judge might have taken something, too." *Note:* Compare especially with Stage 3:Aspect 2. "The judge might have broken the law, too" is unscorable.

2:3 Freedoms

It's not important because "maybe he was forced into it."

2:4 Preferences

(a) "You **don't want** a lawbreaker to harm you."
(b) "Maybe he **wanted** to break the law and go to jail." *Note:* Compare especially with Transition 2/3:Aspect 3.

2:5 Needs

(a) "He may have taken something someone else needed; or (it's not important because) the judge might have broken the law, too, if he **needed** something; or **the lawbreaker needed to do it.**" *Note:* Compare especially with Transition 2/3:Aspect 5. "He didn't have to (break the law)" and "(it's not important because) the judge might have broken the law, too" are unscorable.
(b) "He **needs** to go to jail or to learn that he can't get away with it."
Note: Compare especially with Transition 1/2:Aspect 2 and with Transition 2/3:Aspects 1a and 2.

2:6 Advantages

(a) "So that they won't do it again **right away**, won't be **able** or shouldn't have the chance to do it again (soon), won't get into **more** trouble, or won't go **out** or go **back** and steal again; or (otherwise) he **might** do it again, **might** get in trouble again, will **just** do it again, will **keep** (on) doing it, will do the **same** thing, or will do it **over and over, again and again,** or more than once." *Note:* Compare especially with Transition 1/2:Aspects 1 and 3b, and with Transition 2/3:Aspects 1a and 2.
(b) "(Otherwise) the judge **might** get into **trouble.**" *Note:* Compare especially with Transition 1/2:Aspect 3a.

Transition 2/3

2/3:1 Exchanges/Intrapersonal Approval

(a) "(It will) make them regret it, teach people a **good** lesson, or teach people not to do wrong; or (then) they will **know** not to do it again, they will **think** about what they did, or they will **learn** from their mistakes." *Note:*

Compare especially with Stage 2:Aspects 5b and 6a and with Stage 3:Aspects 3b and 4.

(b) "He **knew** what he was doing, **should** have **known** better, or **should** have **realized** what he was getting into"; or (it's not important because) "maybe he didn't mean to break the law." *Note:* Compare especially with Stage 2:Aspect 1 and with Stage 3:Aspect 4. "He should suffer" is unscorable.

2/3:2 Equalities/Normative Expectations

"He should go to jail like any other lawbreaker; (otherwise) it wouldn't be fair to others (who broke the law and have been punished); or others (who break the law) will **think** they shouldn't be punished, can get away with it, or would have to be let free." *Note:* Compare especially with Stage 2:Aspects 2a, 5b, and 6a. "But it's not fair when innocent people go to jail" is unscorable.

2/3:3 Preferences/Prosocial Intentions

"(Otherwise) the lawbreaker may steal again for someone he **knows** or **loves**; or (it's not important because) maybe he **just** wanted, was only trying, or meant to help someone." *Note:* Compare especially with Stage 2:Aspect 4b and with Stage 3:Aspect 4.

2/3:4 Needs/Empathic Role-Taking

It's important but "**perhaps he feels sorry for what he did** or was desperate; or the judge might feel sorry for the lawbreaker." *Note:* Compare especially with Stage 2:Aspect 5a, and with Stage 3:Aspect 2a and 6.

2/3:5 Needs/Prosocial Intentions

It's important but "he may have had a good reason or motive, or real cause; or he may have needed to **save** or **help someone.**" *Note:* Compare especially with Stage 2:Aspect 5a and with Stage 3:Aspects 2 and 4. "It's important to know why he did it" is unscorable.

2/3:6 Advantages/Empathic Role-Taking/Normative Expectations

"(Then) people won't be scared, afraid, or worried (for their safety); (it will) make things safer, or stop more crimes; (otherwise) the world wouldn't be safe or would be a wreck or (awful) mess; the lawbreaker will hurt or mislead others; people could get hurt or would be in danger; or there would be **more** or a **lot of** crime." *Note:* Compare especially with Transition 1/2:Aspect 3b, with Stage 3:Aspects 2b and 3d, and with Stage 4:Aspect 2d.

The Mature Level

Stage 3: Mutual and Prosocial

3:1 Relationships

(a) "(Otherwise) life would be unhappy."

(b) "The judge would expect to be treated the same way if he had stolen something"—Moral Type B, Balancing.

3:2 Empathic Role-Taking

(a) It's important but "the judge should understand or have a heart (sometimes), would have some feeling, or should put or imagine himself in the situation; the lawbreaker may have been under great strain or pressure." *Note:* Compare especially with Stage 2:Aspect 2b, with Transition 2/3:Aspects 4 and 5, and with Transition 3/4:Aspect 1. "The judge should give people a second chance" is unscorable.

(b) "(Then) people can feel more secure (about not getting their things stolen)." *Note:* Compare especially with Transition 2/3:Aspect 6.

3:3 Normative Expectations

(a) "Judges are supposed to give the sentence people **deserve**; or that is what is expected of judges." *Note:* Compare especially with Stage 1:Aspect 3 and with Transition 3/4:Aspect 3c. "They deserve it" is unscorable.

(b) "It **shows** (lawbreakers) that the law is the law; criminals must be **disciplined** or taught right from wrong; (otherwise) **hard** criminals would get off easily; or everyone would be tempted to become selfish." *Note:* Compare with Transition 2/3:Aspect 1a.

(c) "There is no **excuse** for wrongdoing for breaking the law; or (otherwise) **excuses** (for breaking the law) would become common."

(d) "Laws or judges **protect people**; (otherwise) the country would be berserk, there would be chaos, or **innocent** people could get hurt." *Note:* Compare especially with Transition 2/3:Aspect 6, with Transition 3/4:Aspect 2a, and with Stage 4:Aspect 1.

3:4 Prosocial Intentions

"He **knew** or must have **known** that it was **wrong**; he was acting selfishly; in order to help them **realize** that what they did was **wrong**; (in order) to **show** them or **teach** them that they have done **wrong** or that crime doesn't pay; (otherwise) he might steal again **out of** love or for a **loved one**; or (it's important but) the lawbreaker may have had **good intentions**." *Note:*

Compare especially with Transition 2/3:Aspects 1a,b, 3, and 5, and with Transition 3/4:Aspect 3a,d.

3:5 Generalized Caring

It's important but "the lawbreaker may have saved a **person's, someone's,** or a **human life**"—Moral Type B, Fundamental Valuing.

3:6 Intrapersonal Approval

It's important but "the lawbreaker may have suffered enough already, or has (probably) punished **himself** enough"—Moral Type B, Conscience. *Note:* Compare especially with Transition 2/3:Aspect 4.

Transition 3/4

3/4:1 Empathic Role-Taking/Procedural Equity

It's important but "it **depends** on the **circumstances** or the **case**; the sentence should fit the crime; exceptions may be allowable; there are too many variables for this to be cut-and-dried; or the judge should **consider** the facts or **evaluate** the situation"—Moral Type B, Balancing. *Note:* Compare especially with Stage 3:Aspect 2a and with Stage 4:Aspect 6a. "Depending on what he did, the law, the crime or offense, the criminal, or how bad it was" and "but it depends on the judge" are unscorable.

3/4:2 Normative Expectations/Societal Requirements

(a) "You have to have law or order; or the law is the only order we have; (in order) to keep order or peace or to promote people's accomplishments (in society); (so that) things don't get out of hand or deviant behavior doesn't increase; (otherwise) there would be no sense, point, or value in having laws (if they are not enforced or followed), or there would be anarchy." *Note:* Compare especially with Stage 3:Aspect 3d and with Stage 4:Aspects 1 and 5a.

(b) "The laws **must** be enforced (if they are to work), there **must** be consequences (for those who break the law), or so that there is a deterrent (to breaking the law)." *Note:* Compare especially with Stage 4:Aspect 1. "The law was made to be followed," "to deter others from wrongdoing," and "(because otherwise) there would be no law" are unscorable.

3/4:3 Normative Expectations/Responsibility/Character

(a) "(Then) people won't start thinking that stealing is all right; people will **learn** that they can't (just) do whatever they want; **as an example** (to people) that if you break the law, you must pay the penalty; (otherwise) the law won't be a guideline; or people will lose sight of right and wrong." *Note:* Compare especially with Stage 3:Aspect 4. "(Then) people would do what they want" is unscorable.

(b) It's important if "the person is misguided, or if that way the person can be rehabilitated or become a good citizen; (but) jail may not help the individual, or may do more harm than good; or he may have acted for humane or humanitarian reasons." *Note:* Compare especially with Stage 4:Aspects 2b and 6b.

(c) "A judge's job is to uphold or enforce the law." *Note:* Compare especially with Stage 3:Aspect 3a and with Stage 4:Aspect 3a.

(d) "He **knew** the **consequences, should** accept the **consequences,** or **should** be held accountable or **should** be willing to pay the penalty." *Note:* Compare especially with Stage 2:Aspect 1, with Stage 3:Aspect 4, and with Stage 4:Aspect 3b. "That is the price you pay" and "he should take his consequences" are unscorable.

3/4:4 Normative Expectations/Consistent Practices

(a) "People should not break the law whenever they feel **dissatisfied** or **don't agree** with the law; or (otherwise) other people would break the law and use **that case** as an excuse."

(b) "Judicial leniency is why there is so much crime (in society)."

(c) "Judges should not play favorites." *Note:* Compare especially with Stage 4:Aspect 5b.

3/4:5 Prosocial Intentions/Basic Rights or Values

"The judge should be respected; or (otherwise) people would lose respect for the law." *Note:* Compare especially with Stage 4:Aspect 2d.

3/4:6 Prosocial Intentions/Standards of Conscience

It's important but "he or she may have **felt** or **believed** it was **right,** or may have been doing what he **thought** was **right**"—Moral Type B, Conscience (Relativism of Personal Values). *Note:* Compare especially with Stage 4:Aspect 7.

Stage 4: Systemic and Standard

4:1 Societal Requirements

"The law is the backbone of (our) society; laws are needed to help or **protect society,** government, or humanity; if the lawbreaker is a threat to society; laws must be enforced for the **sake** of **society** (even if a particular law is poor or wrong); or (otherwise) the law is useless to society, or there is no society." *Note:* Compare especially with Transition 3/4:Aspect 2a,b and with Stage 3:Aspect 3d. "Laws protect people" is unscorable.

4:2 Basic Rights or Values

(a) "Some people can't get along with society; or if the lawbreaker is burden to society, or has acted against society." *Note:* "Lawbreakers are dangerous" is unscorable.

(b) It's important if "they can learn to become productive, or to contribute to society (while in jail), or in order to repay society." *Note:* Compare especially with Transition 3/4:Aspect 3b.

(c) It's important if "living together (in society) is to have meaning (for people)."

(d) "People have a **right** to their (own) **property**; they have **invaded**, **violated**, or **infringed upon** someone else's **rights** or the **public right** to **safety** or **security**; for the sake of, or (in order) to respect, rights; (so that) the **rights** of others will be respected; or laws were created to protect rights, or anyone who harms another has no right to live in society." *Note:* Compare especially with Transition 3/4:Aspect 5 and Transition 2/3:Aspect 6.

(e) It's important but "society is composed of individuals, or the individual should be the basis of society."

4:3 Responsibility

(a) "That is the judge's **responsibility**; or the judge has **sworn** to uphold the law, or accepted this **position**." *Note:* Compare especially with Transition 3/4:Aspect 3c.

(b) "The lawbreaker broke the law of his own free will or because of his convictions; or he **must** (be willing to) accept or realize the consequences, or be held responsible or accountable." *Note:* Compare especially with Transition 3/4:Aspect 3d.

(c) "If one lives in, accepts, or benefits from society, one has an obligation or must be willing to live by its rules or accept its restrictions; or the sentence may show people that there must be limitations to freedom, or that there are responsibilities as well as rights"—Moral Type B, Balancing.

(d) It's important but "society may be responsible for crime or criminals."

4:4 Character

This aspect is typically not in evidence with regard to the legal justice value.

4:5 Consistent Practices

(a) "The laws have to be consistent, or standards must be upheld; (in order) to keep society in order, or to avoid setting a dangerous precedent; **inconsistencies** or **exceptions** would lead to subjective actions, lawbreaking, or chaos; or (otherwise) people would take the law into their own hands, or would break the law whenever they feel **justified**." *Note:* Compare especially with Transition 3/4:Aspect 2a. "The law is the law" and "there should be no exception to the law" are unscorable.

(b) "The judge **must** go by the law or **must not** be influenced by his feelings, emotions, or biases; or jail is required by law." *Note:* Compare especially with Transition 3/4:Aspect 4c.

4:6 Procedural Equity

(a) It's important but "the judge **must** recognize exceptions or special circumstances; each case is different or unique, or **must** be considered separately; the law **cannot** always apply appropriately; there **cannot** be set rules for all cases; the judge should interpret the law, should apply the spirit of the law, or can give the minimum sentence; the judge should show wisdom or should use discretion; justice should be tempered with mercy or understanding; or the law or judicial system should or must be flexible or fair"—Moral Type B, Balancing. *Note:* Compare especially with Transition 3/4:Aspect 1.

(b) It's important but "society should search for or must find a better solution (than prison), or should (continue to try to) rehabilitate the offender." *Note:* Compare especially with Transition 3/4:Aspect 3b.

4:7 Standards of Conscience

It's important but "the lawbreaker may have been responding to **God's** or a **higher** or **universal law**"—Moral Type B, Conscience. *Note:* Compare especially with Transition 3/4:Aspect 6.

References

Adelson, J., Green, B., & O'Neil, R. P. (1969). Growth of the idea of law in adolescence. *Developmental Psychology, 1,* 327–332.

Adelson, J., & O'Neil, R. P. (1966). Growth of political ideas in adolescence: The sense of community. *Journal of Personality and Social Psychology, 4,* 295–306.

Alexander, R. D. (1987). *The biology of moral systems.* New York: Aldine de Gruyter.

Ames, G., & Murray, F. B. (1982). When two wrongs make a right: Promoting cognitive changes by social conflict. *Developmental Psychology, 18,* 894–898.

Basinger, K. S. (1990). *Psychometric validation of the Sociomoral Reflection Measure-Short Form.* Unpublished doctoral dissertation, The Ohio State University, Columbus.

Basinger, K. S., & Gibbs, J. C. (1987). Validation of the Sociomoral Reflection Objective Measure-Short Form. *Psychological Reports, 61,* 139–146.

Basinger, K. S., Gibbs, J. C., & Fuller, D. (1991, April). *Measuring moral judgment maturity: The Sociomoral Reflection Measure-Short Form.* Paper presented at the meeting of the Society for Research in Child Development, Seattle.

Bem, S. L. (1989). Gender knowledge and gender constancy in preschool children. *Child Development, 60,* 649–662.

Bigelow, B. J. (1977). Children's friendship expectations: A cognitive-developmental study. *Child Development, 48,* 246–253.

Blasi, A. (1980). Briding moral cognition and moral action: A critical review of literature. *Psychological Bulletin, 88,* 1-45.

Blasi, A. (1984). Moral identity: Its role in moral functioning. In W. M. Kurtines & J. L. Gewirtz (Eds.), Morality, moral behavior, and moral development (pp. 128-139). New York: Wiley-Interscience.

Boyes, M. C., & Walker, L. J. (1988). Implications of cultural diversity for the universality claims of Kohlberg's theory of moral reasoning. *Human Development, 31,* 44–59.

Brandt, R. B. (1959). *Ethical theory: The problems of normative and critical ethics.* Englewood Cliffs, NJ: Prentice-Hall.

Brown, R., & Herrnstein, R. J. (1975). *Psychology.* Boston: Little, Brown.

Burgess, R. L., & Huston, T. L. (1979). *Social exchange in developing relationships.* New York: Academic Press.

Case, R. (1985). *Intellectual development: Birth to adulthood.* New York: Academic Press.

Chapman, M., & Lindenberger, U. (1989). Concrete operations and attentional capacity. *Journal of Experimental Child Psychology, 47,* 236–258.

Colby, A., & Kohlberg, L. (1987). *The measurement of moral judgment: Theoretical foundations and research validation* (Vol. 1). Cambridge, England: Cambridge University Press.

Colby, A., Kohlberg, L., Gibbs, J. C., & Lieberman, M. (1983). A longitudinal study of moral judgment. *Monographs of the Society for Research in Child Development, 48*(1-2, Serial No. 200).

Colby, A., Kohlberg, L., Speicher, B., Hewer, A., Candee, D., Gibbs, J., & Power, C. (1987). *The measurement of moral judgment* (Vol. 2). Cambridge, England: Cambridge University Press.

Damon, W. (1975). Early conceptions of positive justice as related to the development of logical operations. *Child Development, 46*, 301-312.

Damon, W. (1977). *The social world of the child*. San Francisco: Jossey-Bass.

Damon, W. (1988). *The moral child: Nurturing children's natural moral growth*. New York: The Free Press.

Davison, M. L., & Robbins, S. (1978). The reliability and validity of objective indices of moral development. *Applied Psychological Measurement, 2*, 391-403.

Dewey, J., & Tufts, J. H. (1908). *Ethics*. New York: Holt.

Doise, W., & Mugny, G. (1984). *The social development of the intellect* (A. St. James-Emler & N. Emler, Trans.). Oxford: Pergamon.

Edwards, C. P. (1975). Social complexity and moral development: A Kenyan study. *Ethos, 3*, 505-527.

Edwards, C. P. (1982). Moral development in comparative cultural perspective. In D. A. Wagner & H. Stevenson (Eds.), *Cultural perspectives on child development* (pp. 248-279). San Francisco: W. H. Freeman.

Eisenberg, N. (1982). The development of reasoning regarding prosocial behavior. In N. Eisenberg (Ed.), *The development of prosocial behavior* (pp. 219-249). New York: Academic.

Eisenberg, N., Boehnke, K., Schuler, H., & Silbereisen, R. K. (1985). The development of prosocial behavior and cognitions in German children. *Journal of Cross-Cultural Psychology, 16*, 69-82.

Endler, N. S., Rushton, J. P., & Roediger, H. L. (1978). Productivity and scholarly impact. *American Psychologist, 33*, 1064-1082.

Feffer, M. (1970). Developmental analysis of interpersonal behavior. *Psychological Review, 77*, 197-214.

Flavell, J. H. (1985). *Cognitive development* (2nd. ed.). Englewood Cliffs, NJ: Prentice-Hall.

Froming, W. J., & McColgan, E. B. (1979). Comparing the Defining Issues Test and the Moral Judgment Interview. *Developmental Psychology, 15*, 658-659.

Gavaghan, M. P., Arnold, K. D., & Gibbs, J. C. (1983). Moral judgment in delinquents and non-delinquents: Recognition versus production measures. *Journal of Psychology, 114*, 267-274.

Gibbs, J. C. (1977). Kohlberg's stages of moral judgment: A constructive critique. *Harvard Educational Review, 47*, 43-61

Gibbs, J. C. (1979). Kohlberg's moral stage theory: A Piagetian revision. *Human Development, 22*, 89-112.

Gibbs, J. C. (in press-a). Sociomoral developmental delay and cognitive distortion: Implications for the treatment of antisocial youth. In W. M. Kurtines & J. L. Gewirtz (Eds.), *Handbook of moral behavior and development* (Vol. 1). Hillsdale, NJ: Lawrence Erlbaum Associates.

Gibbs, J. C. (in press-b). Toward an integration of Kohlberg's and Hoffman's theories of morality. In W. M. Kurtines & J. L. Gewirtz (Eds.), *Handbook of moral behavior and development* (Vol. 3). Hillsdale, NJ: Lawrence Erlbaum Associates.

Gibbs, J. C., Arnold, K. D., Ahlborn, H. H., & Cheesman, F. L. (1984). Facilitation of sociomoral reasoning in delinquents. *Journal of Consulting and Clinical Psychology, 52,* 37–45.

Gibbs, J. C., Arnold, K. D., Morgan, R. L., Schwartz, E. S., Gavaghan, M. P., & Tappan, M. B. (1984). Construction and validation of a multiple-choice measure of moral reasoning. *Child Development, 55,* 527–536.

Gibbs, J. C., Clark, P. M., Joseph, J. A., Green, J. L., Goodrick, T. S., & Makowski, D. G. (1986). Relations between moral judgment, moral courage, and field independence. *Child Development, 57,* 185–191.

Gibbs, J. C., & Schnell, S. V. (1985). Moral development "versus" socialization: A critique. *American Psychologist, 40,* 1071–1080.

Gibbs, J. C., & Widaman, K. F. (1982). *Social intelligence: Measuring the development of sociomoral reflection.* Englewood Cliffs, NJ: Prentice-Hall.

Gibbs, J. C., Widaman, K. F., & Colby, A. (1982). Construction and validation of a simplified, group-administrable equivalent to the Moral Judgment Interview. *Child Development, 53,* 895–910.

Gilligan, C. (1982). *In a different voice: Psychological theory and women's development.* Cambridge, MA: Harvard University Press.

Gouldner, A. W. (1960). The norm of reciprocity: A preliminary statement. *American Sociological Review, 25,* 161–178.

Grueneich, R. (1982). The development of children's integration rules of making moral judgments. *Child Development, 53,* 887–894.

Haan, N., Aerts, E., & Cooper, B. A. B. (1985). *On moral grounds: The search for practical morality.* New York: New York University Press.

Hammond, G. S., Rosen, S., Richardson, D. R., & Bernstein, S. (1989). Aggression as equity restoration. *Journal of Research in Personality, 23,* 398–409.

Harter, S. (1983). Developmental perspectives on the self-system. In J. H. Flavell & E. M. Markman (Eds.), *Handbook of child psychology* (4th ed., Vol. 3, pp. 275–386). New York: Wiley.

Helkama, K. (1988). Two studies of Piaget's theory of moral judgment. *European Journal of Social Psychology, 18,* 17–37.

Hoffman, M. L. (1983). Affective and cognitive processes in moral internalization. In E. T. Higgins, D. N. Ruble, & W. W. Hartup (Eds.), *Social cognition and social development: A sociocultural perspective* (pp. 236–274). Cambridge, England: Cambridge University Press.

Hoffman, M. L. (1988). Moral development. In M. H. Bornstein & M. L. Lamb (Eds.), *Developmental psychology: An advanced textbook* (2nd ed., pp. 205–260). Hillsdale, NJ: Lawrence Erlbaum Associates.

Kagan, J. (1987). Introduction. In J. Kagan & S. Lamb (Eds.), *The emergence of morality in young children* (pp. ix–xx). Chicago: University of Chicago Press.

Kaplan, M. F. (1989). Information integration in moral reasoning: Conceptual and methodological implications. In N. Eisenberg, J. Reykowski, & E. Staub (Eds.), *Social and moral values: Individual and societal perspectives* (pp. 117–135). Hillsdale, NJ: Lawrence Erlbaum Associates.

Keasey, C. B. (1971). Social participation as a factor in the moral development of preadolescents. *Developmental Psychology, 5,* 216–220.

Keller, M., Eckensberger, L. H., & von Rosen, K. (1989). A critical note on the conception of preconventional morality: The case of Stage 2 in Kohlberg's theory. *International Journal of Behavioral Development, 12,* 57–69.

Kohlberg, L. (1963). The development of children's orientations toward a moral order: 1. Sequence in the development of moral thought. *Vita Humana, 6,* 11–33.

Kohlberg, L. (1966). A cognitive-developmental analysis of children's sex-role concepts and attitudes. In E. Maccoby (Ed.), *The development of sex differences* (pp. 82–173). Stanford, CA: Stanford University Press.

Kohlberg, L. (1971). From *is* to *ought*: How to commit to naturalistic fallacy and get away with it in the study of moral development. In T. Mischel (Ed.), *Cognitive development and epistemology* (pp. 151–235). New York: Academic Press.

Kohlberg, L. (1973). Continuities in childhood and adult moral development revisited. In P. B. Baltes & L. R. Goulet (Eds.), *Lifespan developmental psychology* (2nd ed., pp. 179–203). New York: Academic Press.

Kohlberg, L. (1981). *The philosophy of moral development: Essays on moral development* (Vol. 1). San Francisco: Harper & Row.

Kohlberg, L. (1984). *The psychology of moral development: Essays on moral development* (Vol. 2). San Francisco: Harper & Row.

Kohlberg, L., & Kramer, R. (1969). Continuities and discontinuities in childhood and adult moral development. *Human Development, 12,* 93–120.

Kuhn, D. (1988). Cognitive development. In M. H. Bornstein & M. E. Lamb (Eds.), Developmental psychology: An advanced textbook (2nd. ed., pp. 205–260).

Leahy, R. L. (1983). The child's construction of social inequality: Conclusions. In R. L. Leahy (Ed.), *The child's construction of social inequality* (pp. 311–328). New York: Academic.

Lickona, T. (1983). *Raising good children.* Toronto: Bantam Books.

Livesley, W. J., & Bromley, D. B. (1973). *Person perception in childhood and adolescence.* London: Wiley.

Loevinger, J., & Wessler, R. (1970). *Measuring ego development: 1. Construction and use of a sentence completion test.* San Francisco, Jossey-Bass.

Losco, J. (1986). Understanding altruism: A critique and proposal for integrating various approaches. *Political Psychology, 7*, 323-348.

Maccoby, E. E. (1980). *Social development: Psychosocial growth and the parent-child relationship.* New York: Harcourt Brace Jovanovich.

Maccoby, E. E. (1990). The role of gender identity and gender constancy in sex-differentiated development. *New Directions in Child Development, 47*, 5-20.

Maitland, K. A., & Goldman, J. R. (1974). Moral judgment as a function of peer group interaction. *Journal of Personality and Social Psychology, 30*, 699-704

Marcus, D. E., & Overton, W. F. (1978). The development of cognitive gender constancy and sex role preference. *Child Development, 49*, 434-444.

McColgan, E. B., Rest, J. R., & Pruitt, D. B. (1983). Moral judgment and anti-social behavior in early adolescence. *Journal of applied developmental psychology, 4*, 189-199.

McDougall, W. (1908). *An introduction to social psychology.* London: Methuen.

Miller, J. G. (1986). Early cross-cultural commonalities in social explanation. *Developmental Psychology, 22*, 514-520.

Miller, P. H., & Aloise, P. A. (1989). Young children's understanding of the psychological causes of behavior: A review. *Child Development, 60*, 257-285.

Miller, S. A. (1976). Extinction of Piagetian concepts: An updating. *Merrill-Palmer Quarterly, 22*, 257-281.

Miller, S. A. (1986). Certainty and necessity in the understanding of Piagetian concepts. *Developmental Psychology, 22*, 3-18.

Miller, S. A. (1987). *Developmental research methods.* Englewood Cliffs, NJ: Prentice-Hall.

Montemayor, R., & Eisen, M. (1977). The development of self-conceptions from childhood to adolescence. *Developmental Psychology, 13*, 314-319.

Murray, F. B. (1983). Learning and development through social interaction and conflict: A challenge to social learning theory. In L. S. Liben (Ed.), *Piaget and the foundations of knowledge* (pp. 231-247). Hillsdale, NJ: Lawrence Erlbaum Associates.

Nicholls, J. G., & Thornkildsen, T. A. (1988). Children's distinctions among matters of intellectual convention, logic, fact, and personal preference. *Child Development, 59*, 939-949.

Nunner-Winkler, G., & Sodian, B. (1988). Children's understanding of moral emotions. *Child Development, 39*, 1323-1328.

Page, R. A. (1981). Longitudinal evidence for the sequentiality of Kohlberg's stages of moral judgment in adolescent males. *Journal of Genetic Psychology, 139*, 3-9.

Page, R. A., & Bode, J. (1980). Comparison of measures of moral reasoning and development of a new objective measure. *Educational and Psychological Measurement, 40*, 317-329.

Paris, S., & Upton, L. (1976). Children's memory for inferential relationships in prose. *Child Development, 47*, 660-668.

Pascual-Leone, J. (1970). A mathematical model for the transition rule in Piaget's developmental stages. *Acta Psychologica, 32*, 301-345.

Pascual-Leone, J. (1987). Organismic processes for neo-Piagetian theories: A dialectical causal account of cognitive development. *International Journal of Psychology, 22*, 531-570.

Peterson, C. C., Peterson, J. L., & Seeto, D. (1983). Developmental changes in ideas about lying. *Child Development, 54*, 1529-1535.

Piaget, J. (1965). *Moral judgment of the child* (M. Gabain, Trans.). New York: Free Press. (Original work published 1932)

Piaget, J. (1971a). *Biology and knowledge.* Chicago: University of Chicago Press.

Piaget, J. (1971b). The theory of stages in cognitive development. In D. R. Green, M. P. Ford, & G. B. Flamer (Eds.), *Measurement and Piaget* (pp. 1-11). New York: McGraw-Hill.

Rest, J. R. (1975). Longitudinal study of the Defining Issues Test: A strategy for analyzing developmental change. *Developmental Psychology, 11*, 738-748.

Rest, J. R. (1979). *Development in judging moral issues.* Minneapolis: University of Minnesota Press.

Rest, J. R. (1983). Morality. In J. H. Flavell & E. M. Markman (Eds.), *Handbook of child psychology* (4th ed., Vol. 3, pp. 556-629). New York: Wiley.

Rest, J. R. (1986). *Moral development: Advances in research and theory.* New York: Praeger.

Robert, M., & Charbonneau, C. (1978). Extinction of liquid conservation by modeling: Three indicators of its artificiality. *Child Development, 49*, 194-200.

Sedikides, A. (1989). *Relations between role-taking opportunities and moral judgment development.* Unpublished doctoral dissertation, The Ohio State University, Columbus.

Selman, R. L. (1980). *The growth of interpersonal understanding: Developmental and clinical analyses.* New York: Academic.

Selman, R. L., & Shultz, L. H. (1990). *Making a friend in youth: Developmental theory and pain therapy.* Chicago: University of Chicago Press.

Smedslund, J. (1961). The acquisition of conservation of substance and weight in children: III. Extinction of conservation of weight acquired "normally" and by means of empirical controls on a balance scale. *Scandinavian Journal of Psychology, 2*, 85-87.

Smetana, J. G., & LeTourneau, K. J. (1984). Development of gender constancy and children's sex-typed free play behavior. *Developmental Psychology, 20*, 691-696.

Snarey, J. (1985). The cross-cultural universality of social-moral development: A critical review of Kohlbergian research. *Psychological Bulletin, 97*, 202-232.

Stein, N. L., Trabasso, T., & Garfin, D. (1979, September). Comprehending and remembering moral dilemmas. In S. Goldman, *Understanding discourse: Interactions between knowledge and process.* Symposium presented at the American Psychological Association, New York.

Turiel, E. (1983). *The development of social knowledge: Morality and convention.* Cambridge, England: Cambridge University Press.

Turiel, E. (1989). Domain-specific social judgments and domain ambiguities. *Merrill-Palmer Quarterly, 35*, 89–114.

Vasudev, J., & Hummel, R. C. (1987). Moral stage sequence and principled reasoning in an Indian sample. *Human Development, 30*, 105–118.

Walker, L. J. (1988). The development of moral reasoning. In R. Vasta (Ed.), *Annals of child development* (Vol. 5, pp. 53–78). Greenwich, CT: JAI Press.

Walker, L. J. (1989). A longitudinal study of moral reasoning. *Child Development, 60*, 157–166.

Walker, L. J. (1990, April). The nature and measurement of moral reasoning. In H. Schirp (Chair), *Issues in the measurement of moral development and moral education.* Paper presented at the meeting of the American Educational Research Association, Boston, MA.

Whiteford, M. G., & Gibbs, J. C. (1991, May). *Relations between social role-taking opportunities and moral judgment development during college.* Paper presented at the meeting of the Jean Piaget Society, Philadelphia.

Winer, G. A., Hemphill, J., & Craig, R. K. (1988). The effect of misleading questions in promoting nonconservation responses in children and adults. *Developmental Psychology, 24*, 197–202.

Youniss, J. (1980). *Parents and peers in social development: A Sullivan-Piaget perspective.* Chicago: University of Chicago Press.

Appendix A

The SRM-SF Questionnaire and Rating Form

Social Reflection Questionnaire

Name: _____   Date:_____

Birthdate: _____   Sex (circle one): male female

Instructions

In this questionnaire, we want to find out about the things you think are important for people to do, and especially why you think these things (like keeping a promise) are important. Please try to help us understand your thinking by WRITING AS MUCH AS YOU CAN TO EXPLAIN—EVEN IF YOU HAVE TO WRITE OUT YOUR EXPLANATIONS MORE THAN ONCE. Don't just write "same as before." If you can explain better or use different words to show what you mean, that helps us even more. Please answer all the questions, especially the "why" questions. If you need to, feel free to use the space in the margins to finish writing your answers.

(code #: _____)

1. Think about when you've made a promise to a friend of yours. How important is it for people to keep promises, if they can, to friends?

Circle one: very important   important   not important

WHY IS THAT VERY IMPORTANT/IMPORTANT/NOT IMPORTANT (WHICHEVER ONE YOU CIRCLED)?

_____

_____

_____

_____

2. What about keeping a promise to anyone? How important is it for people to keep promises, if they can, even to someone they hardly know?

Circle one: very important   important   not important

WHY IS THAT VERY IMPORTANT/IMPORTANT/NOT IMPORTANT (WHICHEVER ONE YOU CIRCLED)?

_____

_____

_____

_____

3. How about keeping a promise to a child? How important is it for parents to keep promises, if they can, to their children?

Circle one: very important   important   not important

WHY IS THAT VERY IMPORTANT/IMPORTANT/NOT IMPORTANT (WHICHEVER ONE YOU CIRCLED)?

_____

_____

_____

_____

4. In general, how important is it for people to tell the truth?

Circle one: very important   important   not important

WHY IS THAT VERY IMPORTANT/IMPORTANT/NOT IMPORTANT
(WHICHEVER ONE YOU CIRCLED)?

_____

_____

_____

_____

5. Think about when you've helped your mother or father. How important
is it for children to help their parents?

Circle one: very important   important   not important

WHY IS THAT VERY IMPORTANT/IMPORTANT/NOT IMPORTANT
(WHICHEVER ONE YOU CIRCLED)?

_____

_____

_____

_____

6. Let's say a friend of yours needs help and may even die, and you're
the only person who can save him or her. How important is it for a person
(without losing his or her own life) to save the life of a friend?

Circle one: very important   important   not important

WHY IS THAT VERY IMPORTANT/IMPORTANT/NOT IMPORTANT
(WHICHEVER ONE YOU CIRCLED)?

_____

_____

_____

_____

7. What about saving the life of anyone? How important is it for a
person (without losing his or her own life) to save the life of a
stranger?

Circle one: very important   important   not important

WHY IS THAT VERY IMPORTANT/IMPORTANT/NOT IMPORTANT
(WHICHEVER ONE YOU CIRCLED)?

_____

_____

_____

_____

8. How important is it for a person to live even if that person doesn't
want to?

Circle one: very important   important   not important

WHY IS THAT VERY IMPORTANT/IMPORTANT/NOT IMPORTANT
(WHICHEVER ONE YOU CIRCLED)?

_____

_____

_____

_____

9. How important is it for people not to take things that belong to other
people?

Circle one: very important   important   not important

WHY IS THAT VERY IMPORTANT/IMPORTANT/NOT IMPORTANT
(WHICHEVER ONE YOU CIRCLED)?

_____

_____

_____

_____

10. How important is it for people to obey the law?

Circle one: very important   important   not important

WHY IS THAT VERY IMPORTANT/IMPORTANT/NOT IMPORTANT
(WHICHEVER ONE YOU CIRCLED)?

_____

_____

_____

_____

11. How important is it for judges to send people who break the law to
jail?

Circle one: very important   important   not important

WHY IS THAT VERY IMPORTANT/IMPORTANT/NOT IMPORTANT
(WHICHEVER ONE YOU CIRCLED)?

_____

_____

_____

_____

SRM-SF Rating Form

Code #: _____		SRMS: _____
Rater: _____		Global Stage: _____
Date: _____		
		Moral Type B: Fundamental Valuing _____
		Balancing _____
		Conscience _____
		Number of Moral Type B Components _____

Question	Highest Developmental Level	Aspect Citations	Comments (e.g., Moral Type B components, marginal score, Rules applied)
1. Contract: Friends			
2. Contract: Anyone			
3. Contract: Children			
4. Truth			
5. Affiliation: Parents			
6. Affiliation: Friends			
7. Life: Stranger			
8. Life: Self			
9. Property			
10. Law			
11. Legal Justice			

Space for Calculations

Appendix B

Question Exercises
and Annotated Answer Keys

Note: The sample responses used in these exercises were recorded word-for-word (with the exception of spelling corrections) from actual research protocols. The keys provide complete scoring information for training purposes; all response units have been given a rating, and notations have been made for all Moral Type B components. Where a response yields more than one level of rating, the highest-level rating is underlined in the answer keys. Once trained, the scorer need rate only the highest-level justifications in the SRM-SF Questionnaire responses (see chapter 3).

QUESTION EXERCISES

QUESTION #1 (Contract: Friends)—Keeping promises to friends is important:

1. in this way you demonstrate you can be trusted.
2. because I gave my word to that person, and when I say I'll do something I stick to it.
3. because the friend has trusted me, and he/she believes that I will come through. It is terrible to let down anyone, especially a friend.
4. "Honesty is the best Policy." If they find out that you broke it, then they won't have that special respect for you.
5. because it would not be nice to the people you promised to. And they would not be your friend.
6. because it doesn't matter who it is, a promise is an obligation.
7. you're not much of a friend if you go back on your word.
8. because if you don't they will not trust you or believe you any more when you tell them things.
9. if you want to keep a promise for you, you should keep one for them.
10. I feel that if a relationship has no trust then it is meaningless. I know if my friend made a promise to me I would expect her to keep it.
11. because I wouldn't want someone to not keep a promise that they promised me.
12. because they trust you and if you want to be trustworthy you'll keep a promise.
13. I love them and they love me a promise should not be broken.
14. because I want to keep my friends trust.
15. because friends are people who you respect and treat the same way you would want to be treated. By betraying the trust that had been developed is just asking for trouble.
16. you shouldn't lie to good friends if you don't want them to lie to you.
17. because it's your friends.
18. you want them to like you.
19. because it could be a serious problem.
20. because friendship involves a lot of trust & commitment. When you let a friend down you are hurting the friendship by breaking a trust.
21. some of your friends won't like you any more. Like if you're in a club they could kick you out of it, and make you mad.
22. because you are never supposed to tell.
23. because promises made to friends are very important to me because if they trust me enough to tell me what they are feeling then they deserve me to keep my promises.

24. keeping a promise shows your friendship with that person. Even if that person is not a friend, keeping the promise can show what type of person one is. It shows your integrity and character.
25. people should not lie to a friend.

QUESTION #2 (Contract: Anyone)—Keeping promises to anyone is important:

1. she might beat you up.
2. you want them to trust you.
3. if you needed someone to tell something to the next time, they would keep it just as you did.
4. because a promise is like making a verbal contract with someone and a person's word is very important.
5. (not important) it really depends on who you promise it to.
6. they may need your help and don't no one else.
7. (not important) because I don't think someone (or me) should ever promise something to someone if they know at all before hand that they might not keep it.
8. because if you have made a promise, you have established trust. Breaking that trust would be breaking any type of relationship with that person.
9. it's important to always keep your word so others will keep their's to you.
10. if someone hardly knows you its just as important "first impression" will stick with you as long as they know you.
11. if you don't they will not trust you, thus they won't like or want to get to know you.
12. because I want them to respect me.
13. because it is very important to maintain one's integrity.
14. they are counting on you to do that for them and they would respect you more if you kept your promise.
15. (not important) because I wouldn't be making a promise to someone I didn't know. And if I did you'll never know when you just might meet up with that person he/she could be your next boss.
16. because my responsibility is very important to me. I do a lot and do it well—the key is following through on your word/work.
17. because it won't mean much to you but maybe he might call on you again.
18. (not important) because he might drug you or kill you or do something bad to you.
19. because it's my duty as a member of society.
20. because you never know what they'll do for you.

21. you said you wouldn't tell.
22. that's the way you make friends.
23. (not important) because you might not see that person again so it won't matter.
24. because they would not be your friend. And would not play with you.
25. trust in any relationship is essential for growth and keeping promises is a way to make that a better friendship.

QUESTION #3 (Contract: Children)—Keeping promises to one's children is important:

1. because at this age the children look for you as guidance, lead by example.
2. if you want their trust and respect.
3. if they don't then the children are not going to like their parents, and won't want to keep their promises to their friends.
4. because a child depends on their parents and trusts them. If a parent doesn't keep a promise it would disappoint and hurt that child.
5. so they wont get mad.
6. because a child has to be able to trust their parents.
7. the child may feel that parent don't love them.
8. because children look up to their parents more than anyone and will be deeply disappointed if a promise is broken.
9. because on Sunday he will get a big bag of candy.
10. this is someone the child is going to learn from a type of Role Model. The child should be taught good values.
11. because the child will look forward to that promise and if you don't keep it then they will feel promises don't matter and they'll be hurt.
12. you want them to have trust in you.
13. because you might hurt their feelings and they might take it hard.
14. they might get mad and throw a temper tantrum.
15. if the parent breaks a promise to a child the child might think it's okay to break promises when it's not.
16. because they want you to keep the promise.
17. because kids trust their parents, so they would expect them to keep secrets or promises.
18. the child needs to know they can depend on their parents.
19. because maybe it is a party for him.
20. parents must show that they will be there for their children. It is very important not to place any doubt into a child's thoughts.
21. children are very impressionable, and if their parents can't keep a promise, then the child may never keep promises and he/she may lack integrity in social circles.

22. if you lie to a child they might not respect you.
23. because they will be grouchy and very mad.
24. because the children might their mom doesn't love them anymore or even not love them.
25. if you don't they could run away or do something bad.

QUESTION #4 (Truth)—Telling the truth is important:

1. because you'll feel guilty inside.
2. because people will not like you if you don't.
3. it might be serious or dangerous.
4. if you tell the truth you can gain people's respect, and get more friends.
5. because they might put you in jail.
6. because they will depend one you and plan for it.
7. if you lie people can go around saying he/she is a very big liar and never tells the truth to anyone not even their mom/dad.
8. you will get caught one day, and your lie will catch up with you.
9. if you tell somebody a lie and they get confused they might not depend on you anymore.
10. because it shows character and responsibility. Being honest is the way to go about things when being faced with a dilemma.
11. if someone finds out you may lose some friends.
12. so you can have a clean conscience.
13. if you don't you could get into worse trouble and no one would trust you.
14. because some things are less important than others, but in general honesty is the best policy as well as the safest. Lying causes confusion, lack of communication, not to mention anger.
15. because you get in more trouble if you lie and they find out.
16. no one likes a liar. If you get to be known as one, no one will believe a word you say.
17. honesty helps build trust, and relationships with other people thrive on trust.
18. because lies just cause more pain.
19. if you do tell lies, the truth can come back to haunt you and other people won't trust you!
20. because lying compromises one's integrity and self esteem.
21. but that's not the case all of the time. If someone asks you how their new skirt looked on them, and I thought it looked terrible, I surely wouldn't tell them. Telling the truth is very important, but you should spare the feelings of another too.
22. because you are going to get in trouble and you are going to get punished.

23. because generally when you lie there is no personal satisfaction gained by either party. And in most cases they eventually find the truth and you lose a friendship.
24. people I know who lie are constantly lying. No one can just lie a "little" honesty is the only way you can get to know other people and they can know you.
25. there are many degrees of truth. In some cases telling the partial truth is sufficient. It all depends on the situation.

QUESTION #5 (Affiliation: Parents)—Helping one's parents is important:

1. they've helped you all your life and it's the least you could do for them after all they've done for you.
2. because your parents are the most important thing in your life. You must be there for them as they have been there for you for your entire life.
3. because I love my parents very much and would do everything possible to help them.
4. the spirit of cooperation is important for family life.
5. because they need you. and they would do the same for you.
6. because I feel family relationships are the closest and most important relationships of all. A person should always be able to count on any member of his or her family; they should always be willing to support each other even if no one else will.
7. I would do anything for my parents.
8. you would not like to lose either one of your parents.
9. it is very important to do the job because they do stuff for you like bills.
10. (not important) because my parents do not deserve one thing from me - they think I owe them the world.
11. your mother and father have done a lot for you I see no reason that you should do what you can for them.
12. if you don't help them with something they are going to start yelling.
13. children should help out of respect.
14. because it shows your loyalty and dedication to them. They do more than enough for you. The least the child can do is help them out once in a while.
15. because they are your parents and they're there for you so you should be for them.
16. you are a part of them and it is your duty to help them.
17. one's parent's deserve respect. A child should be obligated regardless of circumstances.
18. because both as one's responsibility as ones you love and want to do for and as a grateful person for the care you have received.

19. because children want parents to think good of them.
20. if you were in trouble your parents would help you. Thus it's very important for you to help your parents whenever they are in need, it's a gift of love.
21. Helping one's parent is important because families are critical to a person's sense of well-being and to societal well-being.
22. if you help them then they'll help you.
23. because your parents have sacrificed their time, money, lives for you and if there is anyway you can repay them you have an obligation to do so.
24. if you don't help them and they die some day you won't have anyone to take care of you.
25. because it teaches the child responsibility and helps earn the trust of the parents.

QUESTION #6 (Affiliation: Friends)—Helping to save a friend's life is important:

1. because you may never have a friend like that again.
2. if you're any type of friend at all you would without a second thought.
3. because they are your friends and they would do the same for you.
4. because I would do everything possible to save a friend's life. If they die a part of me will die also. I couldn't go on knowing I didn't try my hardest to save a life.
5. if I'm the only one who can help - I will!
6. if you really want to keep a friend and other people happy you would help.
7. because why would anyone let another friend die? Friendship is mainly based on honesty and trust and the friend in need should be able to trust his/her friend to help him.
8. because you would want your friend to save your own life, so naturally you should try to save his.
9. because friends are necessary for our survival, so we should do anything we can to keep them in our lives. Friendship involves another kind of love that can definitely be shown through aiding a person's life.
10. friends, good friends, are hard to come by and one should do all one can to help a friend once a good friend is found.
11. in a life and death situation I would do anything I could.
12. because that is one of the greatest things a person can do is to help a friend in dire need.
13. you don't want to lose a friend or watch them die.
14. if you love this person, you must help them. Relationship should be based on selflessness.

15. if the friend is very important to me, I would do anything for them because I wouldn't want to lose them, and have it hurt me in the long run.
16. because you do not want them to die.
17. because some day you're going to need help from that friend.
18. because a friendship is a common bond of helping each other this could also be reversed - This is what life and love is about, whether friend, relative or stranger.
19. because I would not be able to just let my friend die - the guilt would be overwhelming.
20. because they're nice and you might need them one day.
21. judging from the years my best friend and I have been friends and the things we've shared there's nothing in the world I wouldn't do for her. And I'm sure she'd do the same. Having a friend is just as important as being a friend.
22. because some people have done that for you and they might do that for you later on.
23. a life is priceless and if one human being has the ability to help another and don't they have a serious problem.
24. first, to prevent a death or trauma that may be averted; second, to follow-through on a person's own sense of right and wrong, to be consistent with the commitment to the relationship, risking consequences.
25. because you like him and you don't want him to die. He's your friend.

QUESTION #7 (Life: Stranger)—Saving a stranger's life is important:

1. because I would want them to do the same for me!
2. you don't want them to die too.
3. **(not important)** because they could be just saying that to you. So they can do something real bad to you where you will never be found again.
4. because it is important to save <u>anyone's</u> life. Life is to be preserved. The instant you are capable of making a decision to save a life or just stand by and let someone die is the instant you are playing God. Who should live? Who should die?
5. it is very important to save anyone's life to because it's always nice to do something for anyone.
6. because life is very sacred to me—perhaps I should say human life. When you consider that a stranger probably has a family just like yourself, it becomes very critical to help them.
7. it's like the lion and the mouse. The mouse later saved him so you never know. You might need them some time.

8. well I guess that if someone on the streets needed your help I would help them I don't like to see people suffer.

9. still very important to save stranger because all life is valuable—that's how society will survive the best. People must connect with another - help each other. But I probably would not take as great a risk to save a stranger.

10. because everyone's life is important. I would want someone I didn't know to help me if I needed it. Why shouldn't they expect the same?

11. because life is a very precious thing.

12. if someone was dying that I didn't know I would try to do all I could to help him/her and get help.

13. because it is a kind thing to do and it shows you care about them even if you don't know them.

14. I cannot stand to watch or let anyone die.

15. because everyone has the right to live and whether it's friend or enemy shouldn't matter. If you're able to help someone in need, you should.

16. because every one deserves to live and if someone has control over another person's life they don't have the right to let them die.

17. because helping others may even one day help you!

18. again, if I didn't, the guilt would be very strong. Although the person is a stranger to me, he is loved by others.

19. because we have an obligation as part of the human race to care for one another. Whether stranger or friend life is still a precious commodity.

20. Someday you may need this person that you've helped.

21. because you just don't watch people die, it's morally wrong.

22. life has no meaning if you cannot give to others. If I didn't do whatever possible, I would feel so selfish and empty...

23. because any life is important to save. However, family and friends' lives would come before a stranger's.

24. because in this world, people need people. For the survival of the species, we need to help each other. I would expect the same from others.

25. (not important) although this may sound horrible I probably wouldn't be willing to die for a stranger I would though do everything I could for that person to save him.

QUESTION #8 (Life: Self)—Living even when one doesn't want to is important:

1. because they never know what they have to live for until they try. So they should try and live for something.

2. because it is important for them to live so they can get a couple more years of life.

3. (not important) because if that person really wants to die and is in pain, dying is the best thing.
4. but what is the nature of the crisis—emotional or physical? If emotional, help may resolve the crisis and the desire to die dissipate. If physical (Parkinson's, AIDS, Degenerative Heart Disease, Cancer) the decision must rest with the person, with the support of close friends & family.
5. because hopefully people see other alternatives than suicide.
6. they need to be able to do all the things they ever wanted to do.
7. they don't have the right to take their own life. That's only an escape they should face their problems and deal with them differently.
8. because suicide is a very selfish act.
9. (not important) if a person is a vegetable, or only is living on life supports, and he wants to die, he should be allowed to, because he isn't living much of a life anyway. However, if a person is healthy, but just depressed, he should be made to live because things will get better in the long run.
10. because God put us here.
11. because that person can have an impact on a lot of people's lives.
12. (not important) if they don't want to live why should they.
13. because each person must be responsible for his own life. He should be allowed to choose death.
14. life is not ours to lay down.
15. because you have people who care.
16. (not important) if they don't want to live that's their choice.
17. because if they die the people that loved them will be hurt.
18. because they could be famous or have a famous child.
19. but it depends on the situation. If they have or will have something to live for. If they are sick or paralyzed or something and will suffer then I think they have the right to choose.
20. because people need to strive if not for themselves but for the benefit of mankind.
21. because human life is very precious if you don't try to save it then you have killed someone or something.
22. people may want to die but they would miss out on something and many people would miss that person but the person wouldn't know it because he/she was dead.
23. because life is sacred. It should be preserved at all costs.
24. they just think they want to die.
25. because their family loves them and no one wants anybody to die.

QUESTION #9 (Property)—Not taking things that belong to others is important:

1. if everyone took something that didn't belong to them no one wold have anything.
2. because you should ask someone for it and if they say no don't take it or try to trade him or her something for it or buy it from her.
3. because taking things from other people is wrong. If everyone took things from other people, there would be no order in our society. Also, they are violating other people's rights.
4. this is very important because of a basic but strong moral issue for human beings to respect the property of one another.
5. because it's on the same level as promises and telling the truth. It's a personal responsibility.
6. because it isn't theirs and people shouldn't take something that isn't theirs.
7. that's stealing. I don't do it why should others.
8. because that is violating someone else. If you need something you should ask, not just take.
9. because I think other people have worked hard for the object/belonging to keep their possession. So, others should not take things that are not theirs.
10. because stealing is not good because one can't be fully trusted again.
11. you don't want things taken of yours.
12. because they wouldn't want someone to take their stuff.
13. someone worked for that object and no one has the right to take something they didn't work for. They don't deserve to have an easy way for something another worked hard for.
14. respecting other people's property is a law of life. By taking other people's things, you are showing that you do not care about others feelings and do not respect them enough to obey this law.
15. people will get put in jail if they do it.
16. because some items are so special to people, you should never take anything that doesn't belong to you.
17. it is a matter of courtesy and morals not to take things that belong to others. Often possessions carry a sentimental value for a person and when you take it, you take part of the person away with you.
18. one has no right without permission to take anything from anyone else. Chances are the person worked very hard for that thing and it would hurt them very much.
19. because you'll lose people's trust. No one will believe in you.

20. because stealing is something I feel very strongly about. If you've ever had something stolen then you will fully understand the importance of not stealing. It is not trustworthy in any way.
21. if you take someone else's property you have broken a sacred trust.
22. because stealing is wrong. Circumstances may change situations.
23. because if that belonging belongs to someone and you don't have it and you want it and take it, it would be bad because that person would find out sooner or later.
24. it might be a thing that costs over a hundred dollars.
25. because they will make the other person mad.

QUESTION #10 (Law)—Obeying the law is important:

1. because it's safer for others and for you.
2. so that people can live together in society in an effective manner. So that Human Rights of Individuals may be preserved.
3. laws are guidelines for society to follow. If we did not have any laws, there would be many problems.
4. because the law is the law - no doubts - no exceptions.
5. if they don't they will be sent to jail.
6. if everyone were to disobey laws our world would be chaotic. Our world would fall apart and there would be crime.
7. but it depends on what laws.
8. I think that if a law hurts society as a whole that there may be reason to disobey it, but I do think it is important for people to obey the law for society to survive.
9. so that they won't get into trouble.
10. a society cannot be run properly if people didn't obey laws. It would be chaotic.
11. unless the laws go strongly against one's morals.
12. without order, society would be very unorganized and there could be a lot more crime. That's why it's important for people to obey the law.
13. because laws aren't always agreeable to all but we must have some system of conduct to follow.
14. if you want to stay out of trouble.
15. if you don't you can be put in jail or someplace worse.
16. because laws are codes of ethics. It is the only proper way to live and be happy. We must all maintain some code of ethics for harmony. Rebellion & conflict would result without some guidelines. No one could be safe or happy.
17. because laws are the backbone of our country. If we don't follow them we sacrifice the good of all.

18. without laws that people obeyed, everything would be a mess—people would just always do what they wanted without concern of how it could affect others.
19. because you will go to prison or something like that if you don't obey the law.
20. in order to take care of your business and do what you're supposed to do you need to obey all laws. It keeps you out of trouble.
21. the law represents the operational definition of the structure upon which our society is based. However, when "the law" is an insult to one's integrity, self, or conscience, occasionally laws must be broken (1) because society is wrong and (2) grievances must be redressed to the quality of life for all people in society.
22. because you could get hurt like taking drugs or speeding and you could wreck. Because you could get in jail for a long time.
23. the laws were intended to guide us in safety and to solve problems justly and fairly for all parties. Without laws we would probably be in complete chaos.
24. because it is what keeps the whole "system" together and if it is law there is probably a reason it is.
25. you're going to feel guilty and also get yourself into a lot of trouble.

QUESTION #11 (Legal Justice)—Sending lawbreakers to jail is important:

1. but it all depends on what the person did.
2. so that they don't do it again and we don't have to worry.
3. but if the person who broke it couldn't in any way avoid it, and had good intentions, that should be taken into consideration.
4. unless they broke it for a good reason. If they were harming someone or doing it not out of helping anyone then they should go to jail.
5. so they won't do the same thing over again.
6. because though jails may not be an ideal rehabilitation, they do render society safer by removing the criminal. At least keep criminals to a minimum in society. Unfortunately, we can't catch them all.
7. they did it, they pay for it.
8. they need to learn from their mistakes.
9. so that they learn their lesson not to break the law and that you can't get away with anything.
10. if the criminals don't go to jail this sets a bad example for others following a life of crime.
11. because judges need to keep the rights of the innocent victim in mind when sentencing is going on and criminals who do get out and repeat crimes should be brought back to jail for life.

12. I do not feel a person who committed a violent crime should be let loose on society without rehabilitation. It depends on the offense.

13. (not important) because some people should go to jail. Others (murderers, rapists, and those committing treason) should be executed. Most criminals should be put to work to repay their victims.

14. depending on what they did. If they are going to be harmful to society then they should be locked up.

15. because society wouldn't exist if law-breakers weren't punished.

16. because they did something bad.

17. so they won't do it again and to think about what they have done was wrong.

18. because the person that committed the crime knew it was wrong so they should pay the price.

19. some people can't get along with society and they hurt others--they should be the ones who go to jail.

20. they must set examples, then maybe it won't be so "cool" to break the law.

21. because they might think that if the judge lets her off she can go do it again.

22. because lawbreakers need to be punished. If they weren't there would be anarchy.

23. but I'm not sure that jail is always the correct punishment in some cases but in most cases it is important so the offender realizes his wrong doings and perhaps the punishment will prevent him from repeating the same mistakes.

24. if I thought that it helped or rehabilitated the individual I would feel that it would be very important. Unfortunately it does not.

25. if the judge didn't he would go out and steal some more and more and more.

ANNOTATED ANSWER KEYS

QUESTION #1 (Contract: Friends)

1. 3:4b
2. Unscorable. The response is unscorable because of the absence of a justification for the respondent's self-reported practice of "sticking to" his or her "word."
3. 2/3:4a, 2/3:3a. If the characterization had been slightly less vague (e.g., "selfish" or "cruel" instead of "terrible"), the response would have been scorable at Stage 3.
4. 3:3c, 3/4:8a. "If they find out who broke it" is not scored Stage 1 because it merely qualifies the Transition 3/4 justification.
5. 1:4b, 1:4c
6. 4:3a
7. 3:4a
8. 2/3:5b
9. 2:1c. The scorer must recognize that the respondent has inadvertently omitted the word "them" in the middle of the sentence. Interpolations or completions of this sort are acceptable where the intended word or phrase is clearly indicated by context (see chapter 3).
10. 4:2c (Moral Type B, Fundamental Valuing), 3:1d (Moral Type B, Balancing). The Stage 4 match is less than optimal because the reference to relationships ("a relationship") is not explicitly generalized.
11. 2/3:1a
12. 2/3:4a and 3/4:8a
13. 2/3:2a. "A promise should not be broken" is unscorable.
14. 3:1a
15. 3/4:2b, 3:1d (Moral Type B, Balancing), 3:1a, 3/4:1a. The Transition 3/4:Aspect 2b match is marginal: "Friends are people who you respect" is not clearly prescriptive and only implicitly suggestive of the criterion idea that "people . . . deserve respect." One can assume that the referent for "trouble" is the loss of respect and trust.
16. 2/3:5a, 2:1c
17. 1:2
18. 2:6b
19. Unscorable. The response is unscorable because of the vague quality of "serious problem": Is the "serious problem" of a pragmatic nature (cf. "trouble")? Emotional or psychological? A problem for society? Responses that relate equally to Criterion Justifications (CJs) at more than three developmental levels are unscorable, by Rule 3 (see chapter 3).

20. 3:1a, <u>4</u>:3a, 2/3:3a, 3/4:1a. The Stage 3 citation pertains to both "friendship involves a lot of trust" and "you are hurting the friendship [if you break the promise]." In protocol scoring, the only score entered for this question would be the highest level (Stage 4).
21. <u>2</u>:6b, 1/2:2c
22. 1:3a
23. 3:2b,3b
24. 3:1a, 3/4:8a, <u>4</u>:4a. "Shows your friendship with that person" in the response is related to "for the sake of the friendship" in Aspect 1a of Stage 3.
25. Unscorable

QUESTION #2 (Contract: Anyone)

1. 1/2:2c
2. 2/3:4a,5b
3. 2:5a, 2:1b
4. 4:3b (Moral Type B, Balancing)
5. Unscorable
6. 2/3:4a. "Don't no one else" is unscorable.
7. Unscorable
8. 3/4:1a.
9. 2:1b. Although the absolutist expression "always" is suggestive of a Stage 1 rating, the elaboration renders this response scorable at Stage 2.
10. 3:4b
11. 2/3:5b, 2:6b, <u>3</u>:1a
12. 3/4:8a
13. 4:7a (Moral Type B, Conscience)
14. 2/3:4a, <u>3/4</u>:8a
15. Unscorable, 2:6a
16. 4:3a, unscorable. The first sentence of the response is scorable despite its personalized quality. In many cases, however, a personalized response refers merely to psychological attributes with no prescriptive implications, and hence is unscorable. The second sentence of the response is unscorable because "following through on your word" does not provide a justification but, instead, is essentially tautologous to "keeping your promise" (the normative moral value to be justified).
17. <u>2/3</u>:Rule 2, 2:6a. "It won't mean much to you" may refer either to keeping the promise (cf. "it won't matter," Stage 2:Aspect 6f), or to the relationship (cf. "a friend means a lot (to you)," Stage 3:Aspect 1c); hence the Transition 2/3 rating by Rule 2.
18. 1/2:2c
19. 4:3a, 4:4a

20. 2:6a
21. Unscorable
22. 2/3:5b
23. 2:6f
24. 1:4c, 1:5
25. <u>4</u>:1a, 3/4:1a. "Essential for growth" relates to "essential for . . . human development" in the Stage 4 CJ. The latter part of the response goes beyond Stage 3 because it refers to "making" or developing a better relationship.

QUESTION #3 (Contract: Children)

1. 3/4:8c
2. 3:1a, <u>3/4</u>:8a
3. 2:6b, 2:4d
4. 2/3:4a, 2/3:3a, <u>3</u>:2a
5. 1/2:2b
6. 3/4:1b
7. 3:2a
8. <u>3/4</u>:8c, 3:2a
9. 1:5
10. 3/4:8c
11. 2/3:3a, <u>3</u>:4c, 3:2a. "They will feel promises don't matter" is matched to "the children . . . will think dishonesty is all right."
12. 3:1a. "You want" is not scorable as Stage 2, because the referent for the preference is not pragmatic ("to have trust in you").
13. 3:2a
14. <u>2</u>:6b, 1/2:2b. "Might throw a temper tantrum" relates to "might cry."
15. 3:4c
16. 2:4b
17. 2/3:4a, <u>3</u>:3b
18. 3/4:1b
19. 1/2:2b
20. 3/4:Rule 1. The response relates equally to either Stage 3:Aspect 4b or Transition 3/4:Aspect 1b, and hence is given the upper-level rating in accordance with Rule 1 (see chapter 3).
21. 3/4:8c, <u>4</u>:4b
22. 3/4:8a
23. 1/2:2b
24. 3:2a. The scorer must accomplish a completion, i.e., interpolate "feel" or "think" in "The child might their mom don't love them" (see chapter 3).
25. 1/2:2b,c

QUESTION #4 (Truth)

1. 3:6 (Moral Type B, Conscience)
2. 2:6b
3. 2:6c. "It might be serious" is unscorable.
4. 3/4:8a, 2/3:5a
5. 1/2:2c. "Might put you in jail" is matched to "might . . . do something bad to you."
6. 2/3:4a
7. 2/3:6a
8. 2:6d
9. 2/3:4a
10. 4:4a, 3:3c. The Stage 4 reference to "responsibility" is less personalized or more abstract than the Transition 3/4 counterpart ("to show that you are responsible"). The Stage 3 match is marginal.
11. 2/3:5a
12. 3:6 (Moral Type B: Conscience)
13. 2:6d, 2/3:5b
14. 3:3c, 3/4:2a, 2:6b
15. 2:6d
16. 2:6b, 2/3:6a, 2/3:5b. The concern in the response that one may "get to be [known]" as a liar is matched to "the word will get around that you keep your promises" (Transition 2/3:Aspect 6a).
17. 3/4:1a
18. 3:2a
19. 2:6d, 2/3:5b
20. 4:7a, 3/4:10b. The reference in the response to compromising one's integrity implies an intra-individual concern with conscience (Aspect 7).
21. 3/4:5, 3:2a
22. 1/2:2c, 1:4c
23. 3/4:10b, 3/4:5, 3:1a. The reference in the response to a "lack of personal satisfaction" after lying is matched to Transition 3/4:Aspect 10b. An appeal to losing a *friend* (as distinct from friendship or relationship) would be scored Transition 2/3.
24. 2/3:6b, 3:1a. The rating of the first portion of the response as Transition 2/3 represents a marginal match.
25. 3/4:5

QUESTION #5 (Affiliation: Parents)

1. 2/3:1a, 3:1b
2. 3:1b. "Parents are the most important thing in your life" is unscorable, since "parents" does not constitute a *relationship* referent (cf. chapter 4, Stage 3:Aspect 1c).

3. 2/3:5a. The action characterization, "I . . . would do everything possible to help [my parents]," is unscorable.
4. 3/4:1b
5. 2:5a, 2/3:1a
6. 3:1a, 3/4:1b (Moral Type B, Balancing)
7. Unscorable
8. 2/3:2
9. 2:1a
10. Unscorable
11. 2/3:1a. One can infer that the subject intended to write: "I see no reason that you shouldn't do what you can for them."
12. 1:5
13. 3/4:2b
14. 3:3a, 3/4:7b, 3:1b
15. 2/3:1a. "They are you're [sic] parents" is unscorable as Stage 1 because it is elaborated in the full response (see Note associated with Stage 1:Aspect 2a).
16. 3:1a, 4:3. "You are part of them" relates to "a friend is like a part of you" in the Stage 3:Aspect 1a CJ.
17. 3/4:2b, 4:3
18. 4:3, 2/3:5a, 2:4a, 3:1b
19. 3:4c
20. 2/3:1b (Moral Type B, Balancing), 3:2a, 3:4a
21. 3/4:Rule 2, 4:2a. "Sense of well-being" is rated as Transition 3/4 by use of Rule 2, because the phrase is comparably (if marginally) matchable to three adjacent developmental levels: Stage 3:Aspect 6, Transition 3/4:Aspect 9, and Stage 4:Aspect 7.
22. 2:1a
23. 3:1b, 4:3b
24. 2:5b
25. 3/4:7a, 4:6. The Stage 4 match requires considerable inference since its referent is normally the parent rather than the child.

QUESTION #6 (Affiliation: Friends)

1. 2:5b
2. 3:4a
3. 2/3:1b (Moral Type B, Balancing)
4. Unscorable, 3:1a, 3:6 (Moral Type B, Conscience)
5. Unscorable. The statement merely echoes the question.
6. 2/3:2, 2:6a
7. 3/4:1a, 3:2a, 3/4:1b. "Friend in need" is matched to "friend may be in (great) need" under Stage 3:Aspect 2a.

8.   2/3:1b (Moral Type B, Balancing), 3:3d
9.   3:1a, 3:4b. "Friends are necessary for our survival" is unscorable since
     its possible meaning spans more than three developmental levels (Rule
     3, chapter 3): "our" could refer to an aggregate of egoistic selves (Stage
     2) or to interdependent, contributing members of society (Stage 4).
     Better specified justifications might be scorable, for example,
     "Friendships are necessary for society's survival" would be scorable at
     Stage 4:Aspect 1a. "Friendship involves . . . love" is not rated higher
     than Stage 3 because the relevant Transition 3/4 CJ requires a
     specification of friendship as **based on** love (see Transition 3/4 Aspect
     1a).
10. 2/3:7a.
11. 3:5 (Moral Type B, Fundamental Valuing)
12. 3:2a
13. 2/3:2, 3:2b
14. 3:4a, 3/4:1a. "You must help them" is inferred to have a prescriptive
     significance.
15. 2/3:2, 2/3:5c [irregular citation; this CJ is found in the Contract and
     Truth chapter]
16. 2:4a
17. 2:6a
18. 3/4:1b (Moral Type B, Balancing)
19. 2/3:5a, 3:6 (Moral Type B, Conscience)
20. 1:4, 2:6a
21. 3:1a, 2/3:1b (Moral Type B, Balancing), unscorable. "I'm sure"
     signifies a predictive confidence, but not necessarily a prescriptive
     expectation (if the response had been "I would **expect**," it would be
     scored Stage 3). "Having a friend is just as important as being a friend"
     is unscorable.
22. 2:1a
23. 3:5 (Moral Type B, Fundamental Valuing)
24. 3/4:8 (Moral Type B, Conscience [Relativism of Personal Values]), 4:3
25. 2:4a, 1:2a

QUESTION #7 (Life: Stranger)

1.   2/3:1 (Moral Type B, Balancing)
2.   2:4b
3.   2:6c, 1/2:1b
4.   3/4:3. "It is important to save *anyone's* life. Life is to be preserved" is
     unscorable (see note under Stage 3:5a).
5.   1:4a
6.   4:2a (Moral Type B, Fundamental Valuing)

7. 2:5
8. 2/3:5a, 3:2a
9. 4:2b, 4:1b (Moral Type B, Balancing)
10. Unscorable, 2/3:1, 2:5, 3:1a
11. 3:5b (Moral Type B, Fundamental Valuing)
12. Unscorable
13. 3:4a
14. 3:2a
15. 3:2c
16. 3:3a, 3/4:3
17. 2:1
18. 3:6 (Moral Type B, Conscience), 2/3:2a
19. 4:3a, 3:5b (Moral Type B, Fundamental Valuing)
20. 2:5
21. 3:2a
22. 4:2b, 3:4b, 3:6 (Moral Type B, Conscience). "Selfish" is scored Stage 3:4b, whereas "empty" is scored Stage 3:6.
23. Unscorable
24. 4:1b (Moral Type B, Balancing), 3:1a (Moral Type B, Balancing)
25. Unscorable

QUESTION #8 (Life: Self)

1. 3:3b. The "So" beginning the second sentence suggests that the two sentences should be considered together in scoring.
2. 2:6b
3. 2/3:3, 3:2c. "That person really wants to die" in the response is matched to "you **really** (still) want to live" in the CJ.
4. 3/4:2, 3/4:7b
5. Unscorable
6. 2:4a,5,6b
7. 3/4:3, 3/4:4
8. 3:4b
9. 3/4:2
10. 1:1b
11. 3/4:6a
12. 2:3
13. 4:3b, 3/4:7b
14. 3/4:3
15. 2/3:2a
16. Unscorable
17. 2/3:2a, 3:2b
18. 1:2

19. 3/4:2, 3:2b, 3/4:7b
20. 4:2b
21. 3:5b (Moral Type B, Fundamental Valuing)
22. 2:6b, 2/3:2a. The consideration that the person "may want to die" is disavowed and hence unscorable.
23. 4:2a (Moral Type B, Fundamental Valuing)
24. 2/3:3
25. 2/3:2a, 2:4b

QUESTION #9 (Property)

1. 1/2:3b
2. Unscorable
3. 3/4:4a, 4:2d
4. 4:Rule 1. Although the respondent does not explicitly refer to property as a human right (Stage 4:Aspect 2d), he or she does characterize property as a "basic but strong moral issue." Hence, the response is at least as close to Stage 4 as it is to Transition 3/4:Aspect 5b, therefore, it should be given the higher level rating by Rule 1.
5. 4:3a
6. 1/2:1a
7. 1:4, 2:2
8. 3/4:5b
9. 2/3:3
10. 3:4a
11. 2:1b
12. 2/3:1 (Moral Type B, Balancing). "They" in the response is assumed to refer to those who steal, not the prospective victims.
13. 2:3a, 3:3a, 2/3:3
14. 3/4:5b, 3:2a
15. 1:5
16. 3:2a
17. 3:3b, 3:2a
18. 3:2a
19. 3:1c
20. 3/4:9a
21. 4:2c (Moral Type B, Fundamental Valuing)
22. 3/4:3a
23. 2:6b
24. 1:2
25. 1/2:3a

QUESTION #10 (Law)

1. 2/3:9a
2. 3/4:4b (Moral Type B, Balancing), 4:2d
3. 4:Rule 1. Equal 3/4:9b and 4:1a ratings yield the Stage 4 rating by Rule 1.
4. Unscorable
5. 1:5
6. 3:3c, 2/3:9a
7. Unscorable
8. 4:2a, 4:1a
9. 1/2:3a
10. 4:1a. The second sentence is scored at Stage 4 because the referent for "it" in the sentence can be assumed to be "society." An appeal to consequences or chaos in the absence of a reference to society would be scored Stage 3.
11. 3/4:10a
12. 4:1a, 2/3:9a
13. 4:5a
14. 2:4a
15. 1/2:3a
16. 3/4:4a, 3/4:1a, 3/4:9b, 2/3:9a
17. 4:1a, 4:2a
18. 2/3:9a, 3/4:Rule 1 (equal 3:4c and 3/4:8b,9b ratings yield 3/4 by Rule 1), 3/4:2
19. 1/2:3a
20. 1/2:3a
21. 4:1a, 4:7 (Moral Type B, Conscience), 4:2a
22. 1/2:3a, 2:6b
23. 3/4:9b, 2/3:9a, 3/4:1a, 3:3c
24. 4:1a
25. 3:6 (Moral Type B, Conscience), 1/2:3a

QUESTION #11 (Legal Justice)

1. Unscorable. (See 3/4:1 Note in chapter 8.)
2. 1/2:1, 2/3:6
3. 3:4, 3/4:Rule 1. "That should be taken into consideration" relates equally to 3:2 and 3/4:1, and hence is scored Transition 3/4 by Rule 1.
4. 2/3:5,3
5. 2:6a. "Over again" relates to "over and over, again and again" in the CJ.
6. 3/4:3b, 4:1
7. 2:1

8. 2/3:1a. The response is scored as Transition 2/3 even though it partially relates as well to Stage 2:5b.

9. 2:Rule 2, 2:5b. "So that they learn their lesson not to break the law" relates comparably to CJs that span three adjacent developmental levels (1/2:2 and 2/3:1a), and so is rated Stage 2 by Rule 2.

10. 3/4:3a

11. 4:2d. "Rights of the innocent victim" relates to "**rights** of others" in the CJ. Without the reference to "rights," the response would have been scored Stage 3:Aspect 3d.

12. 4:1, 3/4:3b, unscorable (see 3/4:1 Note)

13. Unscorable

14. Unscorable, 4:1

15. 4:1

16. 1:4

17. 1/2:1, 3:4

18. 3:4, unscorable (see 2:1 note)

19. 4:2a, 2/3:6

20. 3/4:3a

21. 2:5b.

22. Unscorable (the response might reflect Stage 2:Aspect 5b or Transition 3/4:Aspect 2, and so is unscorable, by Rule 3); 3/4:2a

23. 3/4:1, 3:4, 2/3:1a

24. 3/4:3b. The rehabilitation consideration is upheld in hypothetical and ideal terms even though it is dismissed as unrealistic. Hence, the response should not be interpreted as a disavowal.

25. 2:6a

Appendix C

Questionnaire Exercises
and Answer Keys

Note: To promote their practical relevance, the responses used in these protocol exercises were recorded word-for-word from actual research protocols. The keys provide complete scoring information for training purposes; all response units have been given a rating, and notations have been made for all Moral Type B components. The highest stage rating for the justifications entailed in each response is underlined in the answer keys. Once trained, the scorer need rate only the highest-level justifications in the SRM-SF Questionnaire responses (see chapter 3).

QUESTIONNAIRE EXERCISES

PROTOCOL 1

1. Keeping promises to friends is very important: because you made that promise and if you breack the promise they may not like you.
2. Keeping promises to anyone is important: they count and trust you.
3. Keeping promises to one's children is very important: because we can get mad and not like are parents.
4. Telling the truth is important: because it might be important.
5. Helping one's parents is important: they can do things for you if you do it for them.
6. Helping to save a friend's life is very important: because there your friennds and you like them.
7. Saving a stranger's life is very important: because you need to help.
8. Living even if one doesn't want to is important: you need to live.
9. Not taking things that belong to others is very important: because if they did it would be stelling and thats a crime.
10. Obeying the law is very important: they can be sent to jail.
11. Sending lawbreakers to jail is very important: because they can do it agian.

PROTOCOL 2

1. Keeping promises to friends is very important: because they might get mad at you and you may loose them as a friend. It might be really personal.
2. Keeping promises to anyone is very important: it's not right to break the promise cause you made it! You have to be trusted!
3. Keeping promises to one's children is very important: because the child may loose trust in them if they braek it!
4. Telling the truth is very important: because the consequences are worse if they find out you lied. You'll feel guilty if you know you lied.
5. Helping one's parents is very important: your parents can't do everything! They also have to work and buy things for you! You should put forth at least some help!
6. Helping to save a friend's life is very important: if your friend died it would take a part of you with him/her. Also I'm sure you'd be doing a favor for other people that have some kind of relationship with him/her.
7. Saving a stranger's life is very important: because everyone is equal. It wouldn't be right (to not save them) if they didn't have anything to do with you!

8. Living even if one doesn't want to is very important: because maybe their life would change if they survived. They can't just think about themselves! Everybody else would be left in misery!

9. Not taking things that belong to others is very important: it's not yours! You didn't pay for it!

10. Obeying the law is very important: if not, the world would be a mess! Everybody would get hurt, physically & mentally!

11. Sending lawbreakers to jail is very important: if not, people would keep on doing it!

PROTOCOL 3

1. Keeping promises to friends is very important: true friendships are based on caring and trust. Keeping a promise to a friend shows you care and are a reliable, dependable person.

2. Keeping promises to anyone is very important: why make a promise if you have no intention of keeping it? The stranger will feel very good about your thoughtfullness, and you will feel good about yourself.

3. Keeping promises to one's children is very important: it is extremely important to keep promises to children. It builds the child's self-esteem and self-confidence. He/she feels worthy & learns to trust other adults & foster good relationships with other children based upon honesty & integrity.

4. Telling the truth is important: under normal circumstances, truth is always best. As the saying goes, "It all comes out in the wash anyway". However, if it causes deep hurt, such as telling someone their spouse is having an affair, I'd think twice.

5. Helping one's parents is very important: children should always "pitch in" to give their parents a hand. They are part of the family and a family is a team - all for one and one for all.

6. Helping to save a friend's life is very important: I can't imagine what kind of a person would turn their back on a situation like this. If you truly care & are a reasonably healthy, normal, well-adjusted person, you will do all you can to ease the pain & suffering of a dear friend.

7. Saving a stranger's life is very important: we should value all human life. When you help a stranger, you feel good about yourself, & that "stranger" may end up helping you someday.

8. Living even if one doesn't want to is very important: because life is a precious gift. No matter how low we feel or how miserable our life is at the time, we never know what tomorrow may bring. One should try to be aware of the unbelieveable suffering loved ones & friends would endure should one so selfishly decide to "end it all."

9. Not taking things that belong to others is very important: well, for one thing, if you're caught, you're in big trouble! Seriously, we all know it just isn't right to steal. Income taxes may be another story.

10. Obeying the law is very important: because utter chaos would be the end result of this. Society, as a whole, could not function without rules & regulations. Children should be taught values & morals to reach healthy, normal adulthood.

11. Sending lawbreakers to jail is very important: murder & rape should be a mandatory life sentence, if not the electric chair. Why let a mentally disturbed person go free to repeat the crime? Possibly to you or your own family. There is no known cure for the criminally insane. Society cannot afford to "mollycoddle" these people because of severely disturbed childhoods or "chemical inbalances" in the genes. We just cannot have a slew of "mental misfits" running around and terrorizing society. Attorneys find too many "loop holes" & judges are too lax & too liberal. However, when it "hits home" it's always a different story.

PROTOCOL 4

1. Keeping promises to friends is very important: so that they will have more trust in you.

2. Keeping promises to anyone is not important: because keeping that promise could hurt you.

3. Keeping promises to one's children is very important: so that the kids will believe in them and trust them.

4. Telling the truth is important: so you don't get in trouble by lying.

5. Helping one's parents is very important: because they help you so much.

6. Helping to save a friend's life is very important: so you can have someone to trust.

7. Saving a stranger's life is important: so that person won't die.

8. Living even if one doesn't want to is very important: because it will hurt the people who love him/her.

9. Not taking things that belong to others is very important: because that person may have worked very hard to get that.

10. Obeying the law is important: so that you don't get thrown in jail.

11. Sending lawbreakers to jail is very important: so that the people don't break the law again.

PROTOCOL 5

1. Keeping promises to friends is very important: because it develops trust in that relationship. My parents taught it that I was to keep promises. My parents modled this for me.

2. Keeping promises to anyone is very important: it will build trust between individuals & thus reflect on communities & all relationships.
3. Keeping promises to one's children is very important: this will be modeling trust for your child. it is very important to the child to develop some sort of sence of trust with someone who is a care giver.
4. Telling the truth is important: because this depends on the situation. At times it may be that it is better to hold back the truth. However, this should be the exeption one should tell the truth almost all the time.
5. Helping one's parents is very important: it is important because it gives the child responsibility, gives them role modles & female/male tasks - responsibilities of life.
6. Helping to save a friend's life is very important: because life is very important. We have a responsibility to help people as much as we can. Life is sacred.
7. Saving a stranger's life is very important: because life is very important. We have a responsibility to help people. Life is sacred.
8. Living even if one doesn't want to is not important: if they do not want to live it is their choice. But if it is possible to help them change their mind it is our responsibility to do so.
9. Not taking things that belong to others is very important: because many times people have worked very hard at achieving what they have/own. It is moroly wrong & Biblically.
10. Obeying the law is important: because it is important in maintaining order and structure with in a society. In some cases though it is not so important to the functioning of society.
11. Sending lawbreakers to jail is important: there needs to be consequences for own wrong actions, for the saftey of others within that society.

PROTOCOL 6

1. Keeping promises to friends is very important: if you donnot keep the promise you might loos a friend and they might be very very mad.
2. Keeping promises to anyone is important: because it is important to keep promises to eanyone if you made a promise and broke it that would be a big lie.
3. Keeping promises to one's children is very important: it is important to keep a promise to a child because they will be grouchy and very mad.
4. Telling the truth is very important: because it is very important to tell the truth because if you told a lie and tell them someone was dieing they would not belive you eany more.
5. Helping one's parents is very important: because it is important to help your mother or father they cant do all the work.

6. Helping to save a friend's life is very important: everyone would be mad at you if you didn't save his or hers life.
7. Saving a stranger's life is very important: because you should save anyone's life you might get a reward or lots of things and everyone would like you for it.
8. Living even if one doesn't want to is important: if you don't no the person they might play a trick on you but I would still go.
9. Not taking things that belong to others is very important: because it might be there favorite thing and it would be bad.
10. Obeying the law is very important: if no one obayed the law id hate and too meany people would get hurt.
11. Sending lawbreakers to jail is very important: because they might go back and keep on doing what ever they were doing.

PROTOCOL 7

1. Keeping promises to friends is very important: if you promised something and don't do it, they'll have no trust in you.
2. Keeping promises to anyone is important: because if you promise someone something they will have trust in you.
3. Keeping promises to one's children is very important: because most kids look up at there parents or brothers.
4. Telling the truth is very important: it could mean matter of a death. Also, they'll have trust in you.
5. Helping one's parents is important: do on to others as you acpect them to do for you.
6. Helping to save a friend's life is very important: because it's a matter of life and death you have to try to save him.
7. Saving a stranger's life is very important: because its a matter of life or death, he might trust, or something.
8. Living even if one doesn't want to is very important: he's got a hole life to live why shouldn't he want to live.
9. Not taking things that belong to others is very important: if you take stuff there going to evenaully find out, then they wont want trust you.
10. Obeying the law is very important: if you didn't obey the law there would be alot of maneacts on the roads.
11. Sending lawbreakers to jail is very important: if everytime you went to see the judge and he didn't send you to jail, there would be alot of criminals.

PROTOCOL 8

1. Keeping promises to friends is very important: because it is very important to keep promises to friend in order to maintain trust and reliability in a relationship. A friend is someone you need to be able to depend on and when he/she breaks a promise that dependency is broken.
2. Keeping promises to anyone is important: broken promises can hurt another person, but there are times when a promise needs to be broken.
3. Keeping promises to one's children is very important: because when parents break promises to their children the trust in them is broken, which breaks up the family bond. In order to maintain a family bond where the child can learn and grow promises are pertinent.
4. Telling the truth is important: because without truth there is no growth or knowledge, but there are ocassion when it's best not to tell the "whole truth" in order not to hurt another person.
5. Helping one's parents is important: helping parents gives children a sense of discipline and responsibility. However, it is not always possible to help parents. Also, helping parents can later lead to helping friends, society, own family, etc. . .
6. Helping to save a friend's life is very important: saveing a friend's life should be done without hesitation (especially if your life is not in danger) or else the person is not really a friend.
7. Saving a stranger's life is important: saveing a life is one of the greatest things a person can do, but when it deals with strangers one does not always know if it is safe.
8. Living even if one doesn't want to is important: because the quality of life is highly valued in our society because it affects everyone around us when a person is lost. Society cannot properly function if the quality of life is not very high.
9. Not taking things that belong to others is important: because a person's belongings is personal and without that sense there is a loss of identity and meaning in a person's life. Of course, minor things should not be judged this strongly.
10. Obeying the law is important: without a sense of law there is chaos and complete disorder. A sense of order is needed that is mutually agreed upon. The conflict arises when law takes advantage of this.
11. Sending lawbreakers to jail is important: because punishment is needed in order to teach and keep order. Otherwise everyone would be breaking the law.

PROTOCOL 9

1. Keeping promises to friends is very important: because they might not like you if you don't keep your promise.
2. Keeping promises to anyone is important: because they might get mad at you.
3. Keeping promises to one's children is very important: ther kids might get mad or wont talk to them.
4. Telling the truth is very important: if you lie you could get into a lot of trouble.
5. Helping one's parents is important: because they might not get it done if you dont help them.
6. Helping to save a friend's life is very important: if they die you wouldn't have a friend if its the only one you had.
7. Saving a stranger's life is important: if you dont help them and somebody noes them they might get mad at you.
8. Living even if one doesn't want to is very important: if you die people might get sad.
9. Not taking things that belong to others is very important: if the police sees you coud get into alot of trouble.
10. Obeying the law is very important: if you dont the police might see you.
11. Sending lawbreakers to jail is very important: if they dont they might get in trouble by the police.

PROTOCOL 10

1. Keeping promises to friends is very important: I think that keeping promises to friends is really important because friendships are based on trust and you should do all that you can so not to betray this trust. A big part of this is following through with that you've told your friend you're going to do.
2. Keeping promises to anyone is very important: because it's important to keep all promises (if possible) because it can damage the persons trust, not to mention credibility of you if you disregard a promise.
3. Keeping promises to one's children is very important: it's important because breaking promises sets bad examples for kids. They see you do it and grow up thinking "mommy & daddy don't do what they say, so why should I?"
4. Telling the truth is very important: this goes back to the issue of credibility. If you're known as a liar, this'll follow you and create a bad image of you for others.
5. Helping one's parents is very important: because your parents are the ones that brought you into the world. Chances are that they didn't ask for you, but they kept you anyway, feeding you, clothing you,

continually doing things for you. If for no other reason, you should at least help them out of respect, but one would think that you'd help them because you love them and want to.

6. Helping to save a friend's life is very important: this is important because you should put yourself in thier shoes; wouldn't you want them to do the same for you? And if they're a friend, one would think that you wouldn't want to see them in trouble and would do all that you could (within reason) to see that they come out o.k.

7. Saving a stranger's life is very important: because human life is the most precious, irreplacable thing on earth and it should be preserved at all cost.

8. Living even if one doesn't want to is important: because I think that most people that don't want to live feel so because they don't think that they have anything to live for. In most cases nothing could be further from the truth. People need to find a reason to live, always keep serching, because if you give up your hope, you've already lost the game of life.

9. Not taking things that belong to others is very important: people work hard to aquire most things. They aquire these things to satisfy their own needs, not those of someone else. Too many people try to freeload today and often people just don't want to put forth the effort to aquire their own things, but when you do it's one of the most rewarding feelings in the world. Noone wants that feeling taken away.

10. Obeying the law is very important: if people didn't obey the law there would be no regulations of right and wrong; people would do what they wanted and there'd be anarchy.

11. Sending lawbreakers to jail is very important: it's important because if those lawbreakers were out on the street they'd be committing more crimes, often hurting innocents. Also, this needs to be done to serve as a lesson to other potential criminals.

PROTOCOL 11

1. Keeping promises to friends is very important: because they depend on you to do something and if you don't you'll go back on your word.

2. Keeping promises to anyone is very important: they hardly know you and they asked you to do something. They wouldn't have asked you if they didn't trust you. If you break your promise they might not trust you again.

3. Keeping promises to one's children is very important: because you might hurt their feelings, and they might take it hard.

4. Telling the truth is important: sometimes you don't want to get your friends in trouble and if you tell the truth they really might get in trouble.
5. Helping one's parents is very important: because they do things for you plus they can't do everything by themselves. Can they?
6. Helping to save a friend's life is very important: because if you don't do anything and they die then you'll be blaming yourself for sorta helping him die.
7. Saving a stranger's life is very important: no matter who they are they really shouldn't die just because you didn't now him and didn't want to help him.
8. Living even if one doesn't want to is important: because later on in life they might be glad they didn't die. They might be in alot of pain and they just want to end their agony.
9. Not taking things that belong to others is very important: it might of meant alot to them or it might of cost alot of money and they liked it alot.
10. Obeying the law is very important: because if they don't they could hurt themselves or someone else or they might get put in jail.
11. Sending lawbreakers to jail is very important: because they shouldn't have broken the law in the first place. This way they might get taught a lesson.

PROTOCOL 12

1. Keeping promises to friends is important: a promise is my word of honor. By keeping a promise I feel good. To do otherwise I would feel depressed and ashamed.
2. Keeping promises to anyone is important: a person who failed to keep a promise to anyone would have less respect for himself. It's a question of being honest or dishonest with others as well as yourself.
3. Keeping promises to one's children is very important: because trust helps to build stronger character and for both children and adults. To be truthful with each other is being honest and helps to build a strong family relationship of reliable trust and respect between child and parent. Family relationship stays with both child and parent throughout a lifetime. Parents must earn the respect of their children. By learning to trust and believe in parents, children will learn to believe and trust themselves.
4. Telling the truth is very important: because people who tell the truth are respected for being honest and of good character. A person who lies is more often than not untrustworthy, a fake, not respected and of low character.

5. Helping one's parents is very important: it is right and healthy for a child to help their parents. Children should have responsibilities from pre-school until they become adults and leave home. Haveing chores at home and working outside of house in their teens helps a child to learn responsibility of work habits, respect for others as well as themselves. Makes the family stronger and benifits all.

6. Helping to save a friend's life is very important: because a true friend is a valuable reward of another person who can be trusted to share your dreams and sorrows. A good friend is a valuable person in your life that should be respected and treasured at all times. When a friend hurts - you hurt - when you are happy they are happy.

7. Saving a stranger's life is very important: life is a gift of God. Its a state of mind. Every effort should be made to save a life even at the risk of death.

8. Living even if one doesn't want to is very important: because when death is imminent - all efforts failed - then we should support the person and family choice of death with dignity. People who have problems created by a state of mind or accident - loss of job - mental exhaustion - physical breakdowns - we should try to help or assist.

9. Not taking things that belong to others is very important: stealing is a crime and should be punishable to the extent of the law.

10. Obeying the law is very important: because the strength of the law is a measurement of the will and needs of the people. We must obey the laws to protect our self respect and our democratic way of life.

11. Sending lawbreakers to jail is very important: when the court judges fail to enforce the law we have a weakening of justice in our society and the democratic system of government may prove to be ineffective or destroyed.

PROTOCOL 13

1. Keeping promises to friends is very important: because it's very important to keep promises to friends because friendships should be based, partly, on trust. And if someone can't trust you to do something you've given your word on, why would he/she want to be your friend?

2. Keeping promises to anyone is very important: because this is very important because your reliability or lack of it greatly affects your credibility. If you make a promise to someone you don't know very well and then turn around and break it, who knows who this person knows that this might get back around to.

3. Keeping promises to one's children is very important: this is very important because parents should be role models for kids.

4. Telling the truth is very important: because if you lie about something it will only hurt you. It's like the saying, what comes around goes around.

5. Helping one's parents is very important: because they didn't have to take care of you all the years that they have. You should want to help them, if for nothing else, out of respect.

6. Helping to save a friend's life is very important: life is one of the greatest gifts God gave us, and we should help preserve it as much as possible.

7. Saving a stranger's life is important: same as 6.

8. Living even if one doesn't want to is important: a lot of the time people want to die for the wrong reasons, and they don't take time to looke to the future and see that things will get better.

9. Not taking things that belong to others is very important: because it's not rightfully yours. I'm sure a person didn't spend 20 grand for a new car just for some thief to come and steal it. It's also a case of "Do unto others. . ."

10. Obeying the law is very important: without laws the world would be in a state of anarchy.

11. Sending lawbreakers to jail is very important: because without proper punishment, they'll just go back and break the law again, and by putting them in jail it says to other would-be lawbreakers, "don't do this or you'll get the same thing."

PROTOCOL 14

1. Keeping promises to friends is important: if you don't keep a promise and you break it you could get into trouble.

2. Keeping promises to anyone is important: cause if you didn't do that thing that you told him you'd do, you break a promise and he might not be your friend any more.

3. Keeping promises to one's children is very important: because if you tell them the children will be mad and wouldn't like it.

4. Telling the truth is important: if it's not true they might get a little mad at you.

5. Helping one's parents is very important: so they can do it faster and it helps them so they can get on to other jobs faster.

6. Helping to save a friend's life is very important: I would get someone and tell them to call their parents.

7. Saving a stranger's life is important: they could be nice.

8. Living even if one doesn't want to is important: maybe I like him and I still want to play with him and he's my friend.

9. Not taking things that belong to others is important: because you could have to pay them and it wouldn't be nice and maybe they'd need it for something.
10. Obeying the law is very important: if your driving the car and you don't have your seat belt on, glass would cut you. If a policeman was behind you, you could go to jail.
11. Sending lawbreakers to jail is important: because if they were someone who breaks into a house, they could steel your stuff.

PROTOCOL 15

1. Keeping promises to friends is very important: well, if it is private you should not tell anyone. Because she or he does not want anyone to know.
2. Keeping promises to anyone is important: it is important to keep promises, because no one wants their promises to be told to anyone.
3. Keeping promises to one's children is very important: because it is very important for keeping promises to there children because they don't want anyone to know.
4. Telling the truth is very important: it is very important to tell the truth because someone could get hurt, lost, or even kidnaped. So you should tell the truth before telling a lie.
5. Helping one's parents is very important: it is very important to help your parents, because they could dround in deep water or even get hurt.
6. Helping to save a friend's life is very important: it is very important to help a friend in any way you can because, if you don't you might lose your only friend you have.
7. Saving a stranger's life is very important: it is important to help a stranger old or young because if they don't die you and them can be friends.
8. Living even if one doesn't want to it important: it is important to live because if you don't want to live because it seems like only bad things happen to you. If you stay alive maybe some good things can happen to you.
9. Not taking things that belong to others is very important: it is very important not to take anything from anyone because the might have got it from a specil person. That might live far away or even died.
10. Obeying the law is very important: it is very important for everyone to obey the law because we would have a bad town if people did not obey the law.
11. Sending lawbreakers to jail is important: it is important for judges to send some people to jail because, it should not happen again from that person.

PROTOCOL 16

1. Keeping promises to friends is very important: so if you need a favor your friend will do you a favor and keep thier promise to do it.
2. Keeping promises to anyone is important: so people will trust you to do something. And they will always like you for it.
3. Keeping promises to one's children is very important: if you lie to a child that child will always rember it and will hold a grudge on you.
4. Telling the truth is very important: when you tell a lie that lie will catch up with you, you might get hurt or hurt some else.
5. Helping one's parents is very important: because your pearents have given up their time to do things for you. They work hard everyday to please, keep you warm and clothed. So you owe it to your pearents.
6. Helping to save a friend's life is very important: because you might be in that situation where you need help and they will rember what you did for them and they might help you if they are your true friends.
7. Saving a stranger's life is very important: because it could be you who needs help one day and that stranger might be able to help you.
8. Living even if one doesn't want to is very important: because if a person decides they don't want to live anymore there is nothing in the world that will change their mind.
9. Not taking things that belong to others is very important: you might get caught and put in jail. No one wants anything stolen from them. It will always catch up with you that you stole something.
10. Obeying the law is very important: if everyone did not obey the law there would be more crime, death, and families torn apart.
11. Sending lawbreakers to jail is important: if the judges let thoes people go they will keep on breaking the law all the time.

PROTOCOL 17

1. Keeping promises to friends is very important: because keeping a promise to a friend shows how strong you feel for their friendship. To be able to trust each other.
2. Keeping promises to anyone is important: because keeping a promise sometimes hurt others try to look for the best way for everyone, especially towards the one you love.
3. Keeping promises to one's children is very important: a child need surcity of trust if parent breaks it the child may not be able in the future to be strong to trust or believe in others.
4. Telling the truth is important: the truth is usually the best way (it comes out in the end). But sometimes it always isn't the answer. Always tell the truth if lying may hurt others.

5. Helping one's parents is very important: when helping parents shows strong bond between other, a family surcity. Build a strong bond for protection.
6. Helping to save a friend's life is very important: when someone is in danger, others should always do their best ability to help. Friendship is a basis of life when friends & family are gone you become weak, unable to do are best because of having to be alone in our hearts, knowing someones there you become strong & willing NEED EACH OTHER.
7. Saving a stranger's life is important: if you can try the best to save a stranger (But never put yourself in danger). That stranger may become a important person in the future to help you.
8. Living even if one doesn't want to is important: if live is given to us we should use it to our fullest. Never give up with live, things should get better.
9. Not taking things that belong to others is very important: because others shouldn't steal, people don't trust them anymore.
10. Obeying the law is important: people should have authority and to obey it. If they didn't the world would go a rappage.
11. Sending lawbreakers to jail is important: but it depends on the crime. Feliny yes, but always find out the reasoning behind the persons motive of crime.

PROTOCOL 18

1. Keeping promises to friends is very important: because if you get a reputation for breaking promises people aren't going to trust you with much & the friend you borke the promise with certainly isn't going to think much of you any more.
2. Keeping promises to anyone is important: it is common curtasy to keep your word. If you don't want to or can't do something, don't promise it to someone in the first place.
3. Keeping promises to one's children is very important: because the child will not trust the parent who breaks there promise to them.
4. Telling the truth is very important: because no one likes a liar. If you get to be know as one, no one will believe a word you say.
5. Helping one's parents is important: depending on how busy the kid is & how much help the parent needs.
6. Helping to save a friend's life is very important: because you would have to live with the guilt that you could have helped them forever.
7. Saving a stranger's life is very important: just do whatever to save whoever or you'll always live with the guilt.
8. Living even if one doesn't want to is important: if the person is just suffering and dieng anyway they might as well be put out of their misery

but if they are just depressed, suicide is the wrong choice & they should seek help.

9. Not taking things that belong to others is very important: stealing is wrong & no one else would want something of theirs stolen.

10. Obeying the law is very important: because that's why the laws were made. If they weren't important, then they wouldn't have been made & they wouldn't be enforced.

11. Sending lawbreakers to jail is very important: depending on the crime should be how long they are in jail. Murderers should also be murdered & so on.

PROTOCOL 19

1. Keeping promises to friends is important: because someone might be counting on you to get some money (or something else) and they don't get the money (that they might need) you'd be mad.

2. Keeping promises to anyone is important: if you promised to participate in a fund raiser and you didn't bother looking at it somebody would loose money.

3. Keeping promises to one's children is very important: a little might be real excited about getting some toy and their parents can't they are really heartbroken.

4. Telling the truth is very important: almost always you get yourself in trouble by telling your mom a lie, your friend the truth and you have to live with it.

5. Helping one's parents is important: because Mom or Dad could have had a bad day at work and they just need a little help now and then.

6. Helping to save a friend's life is important: sure, if you don't get killed in the process, but if there is a car coming at your friend just yell at him. If he/she was sick with a contagios awful disease you could visit him but I wouldn't cure him without any masks, germ catchers, etc.

7. Saving a stranger's life is not important: because it's their fault not yours.

8. Living even if one doesn't want to is not important: if they want to comit suicide it's fine with me (unless they are loved closely).

9. Not taking things that belong to others is very important: it is a crime. Someone takes all your money, can't pay taxes, the FBI will be all over your case.

10. Obeying the law is very important: if someone's drunk and out driving and if they kill themselves, so what? But others?, think again.

11. Sending lawbreakers to jail is very important: because they'll just do it agian.

PROTOCOL 20

1. Keeping promises to friends is very important: because a person's promise is a commitment to do something or not do something. To take that lightly is to show that one cannot be taken at one's word.
2. Keeping promises to anyone is very important: a promise is a promise. In other words, it is a commitment. If one cannot keep the promise, one shouldn't make it, regardless of the relationship.
3. Keeping promises to one's children is very important: a parent needs to set an example and instill values of truth, responsibility, and faithfulness to his or her child.
4. Telling the truth is very important: to not tell the truth is defrauding self and defrauding other. The ramifications affect the private individual (how can one live in the state of a lie?) and on a societal level (if people lie, how will that affect society?).
5. Helping one's parents is very important: because the family unit has important effects on a society. When children take responsibility, as is possible within that unit, their parents as individuals are obviously helped. On a wider scale, if all children do this, society is helped.
6. Helping to save a friend's life is important: God-given life is of value. If I am the only one who can help this person, I should do all that I can ethically and within my means to help.
7. Saving a stranger's life is important: if it is within my power to save someone's life, I should. I must admit that I would be less likely to give my life for someone I do not know. However, if it were in my power to ethically save someone's life (which is of much value), it is important for me to do so.
8. Living even if one doesn't want to is very important: a persons has been given life. It is not for him or her to choose whether or not he should or should not live. This choice is only a divine right.
9. Not taking things that belong to others is very important: a person has a right to his or her own possessions. To take something that does not belong to a person is stealing. This violates the rights of the owner.
10. Obeying the law is very important: because laws are established to protect the rights of the individual and the rights of society. To break the law violates these rights and shows no respect for people.
11. Sending lawbreakers to jail is important: because this is difficult because there are different types of offenses. A speeding motorist should not be sent to jail. Another form of punishment could more easily rectify the situation. However, people who are significantly harmful to others, those who have broken the law and need a strong reinforcement of punishment should be sent to jail.

PROTOCOL 21

1. Keeping promises to friends is very important: because of the trust you place in them and you are disclosing your feelings. When they don't follow through they hurt you & you have a hard time continuing trust in them in future situations.

2. Keeping promises to anyone is important: it's still important because you have made a promise & your word isn't much if you don't follow through with actions. People look at how we treat them & if they place trust in us and they are let down, then we haven't said much for ourselves or who we claim to be.

3. Keeping promises to one's children is very important: because this is a time of learning about promises & how parents treat their children will affect their actions later in life plus it will distort their trust in people if promises aren't kept.

4. Telling the truth is very important: the trust can be helpful or harmful but where it will help the person in the best way they should know. Some people argue about this but I personally would want to know if say something I had on was hidious; but not if just happened to not be the "in" style.

5. Helping one's parents is very important: because this is a bonding process and parents have done so much for kids (most of the time) that the children should show love & respect for them in their help.

6. Helping to save a friend's life is very important: because a friend is someone you should help to all extents - even if they've hurt you. Jesus always helped the less fortunate & we should too. I would give blood for any of my friends right now if they needed it.

7. Saving a stranger's life is important: if there's a situation you shouldn't have to think twice about saving them - like an accident I stopped to see about - all I was worried about is if the people were O.K. - not that I was going to be late to an Orchestra concert.

8. Living even if one doesn't want to is very important: God put us here and He's the only one to decide when we die & the person who doesn't want to live should be taught how to want to live.

9. Not taking things that belong to others is very important: because what we work for we should have if we have rightfully paid for it. I know there are always exceptions but people shouldn't just take things because they don't have them.

10. Obeying the law is very important: without laws the world would be a mess, in fact, laws were probably started because of the mess people started.

11. Sending lawbreakers to jail is very important: if the people have committed a very punishable crime, then they should spend time in a

place aside from the public so as they won't go back out and do it again right away.

PROTOCOL 22

1. Keeping promises to friends is important: because you told them that you would do something
2. Keeping promises to anyone is not important: you don't know them and you won't see them maby.
3. Keeping promises to one's children is very important: because you could hert thers' feellings
4. Telling the truth is very important: because if you liy you will get in more troble
5. Helping one's parents is not important: they can do it their self
6. Helping to save a friend's life is very important: you don't wan't to loos your friend
7. Saving a stranger's life is not important: because you don't know them
8. Living even if one doesn't want to is important: you want them to live.
9. Not taking things that belong to others is important: because thats steling and you could go to jail.
10. Obeying the law is important: so you don't get in troube with the cops.
11. Sending lawbreakers to jail is important: because they did something wrong.

PROTOCOL 23

1. Keeping promises to friends is very important: to establish trust and credability.
2. Keeping promises to anyone is important: importance of relationship determines how important it is to keep promise, magnitude and significance of promise made also primary determing factors.
3. Keeping promises to one's children is important: it is important to keep expressed promises and to be aware of implied promises.
4. Telling the truth is important: it is important to built trustworthyness and confidance in relationship
5. Helping one's parents is important: to be part of a greater whole and to build identity and responsibility.
6. Helping to save a friend's life is very important: if it is within your power to save another, especially those close, you must be a good steward of that power.
7. Saving a stranger's life is very important: determining the need of the stranger, your powers and ability to help, and possible consequences of your actions must all be weighed when determing to help a stranger.

8. Living even if one doesn't want to is important: it is important to the extent that life is a personal choice and if in the case of desiring not to live, when in agreement of family and significant others you choose to end life, you should be able to.

9. Not taking things that belong to others is important: shows honesty, integrity, trustworthiness, responsibility.

10. Obeying the law is important: as long as the law does not violate your conscience and you are willingly and knowlingly ready to accept the consequences of disobeying the law.

11. Sending lawbreakers to jail is important: jail may or may not in some cases be a deterent to future breaking of the law. All avenues of rehabatation should be explored.

PROTOCOL 24

1. Keeping promises to friends is very important: they are your friends.

2. Keeping promises to anyone is not important: you don't really know them.

3. Keeping promises to one's children is very important: so they can think that the world will be nicer for them.

4. Telling the truth is very important: so people will beleive you.

5. Helping one's parents is very important: it shows that you love them.

6. Helping to save a friend's life is very important: because he/she deserves to live.

7. Saving a stranger's life is very important: because he/she deserves to live.

8. Living even if one doesn't want to is very important: if you save them things might turn around for them and they might change their mind.

9. Not taking things that belong to others is very important: so peaple can rely you with something that belongs to them.

10. Obeying the law is very important: they might not be as hard on you when you do break the law.

11. Sending lawbreakers to jail is very important: so they learn their lesson.

PROTOCOL 25

1. Keeping promises to friends is very important: as the physical world is set up w/certain laws on which we count - Gravity, cause & effect physical relations, etc - so are our lives ordered by actions of others. There would be no order in the universe if gravity only worked part of the time. And there is no way to order our lives if you do not know whether a person will keep what he says—there could be no relationships because no one would know if something would happen or not.

2. Keeping promises to anyone is very important: in addition to bringing order, we as people are built on what we do & how we act. If we cannot be trusted to be truthful, & therefore keep promises, our own lives are built on a foundation of deception & there will be nothing solid on which to trust.

3. Keeping promises to one's children is very important: in keeping promises to a child, one teaches him that there are certain absolutes in the world that he can count on. Promises broken will teach a child that actions really do not have consequences (good or bad) & so he may do or say anything without concern for the future. He will also not be able to count on anyone else or know what to trust in life.

4. Telling the truth is very important: if people do not tell the truth, there is no foundation in life. Our actions are based on what we know to be true, & so if those bases are not there, the actions have very different consequences.

5. Helping one's parents is very important: a person's character develops by seeing beyond himself & getting involved in others' needs. A child begins this process by helping parents. As they are taught this concern for others they will be able then to reach out into their world w/ the same help. It also teaches our dependency on others. Parents begin by totally giving to their child; as the child gradually gives back he learns to see the dependency each person has w/ all other persons on earth.

6. Helping to save a friend's life is very important: life itself is something to be valued, so being able to save the life of someone else helps to increase that feeling of value & worth in each person as a sacred being.

7. Saving a stranger's life is very important: life is so valuable, that to be able to have a part in saving someone else's life increases our realization of that value & may increase our sense of both the fragility & sacredness of life itself.

8. Living even if one doesn't want to is important: life is something to be treasured, not only by the individual, but by all others. An individual may not be in a position to realize his worth, & so is important to try to help him life even if he doesn't want to—for his contribution to others, & for the future. However, there may come a time when to prolong life when the person doesn't want to, would destroy all dignity & cause extreme pain & suffering. I think we need to come to the place where we value the individual so much as to allow him to move on to a better life rather than only prolong the physical processes when his "life" has already ended

9. Not taking things that belong to others is very important: in respecting other people's property, we are respecting them as individuals. In our society, we have determined that each person has a right to "own"

"things"—therefore, we are really attacking that person if we take what belongs to him.—and stripping him of some of his dignity.

10. Obeying the law is very important: because obedience to any law creates a sense of order w/in ourselves. Aside from the fact that there would be chaos w/out laws, it is important just for the individual to feel that kind of obligation to others to keep laws whether or not he agrees, or is caught.

11. Sending lawbreakers to jail is very important: because some kind of deterrent is necessary to reinforce the cause-effect idea of breaking, or keeping the law. However, the consequence should be in line with the "crime" - removing people from society may not be in line with all crimes & should only be done when that individual poses a threat to others. In other cases, community services or other consequences would be better deterrents & cause more result in rehabilitation. However, once the deterrent, jail or other, is set, it needs to be enforced—if not is no deterrent at all.

ANSWER KEYS

PROTOCOL 1

1. 2:6b
2. 2/3:4a
3. 2:6b
4. Unscorable
5. 2:1a
6. 1:2a, 2:4a
7. 2/3:5a. This match is marginal.
8. 2:5
9. 1:4. "It would be stelling [sic]" relates to "that's stealing" in the CJ.
10. 2:6b
11. 2:6a

SRMS: 2.00
Global Stage: 2
Moral Type B Components: 0

PROTOCOL 2

1. 2:6b, 2/3:5a, 2/3:3b
2. Unscorable
3. 3:1a
4. Unscorable, 3:6 (Moral Type B, Conscience). "The consequences are worse" is consistent with CJs at more than three developmental levels and thus is unscorable by Rule 3.
5. 2/3:6, 2:1a
6. 3:1a
7. Unscorable. "Everyone is equal" is consistent with CJs at more than three developmental levels, and hence is unscorable by Rule 3.
8. 2/3:3, 3:4b, 3:2b. "Their life would change" relates marginally to "you may find life gets better or things can change" (Transition 2/3).
9. 1/2:1a
10. 2/3:9a, 1/2:3b, 3:2a. "Everyone would get hurt, physically" is matched to "everyone . . . will be . . . killing."
11. 2:6a

SRMS: 2.61
Global Stage: 3(2)
Moral Type B Components: 1 (Conscience)

PROTOCOL 3

1. 3:1a, 3/4:1a, 3:4b, 3/4:8a
2. 3:4b, 3:6 (Moral Type B, Conscience)
3. 3/4:10b, 4:7a, 3:1a, 3/4:1a, 4:4b. Rated as Stage 4 are the references in the response to the child's feeling "worthy" (a marginal match to "sense of self worth," Aspect 7a) and developing relationships based on "integrity" (Aspect 4b).
4. 3/4:5, 2:6d, 3:2a. "Under normal circumstances . . . However, if . . . " is considered to imply "depends on the circumstances" (Transition 3/4).
5. 3/4:1b
6. 3:4a, 3:3d, 3:2a
7. 3/4:[Marginal but equal 3:5a and 3/4:6a ratings yield the Transition 3/4 rating by Rule 1] (Moral Type B, Fundamental Valuing), 3:6 (Moral Type B, Conscience), 2:6a
8. 3:5b (Moral Type B, Fundamental Valuing), 3 (marginal but equal 2/3:3 and 3:3c ratings yield the Stage 3 rating by Rule 1), 3:4b, 3:2b
9. Unscorable. "If you're caught, you're in big trouble" is considered unscorable because the respondent immediately disavows the justification with the comment, "Seriously . . . " (see Chapter 3).
10. 3:3c, 4:1a. The last sentence seems possibly scorable via irregular citation (cf. chapters 4 and 5), but its expression is insufficiently clear.
11. 4:2a, 3/4:4b

SRMS: 3.50
Global Stage: 4(3)
Moral Type B Components: 2 (Fundamental Valuing, Conscience)

PROTOCOL 4

1. 3:1a
2. 2/3:5c
3. 3:1a, 2/3:5b
4. 1/2:2c
5. 3:1b
6. 3. The response is not a close match to any CJ, but relates equally to either Transition 2/3:Aspect 7b or Stage 3:Aspect 1a; by Rule 1, the higher level is scored. Our confidence in this assessment is bolstered by an irregular citation in chapter 6 (Stage 3:Aspect 3c).
7. Unscorable
8. 3:2b
9. 3:2a

10. <u>1</u>:5. "Thrown in jail" relates more closely to the physicalistic "put in jail" (Stage 1:Aspect 5) than to the more pragmatic-sounding "end up in jail" (Transition 1/2:Aspect 3a or Stage 2:Aspect 6b).
11. <u>1/2</u>:1

SRMS: 2.45
Global Stage: 2(3)
Moral Type B Components: 0

PROTOCOL 5

1. <u>3/4</u>:1a, 3/4:8c
2. 3/4:1a, <u>4</u>:2d
3. <u>3/4</u>:8c
4. <u>3/4</u>:5
5. <u>4</u>:3, 3/4:irregular citation. An irregular citation, specifically, Chapter 4 Transition 3/4:Aspect 8c, is used to rate "it . . . gives them role models."
6. <u>4</u>:3, 4:2a (Moral Type B, Fundamental Valuing)
7. <u>4</u>:3, 4:2a (Moral Type B, Fundamental Valuing)
8. Unscorable, <u>4</u>:3. We regard "If they do not want to live it's their choice" as unscorable according to Rule 3: the response relates equally to CJs disparate by more than three developmental levels (Stage 2:Aspect 3 and Transition 3/4:Aspect 7b).
9. <u>3</u>:2a, unscorable
10. 3/4:4a, <u>4</u>:1a, 3/4:3a, 4:1a. "Not so important" is not strong enough to constitute a disavowal of "functioning of society"; hence, this Stage 4 consideration is still scorable.
11. <u>3/4</u>:2b, unscorable. "For the safety of others within that society" is unscorable according to Rule 3: it relates equally (although marginally) to CJs disparate by more than three developmental levels (Transition 2/3:Aspect 6 and Stage 4:Aspects 1 and 2a,d).

SRMS: 3.73
Global Stage: 4(3)
Moral Type B Components: 1 (Fundamental Valuing)

PROTOCOL 6

1. <u>2/3</u>:5a,b, 2:6b
2. <u>1</u>:4b
3. <u>1/2</u>:2b
4. <u>2/3</u>:5b
5. <u>2/3</u>:6
6. <u>1/2</u>:2c

7. <u>2</u>:1a, 2:6a, 2:1a
8. <u>2</u>:6c. The response is scored on the assumption that the respondent still had in mind the previous question (the response is nonsensical in relation to question 8).
9. <u>2/3</u>:6a, 1:4
10. <u>2/3</u>:9a
11. <u>2</u>:6b

SRMS: 2.05
Global Stage: 2
Moral Type B Components: 0

PROTOCOL 7

1. <u>3</u>:1a
2. <u>3</u>:1a
3. <u>3/4</u>:8c
4. <u>3</u>:5c (Moral Type B, Fundamental Valuing), 3:1a
5. <u>3</u>:1c (Moral Type B, Balancing). This match is marginal because of the pragmatic connotation of the end of the response "do for you."
6. <u>3</u>:5 (Moral Type B, Fundamental Valuing)
7. <u>3</u>:5a (Moral Type B, Fundamental Valuing) and 2/3:irregular citation. "He might trust" presumably refers to the to the prospect of being saved. The response can be scored Transition 2/3 extrapolating from, for example, Chapter 4 (Transition 2/3:Aspect 4a).
8. <u>2/3</u>: Rule 2, 2:4a. "Hole [sic] life" in the response is consistent with either "long life" found in Stage 2:Aspect 6b or "full life" found in Stage 3:Aspect 3b. Because Stage 2 and Stage 3 span only three developmental levels, the response is scored Transition 2/3 by Rule 2.
9. 2:6b, <u>2/3</u>:7
10. <u>1/2</u>:3b
11. <u>1/2</u>:3b

SRMS: 2.68
Global Stage: 3(2)
Moral Type B Components: 2 (Balancing, Fundamental Valuing)

PROTOCOL 8

1. 3:1a, <u>4</u>:5, 3/4:1b
2. <u>3</u>:2a, unscorable (see Transition 3/4:Aspect 5 note).
3. <u>3/4</u>:1a, 3/4:3, 3/4:8c. The last Transition 3/4 match is marginal.
4. <u>3/4</u>:8c, 3:2a. The Transition 3/4 match is marginal.

5. <u>4</u>:7 (Moral Type B, Conscience), 4:2a. "Helping parents can later lead to helping . . . society" is marginally scorable to "for the sake of society" at Stage 4.
6. <u>3</u>:4a
7. Unscorable
8. 3/4 (marginal 3:2b and 3/4:7a ratings yield Transition 3/4 by Rule 1), <u>4</u>:1b
9. <u>3</u>:2a
10. 3:3c, 3/4:4a, <u>4</u>:3b (Moral Type B, Balancing). The suggestion in the response that the "need" for "a sense of order" is "mutually agreed upon" relates to the understanding of law as an "agreement" at Stage 4.
11. <u>3/4</u>:2a

SRMS: 3.55
Global Stage: 4(3)
Moral Type B Components: 2 (Balancing, Conscience)

PROTOCOL 9

1. <u>2</u>:6b
2. <u>2</u>:6b
3. <u>2</u>:6b, 1:5
4. <u>2</u>:6d
5. <u>2/3</u> (2:5a and 2/3:6 ratings yield the Transition 2/3 rating by Rule 1)
6. <u>2</u>:5b
7. <u>2</u> (irregular citation, e.g., Affiliation Aspect 6b)
8. <u>2</u>:6d
9. <u>2</u>:6b
10. <u>1/2</u>:3a. "The police might see you" is rated below Stage 2 because the reference to being "seen" by the police represents a physical consequence, that is, to getting caught (reference to an inevitable physical consequence, e.g., "the police *will* see you," would be rated Stage 1).
11. <u>2</u>:6a

SRMS: 2.00
Global Stage: 2
Moral Type B Components: 0

PROTOCOL 10

1. <u>3/4</u>:1a, 3:1a
2. <u>3/4</u>:1a. "Damage the person's trust" relates to "break trust" in the CJ.
3. <u>3/4</u>:8c
4. 2/3:6a, <u>3</u>:4b

5. 2/3:1a, <u>3/4</u>:2b, 2/3:5a, 2:4a
6. <u>3</u>:1c, 2/3;1b, 3:2b. "You should put yourself in thier shoes" relates to "you should take their point of view" in the CJ. The particular expression used in the response is in fact part of the corresponding CJ in chapter 4.
7. <u>3</u>:5b (Moral Type B, Fundamental Valuing)
8. 3:3b, <u>3/4</u>:2, 3:3b. The Transition 3/4 rating pertains to the qualifier "in most cases" in the response, because such a qualifier indicates a sensitivity to situational or circumstantial variations. A simple frequency qualifier, such as "most of the time," would *not* be scored Transition 3/4.
9. 2/3:3, <u>3/4</u>:7, 3:2a
10. <u>3/4</u>:4a
11. Unscorable, 3:3d, <u>3/4</u>:3a. The match to Transition 3/4:Aspect 3a is highly inferential, and should be considered marginal.

SRMS: 3.36
Global Stage: 3(4)
Moral Type B Components: 1 (Fundamental Valuing)

PROTOCOL 11

1. <u>2/3</u>:4a. "You'll go back on your word" is unscorable because it is a simple restatement of breaking a promise (see 3/4:8b note).
2. <u>2/3</u>:4a,5b
3. <u>3</u>:2a. "They might take it hard" should be considered not as a separate scorable justification but instead as an elaboration of "might hurt their feelings."
4. <u>2</u>:4a. The response is scored even though the respondent seems to be justifying why telling the truth is sometimes *not* important. It is also noteworthy that the respondent's appeal to pragmatic preferences refers to the friend, not the self.
5. 2:1a, <u>2/3</u>:6
6. <u>3</u>:6 (Moral Type B, Conscience)
7. Unscorable. It is tempting to score this appeal to fairness, because it is almost certainly more advanced than Stage 2. However, there is insufficient content to determine the response's actual developmental level—arguments could be adduced to score it at any level from Transition 2/3 to Stage 4. Therefore, it is unscorable by Rule 3.
8. 2/3:3, <u>3</u>:2c
9. <u>3</u>:2a, 1:2, 2/3:6a
10. 2:6b, <u>2/3</u>:8a, 1/2:3a
11. <u>1/2</u>:2

SRMS: 2.55
Global Stage: 3(2)
Moral Type B Components: 1 (Conscience)

PROTOCOL 12

1. 4:3a, 2/3:7a, 3:6
2. 4:7a (Moral Type B, Conscience), 3/4:10a (Moral Type B, Conscience)
3. 3/4:8c, 3/4:1a, 3/4:2c (Moral Type B, Balancing), 4:6 (Moral Type B, Balancing), 3/4:8c
4. 3/4:8a, 4:4a, 3/4:8a
5. 4:3, 3/4:7a, 4:7 (Moral Type B, Conscience), 3/4:2a. Whereas "child should have responsibilities" is rated Stage 4, "helps a child to learn responsibility" is rated Transition 3/4.
6. 3:1a, 3/4:2b, 3:2a
7. 3:1b
8. 4:4, 3/4:2
9. Unscorable. See notes under Stage 1:Aspect 4 and Stage 2:Aspect 1d.
10. 3/4:5a, 4:7 (Moral Type B, Conscience), 4:2a.
11. 4:1

SRMS: 3.85
Global Stage: 4
Moral Type B Components: 2 (Balancing, Conscience)

PROTOCOL 13

1. 3/4:1a, 3:4b, 2/3:5a (marginal).
2. 4:4a, 2/3:6a.
3. 3/4:8c
4. 2/3:7a (Moral Type B, Conscience)
5. 3:1a, 3/4:2b.
6. 3:irregular citation (Aspect 1b in chapter 6).
7. 3:1b
8. 2/3:3
9. 2/3:3, 3:1a (Moral Type B, Balancing). The match to Transition 2/3 is marginal. Also, "It's . . . a case of 'Do unto others . . .'" is marginally scorable at Stage 3 (cf. chapter 5, Stage 3:Aspect 1c).
10. 3/4:4a
11. 2:6a, 3/4:3a. The Transition 3/4 match is marginal.

SRMS: 3.23
Global Stage: 3
Moral Type B Components: 2 (Balancing, Conscience)

PROTOCOL 14

1. 2:6d
2. 1/2:2a
3. 1/2:2b, 2:6b
4. 2:6b
5. Unscorable (see Stage 2:Aspect 5a note).
6. Unscorable. This response asserts an action, which is one of the criteria for unscorability (see chapter 3).
7. 1:4a
8. 2:4b, 1/2:2, and 1:irregular citation (Aspect 2a, chapter 5). The respondent evidently still had questions 6 and 7 in mind in answering question 8.
9. 1:4, 2:5b
10. 1:5, 2:6b
11. 1/2:3b

SRMS: 1.78
Global Stage: 2
Moral Type B Components: 0

PROTOCOL 15

1. 2/3, 2:4b. The suggestion that the promise may refer to something "private" relates comparably to either Stage 2:Aspect 3a or Transition 2/3:Aspect 3b; hence, the suggestion is rated Transition 2/3 by Rule 1.
2. 2:4b
3. 2:4b
4. 2/3:4b, 1/2:2b. "Get hurt" in the response is scored Transition 2/3 even though the remainder of the response suggests that its meaning is almost certainly not socioemotional.
5. 1/2:irregular citation (Aspect 3a in chapter 7), 2/3:6.
6. 2/3. "You might lose your only friend you have" relates equally well to either Stage 2:Aspect 5b or Transition 2/3:Aspect 2; hence, the justification is given the higher rating in accordance with Rule 1.
7. Unscorable (see 2/3:6a note).
8. 2/3:3, 2:6b
9. 2/3:6a
10. 2/3:9a
11. 2:6a

SRMS: 2.35
Global Stage: 2(3)
Moral Type B Components: 0

PROTOCOL 16

1. 2:6a
2. 2/3:5b, 2:6b
3. 1/2:2b. "Will hold a grudge on you" relates to "would get mad" in the CJ.
4. 2:6d, 2/3:5c, 3:2a. Although "hurt someone else" is rated stage 3, a reference to someone else *getting* hurt would have been scored at Transition 2/3:Aspect 3a.
5. 2/3:1a,6
6. 2/3:1b, 2:1a, 3:1b
7. 2/3 (2:1 and 2/3:1 ratings yield the Transition 2/3 rating by Rule 1)
8. Unscorable. The early part of the response seems to relate to Transition 3/4:Aspect 7, but overall the respondent's point appears to be practical: "there is nothing in the world that will change their mind" (see 2/3:3 note).
9. 1/2:3a, 2:4b, 2 (1/2:3a and 2:6b ratings yield the Stage 2 rating by Rule 1).
10. 2/3:9a, 1/2:3b. "Families torn apart" is unscorable by Rule 3 because its possible significance spans more than three developmental levels (Transition 2/3 through Stage 4).
11. 2:6a.

SRMS: 2.35
Global Stage: 2(3)
Moral Type B Components: 0

PROTOCOL 17

1. 3:4b,1a, 3/4:1c (Moral Type B, Balancing)
2. 3:2a, 2/3:2a
3. 3/4:1b, 3/4:8c. "The child may not be able in the future to be strong to trust or believe in others" relates marginally to "the child would . . . grow to distrust others" in the CJ.
4. 2:6d, 3:2a. "It comes out in the end" relates marginally to "lies (always) catch up to you sooner or later" in the CJ.
5. 3/4:1b (Moral Type B, Balancing). "Helping parents shows strong bond between other" relates to "common bond of helping each other" in the CJ (one can reasonably complete "between other" as "between each other"). The references to "family security" and "protection" are unscorable.
6. 3/4, 3:2c, 2/3:1c (Moral Type B, Balancing). "Friendship as a basis of life" relates marginally but equally to Stage 3:Aspect 1a and Transition 3/4:Aspect 1a, and hence is given the Transition 3/4 rating by Rule 1.

"When friends & family are gone you become weak, unable to do are [sic] best because of having to be alone in our hearts, knowing someones there you become strong & willing" can be related to "(so that) the parents know they are loved or appreciated, will feel secure (knowing their children are there for them), or will see that the children love them" in the CJ.

7. 2:6a. "Important person" is unscorable.
8. 3:1b, 3:3b, 3/4:4, 2/3:3. "Never give up with live [sic]" relates marginally to "you must have the courage or should have the will (to live or keep on going); you have to learn to bounce back" in the CJ.
9. 2/3:7.
10. 2/3:9a. The misspelled reference to "rampage" in the response ("the world would go [on] a rappage") relates marginally to "crime or constant battles" in the CJ.
11. 2/3:5. "Always find out the reasoning behind the persons [sic] motive of crime" relates marginally to "he may have had a good reason or cause" in the CJ.

SRMS: 3.00
Global Stage: 3
Moral Type B Components: 1 (Balancing)

PROTOCOL 18

1. 2/3:6a, 2/3:5b, 3:4b. "Isn't going to think much of you any more" relates to "people would get a bad image or opinion of you" in the CJ.
2. 3:3b, unscorable (see 1:3a note).
3. 2/3:5b
4. 2:6b, 2/3:6a, 2/3:5b
5. 2/3:6
6. 3:6 (Moral Type B, Conscience)
7. 3:6 (Moral Type B, Conscience)
8. 3:2c, 3/4:2, 3/4:4
9. 2/3:1. The Transition 2/3 match is marginal because the perspective reversal is ambiguous ("no one else would want something of theirs stolen").
10. Unscorable
11. Unscorable

SRMS: 2.83
Global Stage: 3
Moral Type B Components: 1 (Conscience)

PROTOCOL 19

1. 2/3:4a, 2:5b, 2: Rule 2. "You'd be mad" could be intended either as a simple "they'd be mad" (Transition 1/2:Aspect 2b) and as a perspective reversal (Transition 2/3:Aspect 1a). Because the response matches CJs discrepant by only three developmental levels, it is scored Stage 2 by Rule 2.
2. 2/3:4a. "Someone would loose [sic] money relates marginally to "their plans would be ruined."
3. 3:2a. A reasonable completion is "a little kid."
4. 2:6d, 3:6 (Moral Type B, Conscience)
5. 2/3:6
6. Unscorable
7. 2:3
8. 2:3, 3: Rule 1. "Loved closely" relates either to Transition 2/3:Aspect 2a or to Stage 3:Aspect 1c; hence the Stage 3 rating by Rule 1.
9. 2:6b. Note that the theft victim seems to be the referent foro the Stage 2 concern with pragmatic disadvantages.
10. 2:3b, 2/3:9a. Both matches are marginal.   The Transition 2/3 match pertains to "people would or might be hurt" in the CJ.
11. 2:6a

SRMS: 2.50
Global Stage: 3(2)
Moral Type B Components: 1 (Conscience)

PROTOCOL 20

1. 4:3a, 3/4: Rule 1. "Show that one cannot be taken at one's word" relates either to "shows . . .you can be trusted" in Stage 3:Aspect 4b or to Transition 3/4:Aspect 8b; hence the Transition 3/4 rating by Rule 1.
2. 4:3a
3. 3/4:8c, 4:4b
4. 3/4:10a (Moral Type B, Conscience), 4:1a
5. 4:2a, 4:3
6. 3:5b (Moral Type B, Fundamental Valuing). "God-given life is of value" relates generally and marginally to the CJ.
7. 3:5b (Moral Type B, Fundamental Valuing). This match is marginal.
8. 3/4:3
9. 1:4, 4:2d. The Stage 1 rating is almost certainly spurious. Fortunately, in actual protocol scoring this rating would have no effect because only the highest-level rating is counted (see chapter 3).
10. 4:2d, 3/4:5b

11. 3/4:1 (Moral Type B, Balancing), 3/4:2b (marginal rating). Both Transition 3/4 justifications in the response relate only marginally to their respective CJs.

SRMS: 3.73
Global Stage: 4(3)
Moral Type B Components: 3 (Balancing, Fundamental Valuing, Conscience)

PROTOCOL 21

1. 3:1a, 3:2b, 3:2a, 3:1a. The empathic role-taking (Aspect 2a,b) citation presupposes that "you" in the response is intended to refer to another person.
2. 3/4:8b, 3:1a, 2/3:3a, 3:4a
3. 3/4:8c, 3:4c
4. 3:2a
5. 3/4:1b (Moral Type B, Balancing), 3:1b, 3:4b, 3/4:2b
6. 3:3b. The response relates marginally to the CJ.
7. 3:4b
8. 3/4:3
9. 3:3a
10. 2/3:9a
11. 2:6a

SRMS: 3.05
Global Stage: 3
Moral Type B Components: 1 (Balancing)

PROTOCOL 22

1. Unscorable
2. 2:6f
3. 3:2a
4. 2:6d
5. 2:5a
6. 2/3:2
7. Unscorable. "You don't know him" merely repeats the reference to the stranger in the question (see 2/3:6a note).
8. 2:4b. One can reasonably assume that the respondent had questions 6 and 7 in mind in answering question 8.
9. 1:4, 2:6b
10. 1/2:3a
11. 1:4

SRMS: 2.00
Global Stage: 2
Moral Type B Components: 0

PROTOCOL 23

1. <u>3/4</u>:1a
2. <u>3</u>:1a
3. Unscorable
4. <u>3/4</u>:1a,8a
5. 3/4:2a, <u>4</u>:4, 3/4:7a. "To be part of a greater whole" relates marginally to the CJ. "Identity"is matched marginally to "character." "To build . . . responsibility" relates to "taught responsibility."
6. <u>3</u>:1a, unscorable. "Especially those close" relates marginally to "depends on how close the relationship is."
7. <u>3/4</u>:2. The match is marginal.
8. <u>3/4</u>:7b
9. 3:4c, <u>4</u>:4, 3/4:9a, 4:4
10. <u>4</u>:7 (Moral Type B, Conscience), 4:3d
11. <u>3/4</u>:1, 3/4:2b, 3/4:3b

SRMS: 3.55
Global Stage: 4(3)
Moral Type B Components: 1 (Conscience)

PROTOCOL 24

1. <u>1</u>:2
2. <u>2/3</u>:5a
3. Unscorable
4. <u>2/3</u>:4a
5. <u>3</u>:4b
6. <u>3</u>:[irregular citation; chapter 6, 3:3a]
7. <u>3</u>:3a
8. <u>2/3</u>:3
9. <u>3</u>:4a
10. <u>2</u>:6b. This match is marginal.
11. <u>1/2</u>:2

SRMS: 2.40
Global Stage: 2(3)
Moral Type B Components: 0

PROTOCOL 25

1. <u>4</u>:1a,5
2. <u>4</u>:1a, 3/4:1a. This match is marginal.
3. <u>3/4</u>:8c
4. <u>3/4</u>:1a
5. <u>4</u>:4, 3/4:1b (Moral Type B, Balancing)
6. <u>4</u>:2a (Moral Type B, Fundamental Valuing)
7. <u>4</u>:2a (Moral Type B, Fundamental Valuing)
8. 3:5b (Moral Type B, Fundamental Valuing), <u>4</u>:2b, 4:4, 3:2a,c
9. 3/4:5b, <u>4</u>:2d
10. <u>4</u>:7 (Moral Type B, Conscience), 3:3c, 4:3b,5a. The last match is marginal.
11. 3/4:2b, 3/4:1 (Moral Type B, Balancing), <u>4</u>:1, 3/4:1 (Moral Type B, Balancing), 4:6b, 3/4:3b, 3/4:2b. The delineation of different "cases" in the response, like the earlier suggestion that "the consequence should be in line with the 'crime,'" is scored Transition 3/4:Aspect 2a.

SRMS: 3.91
Global Stage: 4
Moral Type B Components: 3 (Balancing, Fundamental Valuing, Conscience)

Index